Creepy Crawlies
and the Scientific Method

Creepy Crawlies

and the Scientific Method

*More Than 100 Hands-On
Science Experiments for Children*

Sally Kneidel

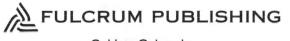 FULCRUM PUBLISHING

Golden, Colorado

Library of Congress Cataloging-in-Publication Data

Kneidel, Sally.
    Creepy crawlies and the scientific method : more than 100 hands-on science experiments for children / Sally Kneidel.
        p.   cm.
    Includes bibliographical references (p. 213) and index.
    ISBN 1-55591-118-8
    1. Animals—Experiments—Juvenile literature. 2. Science—Methodology—Juvenile literature. I. Title.
QL52.6.K58   1993
591'.078—dc20   92–53033
                                                                                    CIP

Printed in Canada

20 19 18 17 16 15 14 13 12 11 10

Fulcrum Publishing
4690 Table Mountain Drive, Suite 100
Golden, Colorado 80403
(800) 992-2908 • (303) 277-1623
www.fulcrumbooks.com

*For Ken, Sarah and Alan (my family), who share my love of animals,
even to the cages on the dinner table.*

*For the children and teachers of Cotswold Elementary in Charlotte, North Carolina,
especially Susan King and Goldie Stribling, whose enthusiasm
motivated me to write the book.*

For my teacher, Sam, who encouraged me to try.

Contents

Preface

Tiffany is a petite and pretty little girl in my daughter's first-grade class. She has a shy smile, big brown eyes usually downcast and tiny little braids with pink bows on the ends. When I met Tiffany she had a severe case of the anticrawlies, meaning she had an extreme aversion to any animal that was smaller than a kitten. Especially the nonfurry ones. This is unusual in children who are that young, but nonetheless Tiffany was so affected. The first time I showed her a critter, a salamander I think it was, she recoiled in horror and begged me not to make her look at it. But the last time I saw Tiffany she was running through the woods, flipping over logs and picking up snails and worms. Ten minutes after that she was showing them proudly to her class like some sort of prize and explaining what they eat. You might say Tiffany underwent a transformation. Although she was a hard-core resister in the beginning, Tiffany was one of the children who helped me develop and put into practice the ideas for nature study that I've presented in this book. Most of the children took to the critters right away. Tiffany took a while to warm up, but her enthusiasm was unsurpassed in the end. I was excited and inspired by Tiffany's progress and by the enthusiasm of the other children as well. I think an aversion to "creepy crawlies" is a cornerstone in children's (especially girls') aversion to science in general. Research has shown that girls tend to have attitude problems with science. Many feel an interest in science is not appropriate socially for their gender; some simply lack confidence in their aptitude for it because of social stereotyping.

The ideas for children and students that I've presented in this book are from the perspective of (1) a mother who keeps an insect zoo in her house and serves as a volunteer roving science instructor at her children's elementary school and (2) a former teacher and scientist (Ph.D.) who spent eight years in graduate school learning field and lab ecology. I drifted into ecology for children gradually. I started off just keeping things in my home for my own children to look at. Their friends' mothers often asked me to show their children the mantises, the tadpoles, the roly-polies, the fruitflies, the slime molds and the worms.

When my daughter started school I found that most of the teachers at her school were open to and interested in bringing "hands-on" science into their classrooms, but were uncertain as to how to go about it. Her first-grade teacher, Susan King, was downright eager to explore whatever I had to offer. Her enthusiasm fed my own. I began taking things in once every week or two: a lizard, a puffball, a bird's nest. The children were fascinated. Slowly the teacher and I began to go from simply "show and tell" to activities and then to experiments. First, jack-o-lantern mushrooms, then slime molds, then roly-polies, then praying mantises. I was surprised that the children so easily understood the concept of the scientific method. What do I mean by "the scientific method"? I mean learning and practicing a five- or six-step procedure that is the underlying format or structure for all scientific experiments in every field from sociology to atomic physics. The scientific method is science. The children became adept at all the steps — coming up with questions, turning a question into a prediction (a hypothesis) and thinking of ways to test the hypothesis. They jumped out of their seats to check the results of their experiments and yelped with excitement when their predictions were right.

I think it's important that we start science early, before children decide that it's too hard or too dull. They need to learn while they're very young that science is in part a process that's fun, not just facts to be memorized. Science is in part finding things about the natural world that interest you and learning how to answer your own questions about them. How could that be dull?

Of all the three basic sciences (physics, chemistry and biology) I think biology is the one children have the most natural attraction for. Think about the zoo and farm animals that even toddlers love. Children's storybooks are absolutely full of animals. It's not a very big leap from zoo animals to the smaller versions that can be found under a log. The main difference is in the attitudes children pick up from their elders. I've learned from working with first-graders as well as college students that most younger children have little aversion to bugs and worms and such. They almost all ask to hold any critter, whereas college students and adults almost never do. If we can preserve their natural innocence and encourage their interest, then studying critters can provide a real jumping-off point for the study of scientific methodology. Children can learn scientific methodology with living things, just as well as with physical or mechanical systems. It makes sense to take advantage of their natural fascination with animals, any animals.

What's great about children's natural interest in animals and about animals' adaptability to scientific study is this: There is a vast array of animals in your own yard, probably in your own house. The last time I took a bug, a dragonfly larva, into my daughter's first-grade class, her classmate Emily asked, "Where do you get all these things?"

"In my yard," I said, "and I don't have a special yard— it's just a regular old yard."

"It *is*?," Emily exclaimed, astonished.

All of the critters I talk about in this book are things that I found in my own yard, and I live on a regular city lot with a sometimes-flowing ditch behind it. This is not to say that I can walk out my front door and find a praying mantis or a caterpillar of a swallowtail butterfly or a slime mold anytime I want to. Rather, it's a matter of looking for things every time I go outside and trying to find a way to make use of what I find. Most times I don't find anything. But sometimes I do. You may find totally different things than I find. But if you can catch it, you can use the principles in this book to adapt it to an experiment. I write in the second chapter about how to provide the basic necessities that will keep most critters alive for several days, long enough to do an experiment. I also give some tips on how to provide habitats outdoors for critters to improve the likelihood of your finding certain types of animals.

I learned to look while I was in graduate school studying for my doctorate in ecology, but not through anything that happened in the classroom. Most of the graduate students were single and we spent all our time together, problem solving. Each of us had a different project with a different animal in a different habitat. Michele studied fish, Ellen and Tim worked with tiny aquatic crustaceans, Phil studied roly-polies, Rich studied beetles, Kiisa worked with salamanders, Judy with aphids, Alan with wasps and so on.

For Michele to work with mosquito fish, she had to know about all the predators of mosquito fish as well as all the smaller animals that mosquito fish eat. She had to understand the interconnection between all the animals in that habitat. If she or someone else needed help setting up pens for her experiments in the field, or help identifying some of the organisms she'd caught, whoever helped her found out all about her ecosystem as well. We learned an awful lot from each other this way.

The upshot of all this was that I learned that there are fascinating little systems of animals everywhere. Judy studied two types of aphids, one red and one green, that live and feed on goldenrod plants. She found that they are able to coexist, or share their resource, only because their predators (ladybug larvae) keep the aphids' numbers so low that the aphids never are in competition for food. Otherwise one species would outcompete and eliminate the other. Ron found that reducing the density of fish in a penned area of a marsh altered the relationship of all their prey species to one another. The dominant prey species were replaced by others. And so on.

I've discovered that a lot of what I learned incidentally in graduate school is of real interest to little kids. It's been too much fun to keep to myself, and it's valuable to the children. Mrs. King says she thinks that if the children remember anything about first grade, it'll be the "hands-on" things we did with crawlies.

If all of our children could learn to regard the tiny and usually unseen residents of our natural areas as creatures worthy of study, maybe we would find in the future more effort devoted to preserving what is left of our undisturbed lands.

This book was written in honor of Mrs. King, my daughter's first-grade teacher, who first planted the seed in my mind, and the many other teachers at Cotswold Elementary who have invited me into their classrooms and provided an audience for me. It's intended for all teachers who have an interest and are looking for the means. I specifically have had elementary teachers in mind, but all of the experiments herein are suitable for secondary schools or college biology labs. Home-schoolers and other parents can use it at home as well. There is no equipment required that would be available only at schools.

Most of the animals in the book can be maintained in the classroom for an indefinite period of time. My approach in classrooms has been to take in one type of creature at a time and spend a couple of weeks on that one, then move on to a different one. I keep many going simultaneously at home, but most teachers find one at a time enough when doing experiments.

Acknowledgments

I want to thank most of all my husband Ken for contributing to every stage of putting the book together. He helped me decide which creatures to use, helped work out ideas for experiments, and "field-tested" several experiments in his high school biology class. His knowledge of insects was a great help at every turn. I thank him also for his editing and feedback on early drafts.

I am grateful to my children Sarah and Alan for helping me collect insects, posing for pictures, for gladly sharing their house with a multitude of bugs, for proudly showing new bugs to the neighborhood kids and in other ways being interested.

The assistance of both children in the classroom was invaluable. Alan was a preschooler and with me full-time when I did most of the classroom work. He carted bugs to and from classes with me and helped feed and water bugs on our daily classroom rounds. Both children passed out materials, contributed information and shared their enthusiasm with other students. Thanks for the excellent teamwork.

I thank all the teachers at Cotswold Elementary in Charlotte, North Carolina, who invited me and my creatures into their classrooms, where I found my inspiration. In particular I thank Susan King and Goldie Stribling, Kelly Bowers, Belinda Cannon, Veronica Carter, Faith Dunn, Emily Gulledge and Margaret Rowe. I am grateful to Elva Cooper, the principal at Cotswold, for her encouragement and support. I thank the other staff and the parents who made me feel welcome.

This book would not have been possible without the students at Cotswold Elementary, who amazed me with their fresh and undaunted interest, their bright eyes and shining smiles, their pudgy little hands so ready to receive worms or bugs or toads and their unending questions and willingness to learn. The steadfastness of their interest surprised me and fueled me every step of the way.

I thank all of the children at Cotswold Elementary who allowed me to photograph them in action, and their parents for giving me permission to use the photographs.

I am grateful to fate for having run me past Sam Watson, whose message to me about writing made a difference. Thank you, Sam, for persisting.

I am indebted to all of the people I knew in the Biology Department and the Ecology Curriculum at UNC at Chapel Hill from 1979 to 1984, who taught me about the natural world and the scientific method. Any errors in the book are my own responsibility.

I want to express my gratitude to my agent Sally McMillan for her efforts in my behalf and for her steady support and interest. I'm grateful too to the staff at Fulcrum Publishing, especially Carmel Huestis and David Nuss, for their guidance, encouragement and editing.

Thanks to my longtime and best friend Kathleen Jardine for her continued faith in me and her appreciation of all the little animals and fungi we examine together on our walks in the woods.

And last but not least, I'm grateful to the insects — the tadpoles, millipedes, spiders and worms — for being there so predictably and for surprising me and amusing me in so many ways.

Introduction

There are a lot of books to help children study nature. But this one is unique in a couple of ways. First of all it contains 114 experiments, mostly behavioral, with animals that are commonly found in nature. Each experiment is a five-step procedure: question, hypothesis, methods, result and conclusion. Chapter 1 is devoted entirely to explaining these five steps, which together constitute the scientific method. So this is more than just an activity book; these are real experiments in the academic sense.

You can, however, use this book as an activity book. The experiments are the last part of every chapter. The first part of each chapter describes the animals (mostly insects), how to find them, how to maintain them and things you can do to encourage observation. There's a lot of enjoyment to be gleaned from just keeping the animals for observation and letting the children hold them in most cases. This is especially fun when each child has his or her own. So each chapter provides the option of stopping short of the experiments if you wish.

A second unique feature of this book is that I have tried to make it more than just an instruction manual. I've tried to convey my own appreciation for these miniature living things. Sharing them with children has helped fuel my own delight in them. Each type of creature is peculiar in its own way. Each is so different from ourselves, yet similar too. They all need food, water and shelter. And even the most lowly is capable of making choices about its habitat or food.

I've included students' reactions when I think they would be useful, and tried to give readers the benefit of my own experience getting things to work out right in the classroom. It's not just an instruction manual — I mean for it to be a map into a tiny wonderland. My small students with their open minds and their ability to marvel at the simplest things have helped me to appreciate that perspective.

My experience with elementary students has all been as a roving volunteer science person. I take the creatures into someone else's classroom, set things up and turn over the ongoing care to the children and their teacher. Then I come back periodically for results and feedback.

The Format of Each Chapter

The format is the same in each chapter except the first two. Below is a list and then a description of the sections found in each chapter.

Introduction
Materials
Background Information
How to Get and Keep the Organism
Field Hunt
The Organism at School
    Getting Ready
    Observations and Activities
    Experiments

Introduction

The short introduction is a summary and also usually tells you what I consider to be the most remarkable feature of that particular animal.

Materials

None of the materials is very expensive, and in many cases you can make do with things you may already have on hand. It will be more fun though and easier if you order a few supplies. The materials I use most frequently are fruitfly culture vials, petri dishes, plastic peanut butter jars and insect sleeve cages. These are described in Chapter 2. They can be ordered from a biological supply company or bought at a science hobby shop.

Although many of the animals in this book can be caught easily outside, most can be ordered too. The materials list or the How to Get and Keep the Organism section in each chapter will tell you if they can be. You'll find a list of biological supply companies in the Appendix. Any place in the book where I suggest ordering something refers to these places, unless stated otherwise.

In those chapters where there are a lot of experiments, or a lot of materials are required, the materials list will tell you which materials are needed for which experiments. Commonly available materials like tape or scissors are not listed.

Background Information

This section tells you about the life cycle and natural history of the chapter's subject. Certain aspects may be interjected later, just previous to relevant experiments.

How to Get and Keep the Organism

Here you'll find out how to go about catching your subjects in nature. I've provided very detailed accounts of how to feed and house the creatures. The daily maintenance of the creatures is probably the most pleasurable aspect of the whole enterprise to me (other than the look of delight on children's faces). I can spend hours rearranging cages and watching animals eat, hours when I'm supposed to be doing other things. But daily maintenance need not take more than a few minutes. Many don't need attention every day.

Field Hunt

This section of each chapter gives information on how to take a class out searching for the particular creature. This can be a fun and worthwhile activity in and of itself, not necessarily leading to classroom experiences. A damp paper towel in the collecting container will keep captive insects and such alive for hours. The inexpensive *Insects: A Guide to Familiar American Insects* by Zim and Cottam will help identify most insects encountered. (See Chapter 12 bibliography.)

The Organism at School

Here I describe how to set up your class to receive the creatures, and usually I explain how I've introduced students to the animals. Where I think it would be useful, I've given children's reactions and questions. I continue to be amazed at the consistency of their enthusiasm and interest. And it's not me — I'm a very quiet and shy person, inept at speaking in front of groups. It's the creatures! Kids love 'em! I took some ant lions to a third-grade class this morning. Lots of kids in the class had worked with ant lions the year before, so I thought they might be indifferent. But it didn't seem to make any difference. They were leaning out of their seats to see, and half the hands in the class were up wagging with comments and questions the whole time I was talking.

The Organism at School section also describes how to encourage observation. With some animals, one option is to let each child have his or her own animal in a small container at his or her desk. With others, like adult praying mantises or water bugs, this is not practical. In some chapters, I suggest activities to help the children notice certain features of the animals.

Next come the experiments. The number of experiments per chapter varies, from 3 to 13, with a total of 114 experiments. Some chapters include tables you can photocopy for the children to fill out, or graphs on which you can plot your own counts or measurements. The Appendix includes a blank graph and table you can photocopy if a chapter does not provide one that fits your needs. In some chapters completed graphs are included to provide examples of how a graph might look. Your graphs may look very different from mine. Conditions vary and animals are not always predictable!

Following Chapter 16 is a Postscript that ties together common threads among chapters. The Postscript includes, at the end, tables and lists of questions that will help students compare results from similar chapters. For example, one table compares responses of under-log creatures, from the first group of chapters. A list of questions compares strategies of different predators, from the second and third sections of the book.

My hope is that reading through the book and trying some experiments will help teachers and students come up with some of their own questions that can be tested. Not just any question can be made into an experiment. I'll elaborate on that in Chapter 1. All it takes is practice to fall into that questioning mode of thinking. Then you're off and running.

The Appendix supplies a list of biological supply companies that provide animals and supplies.

The Scientific Method

Why Do an Experiment?

Why not just keep animals in terraria in your classroom and observe them? I spend a lot of time just watching animals, feeding them, talking to them and in general regarding them as pets. It's fun and it's valuable. I don't routinely do experiments with the animals that live in terraria around my house. I just enjoy them.

The classroom is a different situation. Some children will spend a lot of time watching gerbils or fish in a classroom. Others have less interest. But when a child makes a prediction about that fish's response to something, like covering half of the aquarium with a dark towel, that child invests something of him- or herself in the fish's behavior. It may greatly increase the child's interest in the fish. Say the child then observes that this particular type of fish avoids the dark part of the tank. If the child writes down his or her discovery and shares it with others, the child's going to feel pretty proud. Most of the projects I did as a biology student in college consisted of simply observing captive animals' behavior. I learned a lot from doing that and children will too. But as time goes on, the attention given to a captive wanes. One advantage of doing experiments with animals as opposed to keeping them indefinitely for observation is this: When children make a prediction or a hypothesis about an animal's reaction, they've invested a part of themselves in the outcome. This greatly increases their interest in the animal's reaction.

Another important difference is that posing questions, predicting answers and testing the predictions all develop higher level thinking skills. Experimentation develops the habit of following observations with questions, a trait that adult innovators all possess.

A third and perhaps most important advantage of experimentation over observation is that by conducting experiments, the children learn the meaning of the word science and think of themselves as scientists. I never did any science at all in biology until I got to graduate school. That is, I never did an experiment until then. I read a lot and I learned a lot but I didn't feel like a scientist until I started doing experiments.

What was the big deal about doing experiments? I learned that instead of memorizing stuff other people had discovered, I was creating knowledge. I was contributing to the accumulated body of knowledge. I understood then that science is not an already existing set of facts but an ongoing process of discovery, and I had become a part of this process. By teaching children to do experiments, we give them that feeling too — that science is an ongoing process and they are part of that process. It's an exciting feeling. It ceases to be intimidating and becomes a source of pride.

Okay. But how does a nonscientist develop scientific thinking in a classroom? Science is not necessarily complicated thinking. It's just a method of addressing questions. In my ecology program all of us began by simply picking an area of interest. We then spent time in the field poking around in a pond, or a tree hole or a stream — wherever we were likely to find the creatures that interested us. If we could we'd take several back to the lab to keep in captivity and observe continually. That's how questions occurred to us. If there is no period of observation, then no questions will occur. This can be a fundamental stumbling block if children try to come up with experiments with no prior observation period.

All of the experiments going on in my department at graduate school were simple. (What gives length to the dissertation is the survey of related research and perhaps a series of simple experiments.) Most experiments were based around a simple yes or no question. For example: Do spotted salamanders survive longer with predators if they have weeds to hide in? Yes or no. This was one of my experiments.

This has what seems like an obvious answer. But in science, even an outcome you can guess must be demonstrated experimentally if it is to be accepted by one's colleagues.

Many science projects and many experiments have obvious outcomes, but they are still worth doing. Once you have a simple yes or no question, it's easy to make a hypothesis. Simply state what you think the answer is. Or have the children state what they think the answer is. For example: I think spotted salamanders will survive longer if there are weeds in the water.

Here is an important point: The hypothesis must be testable. The above hypothesis can be tested by putting some salamanders and their predators in an aquarium with weeds and putting others in an aquarium without weeds. Then after a certain length of time, I remove the weeds and count how many are left in each aquarium.

Here is an example of a hypothesis, based on a yes or no question, that is not testable.

Question: Do slime molds like warm dishes better than cold dishes? Hypothesis: Slime molds like warm dishes better than cold dishes.

"Like" is not something we can count or measure. A testable hypothesis must predict an outcome that can be counted, measured or concretely observed in some way. With slight modification, the above can be made into a testable hypothesis: Slime molds survive longer (or grow bigger) in a warm environment than in a cold environment.

These are the steps of the scientific method, as applied to teaching children.

1. **Observation.** Always begin with a period of observation (unless you already have a question). One observation might be, "Roly-polies are found in dark places, like under bricks."
2. **Question.** Get the children to ask questions and focus on one question. For example, "Do roly-polies like to be in the dark?"
3. **Hypothesis.** Get the children to predict what they think the answer to the question will be. For example, "Roly-polies are afraid of the dark." Make sure the hypothesis is testable, which the above is not. Many predictions that young children make spontaneously will not be testable. To test a prediction or hypothesis you must be able to count or measure or concretely observe the outcome. A feeling can't be counted or measured or concretely observed, but most behavior can. The above prediction can be changed to, "Roly-polies will choose light over dark." Most predictions can be modified in some way to be made testable.

   Some teachers prefer that students make predictions as "if" statements. For example, "If I offer roly-polies a choice between light and dark, roly-polies will choose dark."
4. **Methods.** Carry out the experiment. Give the roly-poly a choice. You may want to replicate your experiment (see below).
5. **Result.** State exactly how the roly-poly reacted and which side it chose. For example, "The roly-poly wandered around the light side for five minutes, trying to crawl up the side of the container. Then it entered the dark side and stayed there until the predetermined time to end the experiment."
6. **Conclusion.** Here you state whether your prediction was confirmed or not and try to explain your results.

The Null Hypothesis

Scientists try to make sure their results are not biased by their expectations. One way they do this is to try to disprove the hypothesis, rather than try to prove it. Another way of going about this is to state a "null hypothesis." Instead of stating what effect you think your experimental variable will have on the animal, you state as your hypothesis that the variable will have no effect. For example, a null hypothesis would be, "We think cold will have no effect on the growth rate of mealworms," when actually you expect that cold will make them grow more slowly.

In my experience, young children are more successful at coming up with a hypothesis when they're allowed to say what they think will happen. Trying to convert their natural prediction to a null hypothesis can be confusing; I leave this up to the individual teacher.

Replicates

If you had only one roly-poly and recorded its choice of light over dark only once, you would not have much confidence that roly-polies always prefer darkness. Consider this example. Suppose you drink coffee most mornings, but occasionally you drink tea. An employee of the coffee company calls you Tuesday morning, doing a survey, and asks you if you are drinking coffee or tea. You say tea. If she concluded that you always drink tea she'd be wrong. She'd be even more wrong to conclude from that example that everyone always drinks tea.

It is easier to generalize from one roly-poly to the next than it is from one person to the next. Roly-polies' preferences are genetically programmed so if one of them definitely prefers dark, then probably all of the same species do. But it could be that roly-polies don't really have any preference between light and dark. If not, then giving one roly-poly a choice would be like flipping a coin. You could flip it once. Or you could even flip it three times and get three heads in a row. It's not very likely but it's certainly possible to get three heads in a row by chance. And if you gave your roly-poly a choice between light and dark three times in a row, it could choose dark three times in a row just by chance.

How many times would you have to offer your roly-poly a choice to be sure that your results were not due to chance alone? If I flipped a coin ten times and got heads nine out of ten times, I would wonder if the coin was weighted on one side. If I flipped the coin fifteen times and got heads thirteen out of fifteen times, I would be sure the coin was weighted. I would be sure the results were not due to chance alone. And so, to be sure that my results are really answering the question, I might want to offer the roly-poly a choice ten times.

Each repetition of an experiment is called a replicate, or a trial. The more replicates you have, the more confidence you'll have that your results reflect the truth. With children though, scientific "truth" may not be our highest priority. Sometimes when I get too rigorous with children I lose my audience. We want the children to understand the process and to enjoy themselves. If more replicates become tedious then keep it simple. The concept of how to go about answering a question may be more important than the veracity of the results in some situations. You can always discuss how additional replicates could affect your results and conclusions if you employed them.

It's important too if you're doing a series of experiments to decide before you start how many trials or replicates you're going to do. This is so your results will not be influenced by your expectations. For example, suppose I think my coin is weighted on one side and I want to prove it. I could say, "I'll just keep flipping until I have more heads than tails." Well, during the course of my flipping, the ratio of heads to tails will seldom be exactly 1:1. It fluctuates. After four flips I may have three heads and one tail. But after twelve flips I may have five heads and seven tails. The balance fluctuates. If I choose when to stop after I've already started, I can choose a stopping point that supports my expectations. I'll stop after four flips if I want to prove that the "heads" side is weighted.

Do you see that to be objective I must decide before I start how many flips (or how many replicates) I'll do?

Variability in Results

If you conduct an experiment two times with animals of the same species, same age and same gender under precisely the same conditions, you should get precisely the same results. In an elementary school setting, however, it's difficult to control everything precisely. So your experiences may vary somewhat from those I've discussed in the book. You may use different species whose behavior varies somewhat. Not all roly-poly species react to light the same way. There are several species of crickets called "field crickets." All are territorial but their courtship behaviors probably vary slightly. There are many species of mantises in the United States too.

Small changes in environmental conditions can make a difference. In a particular experiment, your sand may be wetter or dryer than mine. Your aquatic plants may be packed more densely.

The behavior of individual animals can vary too. In Chapter 5 I describe how the level of aggression in a male cricket depends on its recent experiences with territory and other crickets.

Variability can be fruit for discussion and further experimentation. If your results vary from what my comments lead you to expect, help the students speculate about why. It may lead to another experiment: "Let's try it again with dryer sand."

Controls

A control is simply a part of the experiment that gives you something to compare your result to. An experiment where an animal is offered two options, like the one described above with roly-polies, already has a control. If I predict that roly-polies will choose light, then offering dark as well is my control. I can compare their reaction to light with their reaction to dark. If I did not have darkness as an option, I wouldn't know anything about their preference for or aversion to light.

But not all experiments have a built-in control like that one. Consider the experiment I described with the salamanders in the weeds with predators. This requires a control. Suppose you want to know whether salamander tadpoles are able to survive longer with predators if they have weeds in which to hide. Say you put ten salamander tadpoles in an aquarium with pondweed. You added predatory dragonfly larvae. Suppose you had six surviving salamander larvae after a week. This wouldn't tell you a thing about whether or not the weeds helped the salamander larvae escape predation. Some have escaped so far, but why? You don't know for sure. You need something to compare your result to—an aquarium without weeds. If more tadpoles survived in the aquarium with weeds than in the one without weeds, then you'd have some information about the effect of weeds. So the aquarium without weeds is your control. It allows you to attribute your result to the presence of weeds.

The Experimental Variable

It is important that there be only one difference between the control and the experimental setup. In the last example the only difference between the two aquaria is that one has weeds and one has no weeds. In other words, weeds are your "experimental variable" because you are testing a prediction about the effect of weeds. All other factors must be equal between the two aquaria, like size and type of predator, volume of water, illumination, disturbances by little hands, etc. Any factor that could affect the outcome must be the same between the two aquaria—except the experimental variable.

How Is an Experiment Different from an Activity?

An activity is simply watching something, or perhaps interacting with it in some way so as to cause a reaction. For example, feeding a live cricket to a praying mantis is an activity. Many people call activities experiments. But an experiment is an activity that is designed to answer a question and has a control to rule out other interpretations of the result. An experiment is more valuable to a child's learning because it encourages more thinking.

An activity is really part of the observation period and can lead to a question and an experiment. Say we've got a praying mantis in captivity. We've read that it eats insects, so children bring in insects, some alive but mostly dead. The children notice that some things are eaten and some aren't. None of the dead insects are eaten. Some of the live ones, but not all, are eaten. Some insects that sit very still in the cage, like moths, are not eaten. At this point some questions can be asked that lead to experiments. Why does the mantis not eat the dead things? Why does it eat a live cricket but not a live moth? What is the difference between the cricket and the moth? Does the mantis eat crickets because they move more? Coming up with questions like these requires critical and analytic thinking. Children become more proficient at this with experience.

You've got a question now that will invite predictions or hypotheses. For example, a mantis will eat a moving insect before eating a nonmoving one. The method of testing this prediction can be to offer other pairs of moving and nonmoving prey, like a housefly (moving) and a grasshopper (mostly nonmoving in captivity). Or a regular cricket and a cricket that has been chilled for an hour or two in the refrigerator to paralyze it temporarily. Or jiggle a dead cricket with tweezers in front of the mantis.

This can lead to further questions and hypotheses. Will a mantis eat anything that moves? A jiggled piece of ground beef? A jiggled piece of apple? A jiggled piece of paper? How much movement is required, continuous or only once?

Why do an experiment? Why not just offer the mantis a variety of items, record what it eats, look for patterns and generalizations and leave it at that? The value of making predictions is that the children have invested something themselves in the outcome. This greatly increases interest. And by doing an experiment with a control, children learn the process that is the foundation of all our knowledge in science. The children become a part of that process by contributing to that body of knowledge. They become scientists.

CHAPTER 2

Attracting and Maintaining Critters

Some of my best experiences in working with students have been field hunts for critters on the school grounds. The children love it. A field hunt can whet their appetites for keeping animals in the classroom and also helps them relate their school experience to home, where they can explore at leisure. Most chapters have a Field Hunt section that describes how to find in nature the animals focused on in that chapter. What I've described here is not so much how to attract or find anything in particular, but just how to provide fun places to look.

I've described here the cages that I find most useful. Terraria are too big for some things. An interesting cage can motivate even a squeamish child to find something to put in it. Those I suggest for general bug-catching are the same ones you'll need for many of the experiments in this book.

I've divided the chapter into four areas:
1. The Under-Log and Under-Stone Crowd
2. Traps
3. Cages
4. Making a Small Pond

The Under-Log and Under-Stone Crowd

A sheet of plywood or dark plastic left lying (and anchored) on damp ground, preferably with a little dead vegetation underneath, will almost certainly attract something. Among the possibilities are crickets, earthworms, roly-polies, millipedes, centipedes, snails, slugs and small snakes. Spiders are another possibility, so children should be cautioned about not sticking hands into places they can't see into.

Large stones in damp places yield similar results. You may get colonies of ants under large rocks that have been left undisturbed for several weeks or months. If you're lucky you may find a land planarian, a flat, striped, sticky worm with

a triangular head, about 8 inches (20.3 cm) or less in length (see Figure 2.1). My kids find them in our suburban yard about four times a year, usually under bricks or stones. I saw several out in the open once at night on a slate walk when I was a child. Their heads and necks are held up in the air when they're on the move, which is very peculiar looking. They ensnare their prey with slime and leave a slime trail behind them as well.

My biggest success in drawing large numbers of creatures has been with a pile of wet and very rotten (stinking) grass clippings dumped from a plastic bag onto a gravel driveway. The bag had been closed and in the sun for several days. After I dumped it I left it untouched for about three weeks. Then when I looked under it, I found fifty to one

Figure 2.1 — Land planarian. Most encountered in nature are less than 8 inches (20.3 cm) long. They are brown with black stripes running the length of the body. The shovel-shaped head distinguishes them from other worms.

hundred earthworms, crickets, millipedes and beetles. I think the spaces in the gravel enabled them to get under the clippings more easily. But after I'd checked under the pile on three or four successive days, the worms and crickets were all gone. Those not captured had fled.

Frequency of disturbance is a major factor in keeping any under-board type creatures available. They'll leave permanently after being disturbed several times in rapid succession. We used to have a tiny worm snake (the most charming of all the snakes in my opinion) that lived under a concrete slab behind my house. It was there every time we looked as long as I could keep the peeks spaced a month or so apart. But as soon as my kids got big enough to lift the slab, the snake left.

Rotten logs provide a litle more variety than plastic sheets and boards left on the ground. You can look under the log (see Figure 2.2) or inside the log, although a log can be ripped apart only once. You'll see wood roaches and a variety of beetles, as well as all of the same things you see under a board or plastic sheet. Under the bark of rotting logs, termites are common, as are ants. Both travel in tunnels that permeate the log, often the same log, but their tunnels never intersect. I love to watch termites. They look something like white pudgy ants. The ones you see in logs aboveground are all workers and soldiers on foraging expeditions for the queen and her young, who usually live underground. You can distinguish the soldiers and workers easily by the much larger jaws of the soldiers. The soldiers' job is to protect the

Figure 2.2—Alan looking under a log.

workers while they collect food, and they'll try to bite anything that gets in the way. A soldier bit me once as I collected some termites to feed some captive animal, and I had to laugh at its determination. The bite was barely detectable, but the little bugger would not let go! Termites are blind so it had no way of knowing it was biting a 130-pound giant. The bite of a soldier *ant,* on the other hand, can be painful, more like a sting for some species of ants.

A vial and a small paintbrush are useful for collecting termites and ants. Both can be kept in captivity temporarily but only the queens can reproduce. The ant queen may be in the log or on the surface of the ground near a log, and can sometimes be tracked down. But you'll seldom find a termite queen because most are too far underground.

Termites eat rotting wood. Different species of ants eat different things. You can order an ant farm kit from a biological supply company (see Appendix) or buy one at a science hobby shop. Termites are vulnerable to dehydration and must have a damp paper towel to be kept alive for more than a few minutes in a jar.

Keeping Animals in Jars Temporarily

In general, any insect or other invertebrate captive can be kept alive in a jar much longer if you keep a wet (not dripping) paper towel in the jar with it. The paper towel should be crumpled but not balled up, so that the creature can crawl into its nooks and crannies. Most creatures that children collect in jars die of dehydration. The wet paper towel will keep them from losing moisture through their skins or exoskeletons.

Keeping Animals for More Than a Few Days

If you want to keep an animal longer than a few days, try to duplicate its natural habitat in an enclosure. If it was on a stem, put a stem of the same plant in the enclosure. If it was under a rock, put damp soil and a hiding place in the enclosure. If it was in a log, get a piece of rotting log for it. Damp soil and damp leaves or moss instead of a paper towel can help provide moisture in terraria, and at the same time, keep it looking natural. But many animals will need more water than that if you keep them longer than a day or two. Many tiny animals are accustomed to drinking dew drops, so spray the terrarium with a plant sprayer daily. Spray damp-skinned animals, such as amphibians, directly. Birds, mammals and possibly reptiles may drink water from a dish, but most other animals will not.

Most cold-blooded animals (anything but birds or mammals) can go for a week without food with no problem. After that you should let them go where you found them if you know they're not eating. Mammals and birds must eat every day.

Field guides often give information about what particular animals eat and in the introduction often have information about capture and setting up terraria. Most public libraries have an assortment of field guides for identifying animals.

Traps
Drop-Traps

A drop-trap or pit-fall-trap is a can or bucket sunken into the ground so that the top is level with the surface of the ground. It works best if it has a lid on it with a hole in the lid (see Figure 2.3a). The hole should be big enough to leave a lip about 1 inch (2.5 cm) in diameter around the top of the bucket. The lip or overhang keeps animals from crawling out.

The drop-traps I've used that have worked best were about 8 inches (20.3 cm) in diameter and 10 inches (25.4 cm) deep. If your drop-trap is big enough, keep a damp sponge in it to keep animals from dehydrating and from drowning. You can cover the drop-trap with a wood square held off the ground by four rocks to keep rain out (see Figure 2.3a). Some people like to bait drop-traps with food, but this isn't essential.

Smaller drop-traps made with jars or cans without lids can work too. Any trap must be checked every day, because many animals will die if left in a trap longer than a few hours. Moles and shrews may die from stress; amphibians and other animals may die of dehydration.

The success of the trap depends largely on where you put it. The most successful traps are near ponds. If a pond is not accessible, try to put it in an area where you think insects and other small animals are most likely to be, but close enough to your daily path that you'll check it every day even if that means putting it right next to your door. Put a tight-fitting lid on it when not in use.

Figure 2.3a — A drop-trap. This one is a coffee can with a hole cut in the plastic lid to create an overhang. You can cover it with a wood square held off the ground by four rocks to keep rain out.

Funnel Traps

A funnel trap is for flying insects. It consists of a closed container with one opening into which a funnel is fitted, so that the small end of the funnel extends into the interior of the container (see Figure 2.3b). There must be some sort of bait in the container. Bait can be fruit, meat or other food, or at night a flashlight. Flying insects that are attracted to light enter the container through the funnel and then can't get out. With food as bait you'll get mostly flies and flying beetles. A small piece of chicken liver or raw fish will attract a lot of big flies you can use to feed a big mantis. With a light as bait, you'll get moths as well as flying beetles and other insects seen on porches at night.

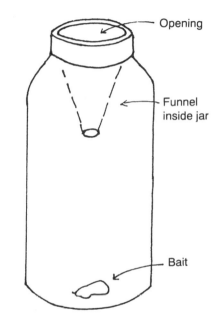

Opening

Funnel inside jar

Bait

Figure 2.3b — A funnel trap. This one is a canning jar with a two-piece metal lid.

Cages

Having an assortment of interesting cages can contribute to children's enjoyment of little wigglies. Petri dishes and fruitfly culture vials are useful for almost anything in the less-than-1-inch (2.5 cm) range (see Figures 2.3c and 2.3d). Both can be ordered from a biological supply company (see Appendix) or found at science hobby shops. Petri dishes come in various sizes, either glass or plastic. I prefer the 3 1/2-inch (9 cm) size in plastic. Fruitfly culture vials are about 4 inches (10.2 cm) tall, plastic and they come with foam rubber stoppers. Whenever I refer to vials in this book, I mean fruitfly culture vials. Children will enjoy using these two all-purpose containers to house anything and everything—a small slug from the bus, a roly-poly from under a brick, a tiny spider from the wall. Both petri dishes and fruitfly vials are clear for good visibility and shatter-proof (petri dishes will crack with

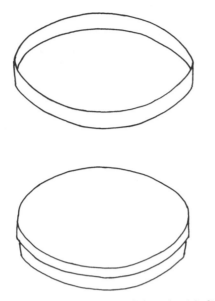

Figure 2.3c — Petri dish without lid and with lid. Clear plastic, about 3 1/2 inches (9 cm) in diameter.

Figure 2.3d — Fruitfly culture vial. About 4 inches tall.

Children can make a bug house by cutting a window in a milk carton and covering the window with window-screen mesh or plastic wrap. They can clip the top closed with a clothespin or paper clip, but a lot of small bugs can still escape from these milk carton cages.

A handy cage to have for flying or jumping insects is the *insect sleeve cage*, which is about the size and shape of a hat box (see Figure 2.3e). This can be ordered from a biological supply company (see Appendix). I have three and all three are always in use. You can stick your hand in through the cloth sleeve to feed and water the animals, without allowing any escapes. You can make one by cutting a circular hole in the side of a plastic bucket and stapling a sleeve around the opening of the hole. If you cover the top with plastic wrap, the animals can still breathe through the sleeve. Those you buy come with a removable mesh top, which I sometimes replace with plastic wrap. Insect sleeve cages have handles and are lightweight for easy transporting.

A terrarium is hard to move around, but is preferable to the insect sleeve cage in terms of visibility. (Animals in the insect sleeve cage must be viewed from above.) A terrarium is probably the better choice for animals that won't escape easily and don't need to be moved often.

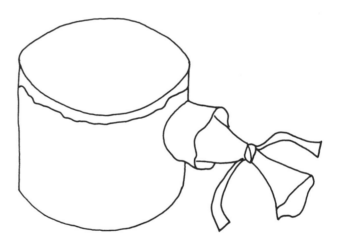

Figure 2.3e — Insect sleeve cage. The top is mesh with an elastic border. A hand can go into the cage through the cloth sleeve, which stays tied shut when not in use. The cage is about 1 foot (30.4 cm) in diameter.

pressure though), and they can be easily slipped into a pocket. A rubber band will keep the petri dish closed. Some children are more interested in the cage than the bug! But that's okay — scientists are sometimes the same way! Enjoying the paraphernalia is part of enjoying any job or hobby.

If you can provide one or two petri dishes and one or two empty vials and stoppers for each child, you'll be well prepared for many of the experiments in this book.

For animals too big for petri dishes or vials I use clear plastic peanut butter jars, the 1-quart or 1-liter size. A cloth lid secured with a rubber band over the top permits air flow.

Making a Small Pond

I'm talking about tiny ponds here, about six feet in length. Many animals will come to any body of water on their own. If you have some vegetation in the pond, aquatic beetles and bugs may fly in and lay eggs. Water striders and dragonflies may too. Frogs and toads and even salamanders may come if you're not located in town. Birds will come to drink and bathe. Mosquitos will almost certainly lay their eggs in your pond. The pond gets interesting faster, however, if you stock it with

Figure 2.4 — A bullfrog on its perch in the middle of a small homemade pond.

whatever you can catch with a net on the edge of a well-established pond. Animals that can't fly or can't live on land at all, which is most of the animals in a pond, have no other way to get there except a flood or as passengers on other animals.

What I've enjoyed most about the small pond in my backyard is the bullfrogs we've had as guests (see Figure 2.4). They all migrated to the pond on their own, although it's in a densely populated suburban neighborhood. Most of the frogs are rather timid, but one has become tame enough to take food from our hands. He's not very precise; sometimes he gets fingers too. The children usually move too fast to be able to feed him (it requires stealth), but they like watching me feed him.

Figure 2.5 — Alan dipping fish, tadpoles and more out of a homemade pond.

One of the best things about having a pond is the potential for exploration (see Figure 2.5). The children in my neighborhood spend hours fishing around in my pond — a pond about the size of two bathtubs — with pet store fish nets. They dump their captives into buckets or jars and compare counts. When it's time to go home, the creatures go back into the pond.

If you stock your pond well to begin with, it will maintain itself. We stock our pond once a year or so, because the fish wipe out some of the other animal populations. (You don't have to have fish.) To stock it we sweep a dip net through the weeds in a well-established pond and put whatever we catch in our pond (see Figure 2.6). You can order specific items from a biological supply company, if you prefer that to the luck of the draw. In the following sections I'll describe how you can make and stock your own pond.

Figure 2.6 — Justin catches tadpoles from a pond.

How to Make a Pond

Dig a depression in the ground the size you want the pond to be. Mine at home is about 1 foot (30.4 cm) deep, 7 feet (2 m) long and 60 inches (1.5 m) wide. Clear the bottom of the bed of all sharp stones or sticks that might puncture the liner. You can buy pond liners from a swimming pool supply store, but they are expensive. We use instead an inexpensive sheet of black plastic or a blue tarp from the local hardware store. Black plastic looks better but the blue tarp lasts longer. If you're careful not to puncture it, the black plastic will last a year or two; the blue tarp will last five years or more.

Before you put the water in, set up perches for the frogs that will hopefully migrate to your pond. Put them near the center so cats can't get to the frogs. We use an inverted flower pot with a flat rock or two on top that protrudes from the water.

Fill the pond with water from a garden hose. Let the water sit for a couple of days to give the chlorine a chance to vaporize before you add creatures. Don't trim the edges of the plastic or tarp to fit the pond until after you've put it in place and filled it with water. The weight of the water will push the liner into every little space and consequently pull the edges farther down than you might predict.

To change the liner, we transfer everything we can see in the pond to a metal tub or child's wading pool, with enough water to cover it. We then siphon the remaining water onto the ground with a length of garden hose. You can put a piece of mesh at the far end of the hose to catch creatures.

We've planted monkey grass (*Liriope*) around the pond's edge to hide the edge of the plastic sheet and give the pond a more natural look. Unfortunately, the monkey grass may shield cats from the frogs' view and give the cats an advantage. But as long as the frogs' perch is 2 feet (61 cm) or so from the edge, they seem to be safe.

You can use a child's wading pool, aboveground or sunk into the ground, instead of digging a pond. In that case all you have to do is make the perches and fill it.

How to Stock Your Pond

Plants

Get plants that can survive without being rooted, unless you want to put soil in the bottom of your pond, which there's no need to do. Most pet stores that carry fish will carry aquatic plants. You need only a small amount because they reproduce rapidly in the pond. We have *Elodea,* hornwort and duckweed. Duckweed floats and really adds to the charm of the pond, the other two stay submerged. *Elodea* is available from biological supply companies (see Appendix) and others may be too. Any unrooted aquatic plant you find in a pond or lake will do.

None of the animals I've suggested eat these plants. But algae will grow on the plants and some eat algae. The plants are mainly to provide habitat—places to hide and hang out.

Food for the Animals

If possible add to your pond about a bucketful of rotting vegetation from an established pond a couple of weeks before adding animals (see Animals section), to allow bacteria to build up. Bacteria and other microorganisms are the food source for some of the plankton and the mosquito larvae (group 1—see Animals section). The same bucketful of rotting vegetation will provide food for the scavengers (group 2). Your algae-eaters (snails and tadpoles, group 3) will need a few algae-covered leaves (the leaves feel slick) from an established pond. The predators (group 4) will eat all the other animals, except for the water striders, which eat insects that fall on the surface of the water.

Animals

All of the animals described below can be ordered from a biological supply company (see Appendix), at least at the time of this writing, except whirligig beetles and water striders. (Many are not available for order in mid-winter.) With persistence, all of them can be collected from a well-established pond. An aquatic dip net with a net opening of 1 foot (30.4 cm) works best. The net can be ordered from a biological supply company too or bought at a hobby shop. Choose a pond with some weeds around the edges. The animal life will be much more dense in weedy areas. Move the net quickly through the weeds, bumping it along the bottom as you go and then quickly pull it up. Invert the net over the mouth of your jar or bucket, emptying all the contents into the container even if you don't see any animals. Then move to a new area.

It's worth buying or checking out from the public library *Pond Life,* an inexpensive pocket-sized paperback in the Golden Field Guide series. Everything here—and more—is described and pictured more thoroughly there.

Following is a brief description of the most common and/or easily recognized pond animals. I've divided them into four groups: (1) those that eat microorganisms, (2) scavengers, those that eat dead plant and animal matter, (3) herbivores, those that eat living plants, algae in this case and (4) predators, those that eat other living animals.

You may want to stick to plankton, scavengers and herbivores. If you add predators, they may drastically reduce or eliminate populatons of other animals. At any rate, you don't need all of these animals. Those most likely to be caught in your tiny pond by the children are fish, tadpoles and snails. Frogs will leave if they are caught too often.

ANIMALS THAT EAT MICROORGANISMS

Mosquito larvae and pupae (see Figure 2.7). These are the aquatic stages of the mosquito life cycle. The larva is 3/16 inch (4.8 mm) long or less, caterpillar-shaped and hangs from the surface of the water. When disturbed, it sinks rapidly, jerking erratically. The pupae look and behave similarly except that the head and thorax are fused to look like a big knob on one end of the body. The larvae eat microscopic organisms.

Plankton. Plankton are small aquatic plants and animals about the size of the period at the end of this sentence. Many are crustaceans. I use a plankton net from a biological supply

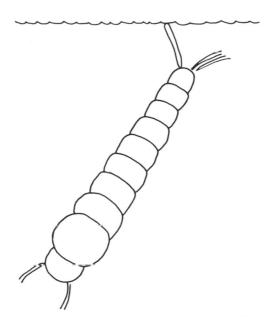

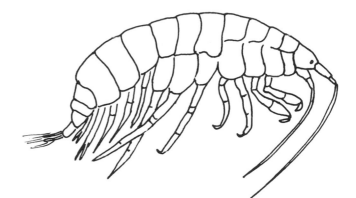

Figure 2.8a — Amphipod. They are 1/8 to 3/8 inch (.3–1 cm) in length.

Figure 2.7 — Mosquito larva. They are between 1/8 and 1/2 inch (.3–1.3 cm) in length. Most are about 3/16 inch (4.8 mm). The pupae are similar but shorter, with a huge knob at the head end of the body.

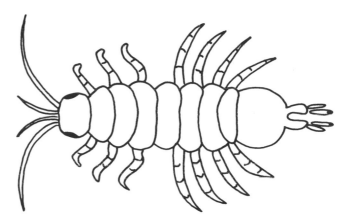

Figure 2.8b — Aquatic isopod. They are 3/16 to 7/8 inch (.5–2.1 cm) in length. The one shown is a female. Males look slightly different, but both are flattened from top to bottom.

company to catch plankton, but it's relatively expensive, so you probably don't want to buy one for infrequent use. A plankton net is made of very fine mesh, cloth really, that water can pass through but plankton cannot. You can improvise by making some sort of circular or square rim (of clothesline wire or wood or plastic), then fastening the edges of a large piece of cloth around the rim to make a deep bowl. Pour buckets of pond water through the cloth bowl slowly. After each pour, invert your "bowl" into a collecting container with some pond water in it. You may have to experiment a little to find a cloth that lets water through quickly.

You can, of course, just take a bucket of pond water with a few plankton to your new pond. They will reproduce quickly if you leave them in the pond for awhile before adding any predators. They'll reproduce faster if you've added rotting vegetation well in advance to allow bacteria to build up for the plankton to eat. But you can get a lot of plankton quickly and with less lugging if you concentrate them first with the net.

Some plankton have chlorophyll and make their own food by photosynthesis like plants. They are called phytoplankton. Some plankton consume other organisms and are called zooplankton. You can order from a biological supply company assorted unidentified plankton or three particular types of zooplankton: ostracods, copepods and *Daphnia*, all of which are tiny crustaceans.

Figure 2.8c — Aquatic planarian. They are 1/2 inch (1.3 cm) or less in length and dark brown in color.

Scavengers (see Figure 2.8)

Amphipods. Amphipods resemble tiny shrimp, usually 1/8 to 3/8 inch (.3–1 cm) long, with legs that project downward. Their bodies are somewhat flattened from side to side. They

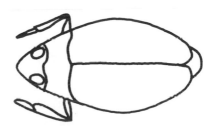

Figure 2.8d — Whirligig beetle. They are about 1/2 inch (1.3 cm) in length. Their middle and hind legs are short and flattened for swimming. They can be distinguished from similar insects by the fact that they live in groups, whirling around on the surface. Each eye is divided into two parts so they can see underwater and above water at the same time.

are common on pond bottoms, so you have to bump the net along the bottom to get them. They scuttle backward like crayfish, and in late winter many are bulging with pink egg sacs. The smallest ones are almost invisible in the bottom of a net, except for their movement.

Isopods. Aquatic isopods resemble roly-polies (pill bugs) somewhat, because roly-polies are terrestrial isopods. The aquatic isopods are between 3/16 and 7/8 inch (.5 cm–2.1 cm) in length. They can be distinguished from amphipods in that their bodies are flattened from top to bottom, as though a finger from above flattened them against a table. Also their legs stick out sideways rather than downward. They are less common in ponds than are amphipods.

Both isopods and amphipods are mainly scavengers, which means they eat dead animal and plant material. Both are crustaceans.

Aquatic planarians. Aquatic planarians are very small flatworms, usually about 1/2 inch (1.3 cm) or less in length. They are related to the land planarians. The aquatic planarians are found in shallow water, usually under objects or plant debris. They can be considered scavengers because they eat dead animal matter, but they also eat very small living animals. Ditches and ponds can be "baited" for planarians with small pieces of raw beef. After fifteen minutes to twenty-four hours, examine the meat and shake any planarians off into a dish of pond water. In a dish they can be fed a tiny (pinhead size) bit of yolk from a hard-boiled egg, a drop of blood or a tiny piece of meat. Don't let the food rot in the water.

I have caught planarians with bait, but I've been equally successful at catching them just by examining the undersides of plant debris or by netting. They can be hard to recognize the first time. When disturbed or removed from water they retract into a small gray blob, but will stretch out again when placed in still water.

Whirligig beetles (Family Gyrinidae). Whirligigs are found in groups, usually on the surface of ponds. They glide around each other or float quietly. When disturbed they move fast, but can be caught with a net. Adults are about 1/2 inch (1.3 cm) in length and are considered scavengers, although they also eat live insects that fall on the surface of the water. They cannot be ordered.

HERBIVORES (see Figure 2.9)
Aquatic snails. Aquatic snails are abundant on vegetation in ponds. If you get weeds, you'll probably get snails too. Their eggs look like a small flattened mass of clear jelly on submerged leaves, easily visible in warm weather. Snails eat the coating of living algae that covers most underwater surfaces and sometimes dead material.

Tadpoles. These can be caught by sweeping a net through the weeds at a pond's edge, as can most of the above. (See Chapter

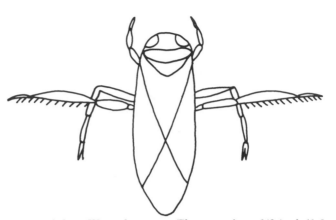

Figure 2.9a — Water boatman. They are about 1/2 inch (1.3 cm) long. The hind legs are flattened for swimming. The front legs are often not visible from above.

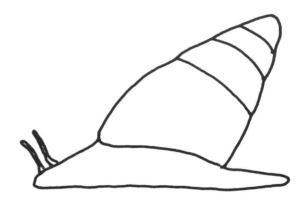

Figure 2.9b — Aquatic snail. This one is about 1/2 inch (1.3 cm) in length.

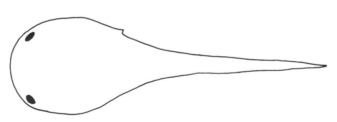

Figure 2.9c — Tadpole. They range in size from 3/8 to 4 inches (1–10.2 cm). Tadpoles have a spoutlike opening on the side for breathing, called the spiracle.

8 for more information on catching tadpoles.) Most tadpoles eat the thin film of algae that covers submerged objects.

Water boatmen (Family Corixidae). These insects resemble beetles somewhat but are really "true bugs" or hemipterans. Most are about 1/2 inch (1.3 cm) long. Water boatmen have one pair of long oarlike legs and two shorter pairs. They are herbivores or scavengers and do not bite. They can be caught by sweeping a net through aquatic vegetation. Adults fly and may come to the pond on their own.

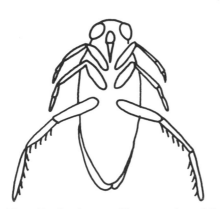

Figure 2.10a — Backswimmer. Most are about 1/2 inch (1.3 cm) long or shorter. They can be recognized by the fact that they swim on their backs, belly up. The back is keeled like the bottom of a boat. Their hind legs are much longer than their middle and front legs.

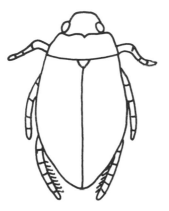

Figure 2.10b — Diving beetle. They are about 1/2 inch (1.3 cm) in length. They often hang head down from the surface of the water, with the tip of the abdomen out of the water. They have long "hair" on the hind legs for swimming underwater.

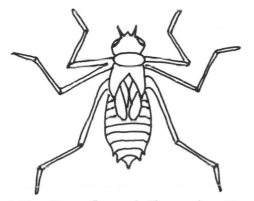

Figure 2.10c — Dragonfly nymph. They are from 1/2 to 1 3/4 inches (1.3–4.4 cm) in length, depending on species and age.

PREDATORS (see Figure 2.10)

Backswimmers (Family Notonectidae). Backswimmers are aquatic insects that may be mistaken for beetles, but are, like the water boatmen, really in the order of "true bugs" (*Hemiptera*). They range in length from 3/16 to 5/8 inch (.5–1.5 cm) and have one pair of long oarlike legs plus four shorter legs. They swim upside down, underwater and rest upside down at the surface, which makes them easy to recognize. They prey on small fish, other aquatic insects and small tadpoles. They have a painful, stinglike bite.

Diving beetles (Family Dytiscidae). These beetles are predatory as adults and as larvae, eating small fish, other aquatic insects, snails and tadpoles. The adults are 3/8 to 1 1/2 inches (1–3.8 cm) in length (depending on the species) and are found in ponds with aquatic vegetation. They can be easily collected by sweeping a net over the pond bottom. Their legs are modified for swimming underwater, although some do leave the water and fly. A lamp near water at night will sometimes attract them. They eat tadpoles, fish, dragonfly larvae, etc., but will also eat cooked or raw meat. They may bite, but probably not painfully. Adults fly and are attracted to light. They may come to the pond on their own.

Dragonfly nymphs (Order Odonata). Dragonflies are large, handsomely colored insects that are usually found flying over bodies of water. Their young, called nymphs, live in water on submerged vegetation or on the bottoms of ponds or ditches. They range in length from 1/2 to 1 3/4 inches (1.3–4.4 cm), and are not very attractive creatures. All are predatory. I've kept them in jars on occasion and have watched them eat tadpoles, salamander larvae, other aquatic insects and small fish. I don't catch them as predictably as snails or amphipods but with persistence they can be caught by sweeping a net through aquatic vegetation. They may bite, but the bite is a pinch not a sting.

Fish. I use *Gambusia*, commonly called mosquito fish, which are quite small — 1/2 to 1 inch (1.3–2.5 cm) and can be ordered from a biological supply company (see Appendix). They are also common in ponds. You can catch tiny fish along the margin of any sizable pond or lake by sweeping a net through weeds along the pond's margins. Look in an area that offers the fish protection — a shallow area with weeds in the water is ideal. Small fish stay away from open areas to avoid being eaten by birds and bigger fish.

Mosquito fish are predatory, but will also learn to eat commercial fish food after a week in captivity with nothing else to eat. Of course, the fish you catch may not be predatory. Most fish reproduce rapidly, and if they are predatory can substantially alter the species composition of your pond, so you may want to add fish after you've explored the other species, or not at all. Read the experiments before making that decision. Mosquito fish do help control or eliminate mosquito larvae, which is a plus.

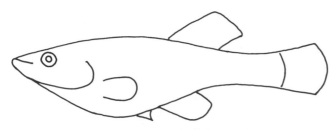

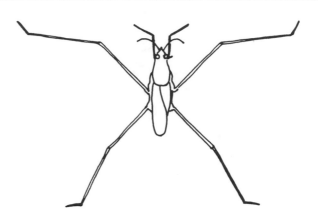

Figure 2.10d — Mosquito fish or Gambusia. *They are about 2 inches (5 cm) long when mature, but most caught in nature are between 1/2 to 1 inch (1.3–2.5 cm).*

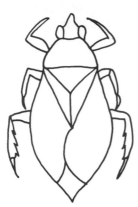

Figure 2.10f — Water strider. Adults are about 4/5 inch (2 cm) long. They skate on top of the water, with the ends of their legs resting on the surface tension and their bodies suspended above the water.

Figure 2.10e — Giant water bug. Adults are 1 to 2 inches (2.5–5 cm) in length, although those ordered from biological supply companies are often nymphs and are smaller.

Giant water bugs (Family Belostomatidae). These are large bugs at 1 to 2 inches (2.5–5 cm) long. They are hemipterans. Like the water boatmen and the backswimmers, the giant water bugs resemble beetles somewhat. The hind legs are flattened for swimming. They're found in aquatic vegetation and prey upon other insects, tadpoles, fish and small frogs. Adults fly and may come to the pond on their own. They have a painful, stinglike bite.

Water striders (Family Gerridae). These insects will probably arrive at your pond without your help. They are also in the group of "true bugs" (Hemiptera) and are predatory, but look nothing like beetles. They have frail-looking bodies and long thin legs. Adults are about 4/5 inch (2 cm) long. Water striders eat insects that fall on the surface and will not affect the density of pond organisms. They cannot be ordered.

See Chapter 9 for activities and experiments involving these pond animals in the classroom.

CREATURES FOUND IN AND UNDER LOGS

CHAPTER 3

Roly-Poly or Pill Bug Science

Introduction

Roly-polies' or pill bugs' claim to fame is the ability to roll into a tight little ball when disturbed. Both common names derive from this talent. The rolling up behavior alone is enough to charm most children.

Roly-polies are commonly assumed to be insects but are actually crustaceans. Because they have descended from aquatic animals, their bodies are not designed to retain water very well. This chapter describes experiments to show how roly-polies reduce their water loss behaviorally. It also describes how to maintain a thriving population of roly-polies in a container indefinitely for exploration.

After you've done the experiments in this chapter and in Chapters 4, 5 and 6, refer to the table in Figure 1 in the Postscript, which provides a comparison of the results for the experiments in these chapters. Figure 2 in the Postscript is a blank table that can be filled out with the results of your experiments, for comparison.

Materials

1. Roly-polies or sow bugs. (Sow bugs are similar but don't roll up.) These can be found easily under stones or logs, or can be ordered (see Appendix).
2. Petri dishes and lids. Three-and-one-half-inch (9 cm) diameter dishes work well. These can be bought at a science hobby shop or ordered by mail (see Appendix). One dish per child or per group is enough. Kitchen saucers with plastic wrap lids will do as well.
3. Filter paper or paper towel circles. You need one sheet per dish, the same diameter as the dish.
4. One small apple or potato chunk — approximately 1/3 inch (.8 cm) square — for each dish.
5. Enough sand to fill half of each dish for Experiment 1.
6. A sheet of dark paper (construction paper works well) for every two dishes for Experiment 2.

7. Two fruitfly vials (see Chapter 14) or Play-Doh or something else for making crevices or tunnels for Experiment 4.
8. Fabrics, paper, soil, etc., for offering different textures for Experiment 5. You'll need a container larger than a petri dish if you use vials to make tunnels.
9. Cups to hold roly-polies while experimental conditions in the dish are being altered.

Background Information

My four-year-old son loves to find roly-polies around the edges of the sidewalk and show them to anyone who'll look. He thinks there's something magical about them because of the way they roll into balls. Roly-polies are one of the easiest animals in this book to find, so most children will be familiar with them. On log-flipping expeditions, they are one of the first animals to be grabbed because they look so harmless.

Rolling into a ball is the pill bug's only way of protecting itself from predators (see Figure 3.1). I've watched praying mantises try to eat them and fail because

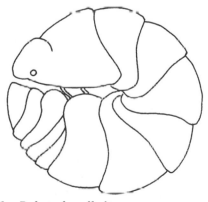

Figure 3.1 — Roly-poly rolled up.

their jaws apparently couldn't penetrate the rolled up armor. *Armadillidium* is the genus name of the common roly-poly in my area, and that seems appropriate. The rolling up is interesting, but not nearly as interesting to me as the array of behaviors that roly-polies have evolved to cope with the problem of dehydration.

Dehydration

Life began in the ocean, and so the life processes that keep us all alive developed in a watery environment. All living cells are full of water that is essential to their functioning. Because air has a drying effect, keeping cells full of water is one of the major challenges of land animals. Insects were among the first invaders of land, so they have had time to become finely tuned for life on land. They've evolved a number of physiological adaptations for preserving their bodies' water content. And insects have consequently invaded every corner of the earth, including the driest deserts. Efficiency of water conservation is not the only reason insects have been so successful, but it's one of them.

Roly-polies are not insects, but crustaceans. Most crustaceans (crabs, lobsters, crayfish, etc.) are aquatic. The roly-polies' move onto land has been recent, in evolutionary time, so they have not had time to evolve the complex physiological adaptations to a dry environment that insects have — adaptations that involve the respiratory system, excretory system and more. For example, insects breathe by means of a system of internal tubules that run throughout the body. The tubules can be closed to reduce water loss. In contrast, roly-polies have gill-like breathing structures that must stay moist and lose a lot of water by evaporation. Insects also have a waxy covering that reduces water loss through the skin. Roly-polies lack this waxy cuticle and constantly lose water through the skin, especially when the humidity is low. In the animal kingdom, behavior is often the first line of adaptation to a new environment. Since roly-polies lack physiological adaptations for conserving water, they compensate with behavioral adaptations. That is the subject of most of the experiments I do with roly-polies, which show how roly-polies cope with one of the major challenges of living on land.

How to Get and Keep Roly-Polies

Roly-polies are abundant in most areas of the United States. I find dozens when I look under the edges of the black plastic liner to my tiny backyard pond. I find them under bricks, under stones, under logs, under leaves, in the cracks between the cement porch and the brick wall of my house or under a sheet of black plastic over my compost pile. I can collect fifty in a half-hour without leaving my yard. I find sow bugs, which look similar but don't roll up,

in the same places. They are also crustaceans, though, and their behavior is similar, so they'll do.

Keeping a thriving population in captivity is even easier than finding them. I keep them in a plastic rectangular food-storage container about 10 inches (25.4 cm) long, with a floor of 1 inch (2.5 cm) of damp sand. I also keep some in large margarine containers with damp soil. A damp piece of rotting log covers much of the surface of the sand. I throw in an apple core or slice of potato every week or so. They eat fruit as well as rotting plant material, fungi and seedlings. I use a plastic lid or wax paper and rubber band lid, with a few holes, to keep the dampness in. The roly-polies reproduce like crazy in the containers. They stay in all the nooks and crannies of the piece of wood, and many burrow under the sand. They live up to four years — I have oldsters as well as tiny youngsters. The young look like miniature adults (there is no larval stage), except they're lighter in color. As they age they darken to a brownish gray. Rummaging around in a container like this will keep a child entertained for quite a while. It seems to be teeming with life. I keep a few other rotten-log creatures in there to make it more amusing: crickets, millipedes or a few snails. I find them in the same places I find roly-polies.

Field Hunt

A class field hunt for roly-polies is fun and easy. Let each child take a milk carton or other container for captives. A group of five or so works well for me, if I'm flipping the logs and the children are looking for the insects. In addition to logs, flip over bricks, boards, rocks or anything. Look in cracks and crevices around sidewalks. Make the point that we should always leave logs, bricks, etc., in their original position so that the damp places will stay damp. Otherwise on the next field hunt, there'll be no critters left.

Roly-Polies at School
Getting Ready

I use petri dishes for most experiments with roly-polies, although any small flat plate will do. Whatever you use must have enough of a rim to contain sand and to support a (transparent) lid. The dishes, the animals and something to hold moisture are all you need to get started.

Observations and Activities

Before you do any experiments you can get the children involved by letting them set up their own dishes. Give each child or group a dish and a piece of filter paper or paper towel cut to fit the bottom of the dish. Let them moisten the paper with a spray bottle or by dripping water on it. Each dish will need a piece of apple or potato.

Children enjoy choosing their own roly-polies from the big container, and most will enjoy letting the roly-polies

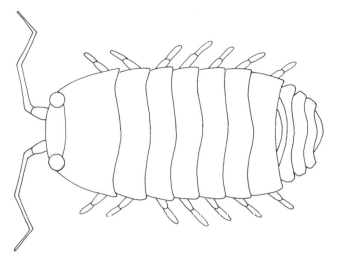

Figure 3.3 — Roly-poly at rest.

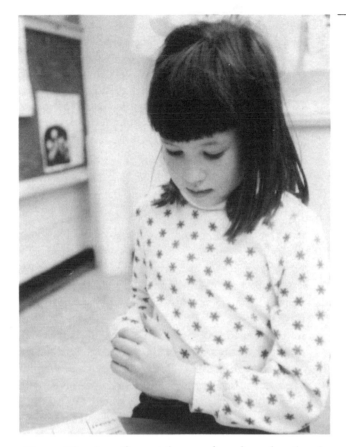

Figure 3.2 — Jennifer watches a roly-poly on her thumb.

crawl on their fingers (see Figure 3.2). Occasionally a child will have an aversion to touching them or even looking at them. My experience is that if I respect the feelings of reluctant children and don't try to coax them into looking or touching, they often will come around on their own. It helps to let them see my and others' enthusiasm, and to give praise for any positive interest they may have. Tiffany, the little girl I described in the Introduction, was absolutely revolted by roly-polies at first. But after a morning of picking through rotten logs outside, she was the most ardent enthusiast of all. They say reformed smokers are the most zealous anti-smokers, and I guess the same logic applies here.

After each child has a roly-poly settled in a container, ask them as a group to describe it to you. Then ask them to describe what the roly-poly is doing. Some will be running laps around the dish, some will be on the apple piece. If there are any blips along the edge of the filter paper, the roly-polies probably will crawl under it because they like to burrow.

While the children are watching is a good time to lead them to notice that roly-polies are not insects by asking them about the characteristics of an insect (six legs, three body parts) (see Figure 3.3). You can tell them then that rolies are crustaceans and ask them where other crustaceans live, like crayfish and lobsters and crabs. (Most of them live in the water.)

Roly-polies are attracted to dampness, and moving about until they've found a damp spot is one of the behaviors that helps them survive in a terrestrial environment, in spite of inefficient physiological mechanisms for water retention. If you ask children to describe where they found the roly-polies, they'll say under bricks, in cracks, under a sheet of plastic, etc. Ask them what it's like under those places. They're unlikely to say "damp" at first because they haven't yet learned to think in terms of what features of the hiding places might be important to an animal. They're more likely to say yucky, hard and dirty. Here's where you may need to lead them, by asking, "Was it damp or very dry?" Most will say damp. "Was it dark or light?" Dark. "Was it close and cramped, or roomy and airy?" Close and cramped. "So what kinds of places do you think roly-polies like?" Damp, dark, close and cramped (and maybe dirty, yucky and hard too!).

At some point you may want to talk to the children about what features of any place are important to an animal. Most little animals are interested only in staying alive, and what they look for are features most likely to keep them alive. What do they need to stay alive? Food, water and safety from predators. Aesthetics (yucky and dirty) are irrelevant to most animals. The risk of death is so great in small, vulnerable animals that avoiding death is really their only concern. A mouse or an insect that takes a stroll to find a cleaner and more attractive home is likely to get eaten or find itself with no home at all. Gorillas or lions, perhaps; their risk of death is much lower. They can afford to enjoy themselves, while a roly-poly cannot.

The first two experiments are designed to determine if the generalizations you and the children have made about what kinds of places roly-polies like are valid. Or is it something else that leads them to hang out under rocks? Maybe they're just hiding from predators or looking for supper.

Experiments

Remember that the hypotheses I give are just examples. Most are written in the "if ... then" format, but they don't have to be. Your hypotheses will be the predictions made by the class or a particular child. Your result for each experiment will be a statement of how your animals reacted to your experimental setup. Your conclusion is a statement of whether your prediction was confirmed or not. For each experiment, adding replicates increases your confidence in the validity of your conclusion, but they may be omitted if tedious for young children.

Experiment 1

You've gotten the children so far to notice that all the places they found the roly-polies were damp. Now it's just a short jump to get them to propose the experiment itself. You could start by saying something like, "You children have said you think roly-polies may be attracted to damp places. What kind of choice could we offer the roly-polies to see if that's really true?" Someone may eventually suggest that you make one side of the dish damp and one side dry.

You can let each child who's interested do the experiment in his or her own dish, or do it as a class with one or several dishes.

Question: Are roly-polies attracted to dampness?
Hypothesis: If we offer roly-polies a choice between damp and dry, they will choose damp.

Methods: There are several ways to make a damp side and a dry side in each dish. You can use two half-circles of paper, one damp and one dry for each dish. Or you can use sand, dry on one side and damp on the other. Because very young children can set it up themselves, I use damp sand on one side and bare plastic on the other. Damp sand packed hard holds its shape very well. Each child can scoop the sand into his or her own dish and shape it into one half of the dish. The filter paper and apple or potato chunk that was in his or her dish can be set aside in a cup with the roly poly while the sand is put in. I save yogurt cups for this purpose.

One problem with using damp sand on one side and bare dish on the other is that you can't be sure whether the roly-polies are reacting to the dampness or to the texture of the sand. They do like to burrow. To control for this, you really need to put dry sand on the other side. But then you have to deal with the problem of the dry sand wicking moisture from the damp sand. A strip of aluminum foil or plastic on edge between the two sides will help that. There's the same problem if you use wet and dry paper, but it can be solved with either a low barrier or a space to stop the wicking.

After the dish or dishes are set up, put a roly-poly in the center of each one. Put only one roly-poly in each dish because they influence one another's behavior when together. Make sure it can cross freely from one side to the other. Decide at the beginning how long you're going to wait to check the roly-polies' choice of sides. Give the roly-polies several hours to settle down. The more roly-polies you test, the greater will be your confidence in your results.

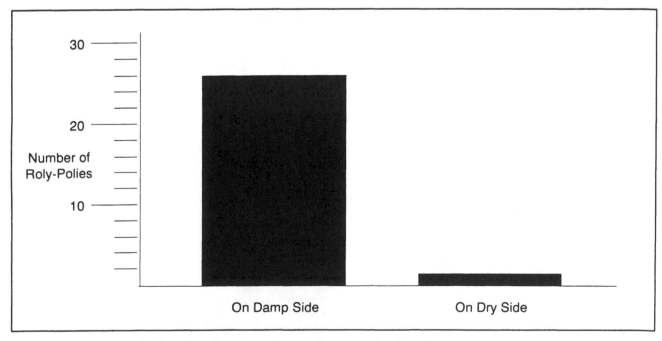

Figure 3.4 — Number of roly-polies choosing a damp substrate and a dry substrate.

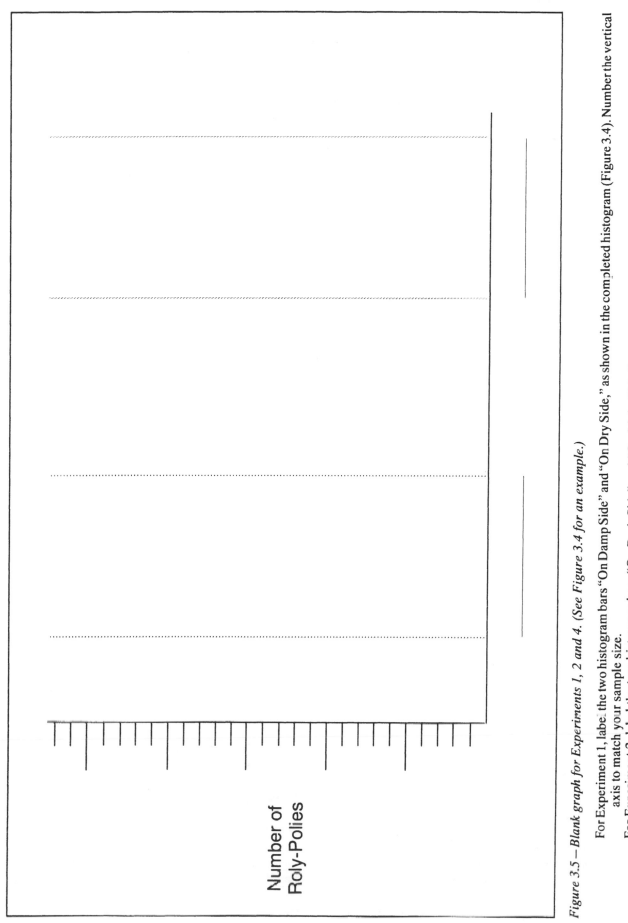

Number of
Roly-Polies

Figure 3.5 — Blank graph for Experiments 1, 2 and 4. (See Figure 3.4 for an example.)

For Experiment 1, label the two histogram bars "On Damp Side" and "On Dry Side," as shown in the completed histogram (Figure 3.4). Number the vertical axis to match your sample size.

For Experiment 2, label the two histogram bars "On Dark Side" and "On Light Side."

For Experiment 4, label the two histogram bars "In Closed Space" and "In Open Space."

Result: Your result is a description of your roly-poly's behavior during the experiment and its location (damp or dry) at the end of the experiment. You can use a histogram or bar graph to record your results (see Figure 3.4). A blank graph is provided for your results (see Figure 3.5).

Conclusion: If offered a choice between damp sand and dry plastic, roly-polies will almost always choose the damp sand. The prediction is confirmed.

Experiment 2

Approach this one the same way you approached Experiment 1, by getting the children to state their observations about where you find roly-polies. If someone mentions dark places, then ask what kind of choice you might offer to see if they really do prefer dark places.

Each child who's interested can do the experiment in his or her own dish, or you can do it as a class.

Question: Are roly-polies attracted to darkness?

Hypothesis: If we offer roly-polies a choice between light and dark, they will choose dark.

Methods: The bottom of the dish should be uniformly damp. Paper is probably preferable because the roly-poly may burrow in sand and thereby avoid the light. If you use dry paper you may get a quicker response to the light, but be aware that your roly-poly may dehydrate and die quickly without dampness in the dish.

I create darkness for the roly-poly by taping a piece of black construction paper over one half of the dish, enough to extend beyond the edge of the dish (see Figure 3.6). This shades the edge too, making the inside darker. Put the roly-poly in the middle of the dish, put the lid on and leave it for a predetermined interval of several hours. If your roly-polies show no preference try putting the dishes close to a light bulb.

Result: Your result is a statement of the behavior of the roly-polies in the dark/light dish. You can use a histogram or bar graph to record your results (see Figure 3.4). A blank graph is provided for your results (see Figure 3.5).

Conclusion: If offered a choice between light and dark, most roly-polies choose dark. The prediction here is usually confirmed.

There are, however, several species of roly-polies and sow bugs and some react to light differently than others.

It may not be obvious to a child that light, and the heat usually associated with it, can be drying. You may need to prompt this realization by asking what would happen to various items left out in the sun. Have they ever seen a dried up earthworm on the sidewalk? How does a grape become a raisin?

Figure 3.6 — Claire peeking at her roly-poly on the dark side of the petri dish in Experiment 2.

You can do an experiment to determine whether roly-polies have a preference for warmth or coolness, unrelated to lighting. You can heat and cool opposite ends of a tray by following the procedure described in Chapter 4, Experiment 2, for earthworms. Roly-polies and most other crawlies prefer the cool end.

Have you ever huddled against another person when it's cold? Or crouched into a ball with your arms crossed tightly against your chest? We do this instinctively to reduce our surface area when it's cold. By making contact with other warm skin over at least part of our body's surface, we reduce the amount of heat that radiates from our bodies.

Roly-polies are not concerned about loss of heat because they're not warm-blooded animals. But they do need to conserve moisture, and huddling together works the same way to reduce water loss. By making contact with other roly-polies or really by making contact with any surface, roly-polies can reduce the amount of surface area exposed to the drying effects of air.

Experiment 3

Question: Will roly-polies bunch to reduce water loss?

Hypothesis: Roly-polies will bunch, or huddle together, when in a dry environment.

Methods: You'll probably have to do this as a class, unless everyone has two dishes and several roly-polies. Set up one dish with a damp floor of sand or paper and another with a dry floor. Put several roly-polies (ten or so) into each dish. Wait for a predetermined interval (several hours) and then check their position. Are they in contact with each other (or very close) in either dish? If not, wait longer until the ones in the dry dish begin to dehydrate.

Result: Your result is a statement of how each group of roly-polies behaved in response to their dish.

Conclusion: Roly-polies in a dry dish will aggregate, or bunch, to reduce water loss, so the prediction is confirmed. Those in a damp dish may too, but not as much. Does it work? Does bunching reduce water loss? Children may find this unacceptably cruel, but one way to find out if bunching improves the survival of roly-polies is to compare the survival of several that are allowed to bunch to the survival of one in isolation. The dishes should be equally dry. If bunching helps reduce water loss, then the several roly-polies together should survive longer than the one in isolation, which will probably die pretty quickly in a dry dish.

Experiment 4

Moths fly toward a light source. In the study of animal behavior, any innate tendency to move toward or away from a particular kind of stimulus has a name. For example, the tendency to move toward light is called phototaxis. So moths are phototaxic. Movement away from light is photophobia. A tendency to movement toward heat, as in the dog tick, is thermotaxis. Roly-polies, in addition to being hydrotaxic (attracted to moisture) and usually photophobic (avoid bright light), have a third tendency with an odd name: thigmotaxis. A thigmotaxic animal will seek out a position where its body has contact with something besides air on all surfaces. One of the first things a class of first-graders noticed about their roly-polies in petri dishes, each with a damp piece of filter paper, was that many crawled under the filter paper if there was a wrinkle that made a small tunnel. Thigmotaxis could be responsible for that, although it was probably more humid under the paper too. Thigmotaxis is responsible for bunching behavior. If no other roly-polies are available, how else might roly-polies satisfy their thigmotaxic urges?

Question: If we offer a roly-poly a crevice or some other enclosed space, will the roly-poly seek out that spot? Is a roly-poly in a dry environment more likely to do so?

Hypothesis: A roly-poly in a dry environment will seek out a crevice, while one in a damp environment may not.

Methods: The children can volunteer their roly-polies for one of the two "treatments," damp and dry. In both types of dish, supply some sort of crevice the roly-polies can crawl into. You can make a trough of Play-Doh or clay or plastic, just wide enough for the roly-poly to get into, about 1 to 2 inches (2.5–5 cm) long. Leave it open at the top to be sure the attraction isn't darkness. Or, in a dish bigger than a petri dish, submerge a transparent fruitfly vial (see Chapter 14) horizontally

in damp sand, so that the protruding side is only 1/4 inch (.6 cm) off the sand. The inside of the vial should contain sand at the same level as outside the vial. This creates a long, low-roofed tunnel for the roly-poly, which is light inside, to rule out the effects of darkness. Set up another vial the same way in dry sand. Put one roly-poly in each dish and give them a predetermined amount of time to settle themselves (several hours). To add replicates, repeat the procedure with more individual roly-polies, one at a time. Do any roly-polies go in the crevice or the tunnel? Are those in the dry dish more likely to than those in the damp dish? Do the roly-polies in the tunnel (fruitfly vial) stay where the roof slopes into the sand, where the roof is low enough to touch their backs?

Result: Your result is a description of how the roly-polies responded to the setup in each dish. You can use a histogram or bar graph to record your results (see Figure 3.4). A blank graph is provided for your results (see Figure 3.5).

Conclusion: If we offer roly-polies a crevice or a tunnel in a dry environment, they'll go in. They are thigmotaxic. If we offer roly-polies a crevice or tunnel in a damp environment, they may go in but not as often. They show less thigmotaxis in dampness.

Experiment 5

Question: Do roly-polies prefer some textures over others? Do they prefer substrates that allow burrowing? Does humidity affect any preferences?

Hypothesis: Roly-polies prefer substrates that are not perfectly flat and smooth, but are bumpy and conform more to their bodies. They particularly like substrates into which they can burrow.

Methods: Offer the roly-polies a variety of substrates in pairs, two half-circles at a time in a petri dish. Offer damp choices and dry choices. You can try wax paper, unwaxed paper, wool, flannel, other fabrics, sand, soil, etc. The papers and fabrics may need to be taped down. Give the roly-polies time to settle down, and check their location. Can you make any generalizations?

Result: Your result is a description and tally of your roly-polies' choices.

Conclusion: Roly-polies tend to prefer irregular surfaces and avoid slick surfaces. They especially prefer substrates that allow burrowing. These preferences seem to be related to their thigmotaxis, and are less pronounced when humidity is high.

These experiments are all related. A table may help the students tie it all together. Figure 3.7 provides a sample table. Figure 3.8 supplies a blank table on which to record

Stimulus	Rolies' Choice		Effect of Choice on Rolies	
	Attraction	Avoidance	Drying	Keeping Damp
Dampness (Experiment 1)	✔			✔
Light (Experiment 2)		✔		✔
Heat (see Experiment 2, Chapter 4 for directions)		✔		✔
Other Rolies (Experiment 3)	✔			✔
Crevices (Experiment 4)	✔			✔
Rough Textures (Experiment 5)	✔			✔
Substances That Allow Burrowing (Experiment 5)	✔			✔

Figure 3.7 — Sample table summarizing the choices of the roly-polies.

your results. Your results may all show that rolies avoid the drying effect of air and heat any way that they can. Or you may have mixed results. Experiments don't always turn out the way you think they will, which is in itself a valuable lesson about how progress is made in scientific research. You may have a species that responds differently from most of the others — for example, roly-polies that don't respond negatively to light. The students can speculate about why you got the results you did (see Figure 3.9). They may conclude that we can't always explain our results, which is a fact of science.

It might be interesting to repeat one or all of these experiments with an insect that you know to be more tolerant of dry conditions, maybe a beetle or a small grasshopper. You may get some of the same results. My daughter compared the behavior of *Tenebrio* beetles (see Chapter 16) in dry dishes to that of roly-polies in dry dishes. To our surprise, she found that the beetles bunched too. We couldn't explain the results, but she won first prize for the second-grade science fair anyway just because she was the only one who did an experiment.

Figure 3.9 — Craig ponders the meaning of his observations, trying to tie it all together.

Stimulus	Rolies' Choice		Effect of Choice on Rolies	
	Attraction	Avoidance	Drying	Keeping Damp
Dampness (Experiment 1)				
Light (Experiment 2)				
Heat (See Experiment 2, Chapter 4 for directions)				
Other Rolies (Experiment 3)				
Crevices (Experiment 4)				
Rough Textures (Experiment 5)				
Substances That Allow Burrowing (Experiment 5)				

Figure 3.8 — Blank table on which to record your results.

Wiggly Earthworms

Introduction

Children love to hold slippery, slimy, wiggly worms, especially the big nightcrawlers (see Figure 4.1). Both older and younger children enjoy predicting the worms' preferences in terms of living conditions. Do the worms like heat or cold, dampness or dryness, light or dark? Earthworms can be tied into a study of soil and our dependence upon soil and plants. They have a tremendously beneficial effect on soil. Their tunnels aerate the soil and allow water to penetrate better. They mix the soil layers and increase the volume of soil. They improve soil texture and nutrient content. Several experiments explore these effects.

The maze (Experiment 9) is probably children's favorite exploration, other than just handling the worms. Can the worm find the right door?

After you have done the experiments in this chapter and Chapters 3, 5 and 6, refer to the table in Figure 1 in the Postscript, which provides a comparison of the results for the experiments in these chapters. Figure 2 in the Postscript is a blank table that can be filled out with the results of your experiments, for comparison.

Figure 4.1 — Felicia dangles a worm for inspection.

Materials

1. Earthworms can be bought at a fishing supply store, dug up at home or ordered from a biological supply company. Other types of worms are available for order too, for the sake of comparison.
2. A tray and paper towels for Experiments 1 to 5.
3. A heating pad and bowl of ice for Experiment 2.
4. A lamp, dark paper and a dish for Experiment 3.
5. A flashlight and red and blue (or other second color) cellophane for Experiment 4.
6. Dark loamy soil, like potting soil or good garden soil for maintaining the worms.
7. Experiments 5 and 6 require sandy soil and clay soil or other soil types in addition to your loamy garden soil.
8. A worm-viewing cage for Experiment 6 (see Figure 4.2).
9. A medium-sized jar and sand for Experiment 7 and several worm foods for Experiments 7 and 10.
10. Two potted plants for Experiment 8.
11. A Y-shaped tube for Experiment 9. You can order one from a biological supply company (see Appendix) or make one (see Figure 4.13).

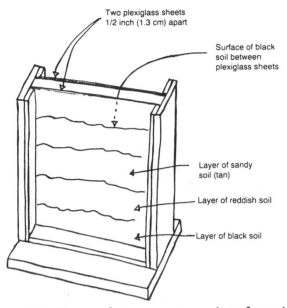

Two plexiglass sheets
1/2 inch (1.3 cm) apart

Surface of black
soil between
plexiglass sheets

Layer of sandy
soil (tan)

Layer of reddish soil

Layer of black soil

Figure 4.2 — Homemade transparent containers for seeing earthworms' tunnels.

Background Information

Earthworms in Relation to Other Worms

The word *worm* is used as sort of a catch-all term for any long and thin and more or less legless creature that isn't a snake. Caterpillars are often called worms although they're really larval butterflies or moths. There are three large groups or phyla of real worms, which are only distantly related to each other. One group is the flatworms, which includes tapeworms. They're all more or less flat and are not all parasitic like the tapeworms. Land planarians are flatworms that I find under rocks in my yard occasionally. They're 4 to 6 inches (10.2–15.2 cm) long and have triangular heads. I can catch aquatic planarians, about 3/8 inch (1 cm) long, by leaving a piece of raw meat in the few inches of water in a ditch behind my house. They look like a tiny black blot on the meat but will stretch out and swim around if you put them in a dish of pond water.

Another group or phylum is the roundworms. They're all round in cross-section and smooth-bodied. Some are parasitic, some are tiny and live in the soil (nematodes).

The third group, to which earthworms belong, is the segmented worms or annelids. They are round in cross-section too, but their bodies are obviously ringed, or segmented. This distinguishes them from the roundworms. (You can order representatives of any of these three groups of worms, dead or alive.)

Lots of people react to worms with disgust, and some of them are revolting, like the intestinal parasites. But earthworms are completely harmless and clean, fascinating to children and tremendously beneficial to humans through their effect on soil (see Earthworms and Soil section). I find that very few children, if any, react to

worms with real distaste. Many are cautious and only want to look at first. They look to the teacher and others for cues as to how to react. With calm encouragement, but not pressure, most will want to hold the worms within five minutes.

I've used worms with younger children (kindergarten and first grade) as an introduction to a creature very different from ourselves and as an exploration of how its differences suit it. I like the children to see that even an animal as base as a worm (no head, no legs, no apparent body parts of any kind) can have preferences and make decisions.

Earthworms and Soil

Earthworms can easily be tied into a study of the environment because they greatly improve the quality of the soil. There are a number of ways to explore this effect through experiments. All earthworms create tunnels underground. Their tunnels help air and water to penetrate the soil, which is helpful to plant roots. Their tunneling also mixes the different layers of soil, bringing minerals up from lower layers and taking the organic top layer down below.

Most important perhaps is that worms ingest dead leaves and other organic matter and convert it into nutrient-rich castings, which vastly improve both the texture and the nutrient content of the soil. Soil that is rich in castings holds together better and holds water better. The children can see the effects of the worms on the soil and how plants react to the improved soil.

I think it's good for children to see how humans can benefit from the normal activities of a creature as lowly as the worm. It gives them a feeling of the interconnectedness of all creatures. Even our most advanced technology can't do for our soil and ultimately our vegetables what the little earthworm can do. By aerating the soil, mixing layers and converting leaves into nutrient-rich castings, earthworms do more to improve the soil than all other soil animals put together, and soil is full of tiny organisms. We need worms!

The Body Parts of a Worm

The external anatomy of a worm is quite simple (see Figure 4.3). There is a "head" end, with a mouth at the tip. About one-third of the way from the head to the tail is a smooth band around the body, called the clitellum. I identify the head end by finding the clitellum, since it is closer to the head. The segments of the body are conspicuous. A segment is the space between two rings.

If you rub the worm gently between two fingers from the tail end toward the head, it will feel rough. You're feeling tiny hairlike projections called setae (pronounced see-tee) that help the worm hold on to the sides of the burrow.

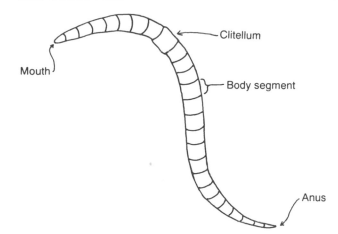

Figure 4.3 — External anatomy of the earthworm. Length varies tremendously with species.

Inside its body the worm has a long tubular digestive tract. Normally a worm likes leaves and similar organic matter to eat, but it can eat its way through soil that is too dense to push through. The leaves or soil are ground up in a muscular part of the digestive tube called the gizzard. The undigested part passes out the tail end as castings. The castings are technically feces but are not decayed or foul-smelling. The castings are essentially just enriched soil.

A Worm's Unique Muscle System

The muscles of a worm are interesting for children who are old enough to understand that animals move by muscle action and that a muscle shortens when it contracts. If you handle a worm or watch it move across the table top, it's obvious that the worm can draw its body up to become short and thick. It does this by contracting the muscles that run the entire length of the body, under the skin. They're called longitudinal muscles.

But the worm can also extend its body to become long and thin. It does this by contracting muscles that encircle its body from head to tail. They are called circular muscles. The worm moves by contracting these two sets of muscles alternately, in different parts of its body. For example, it can extend the head end by contracting the circular muscles in the head end. (This increases the pressure in the fluid-filled body cavity, thus causing the squeezed segments to lengthen.) Then while resting the head end on the ground, it draws the tail end up to meet the head end by contracting the longitudinal muscles in the tail end.

This squeeze–extend type of movement is very different from the movement of a snake, which lacks the sets of opposing muscles. Snakes move in several different ways, but generally by pushing against the ground with curves in their bodies. A snake's body does not change in either length or circumference as the worm's does. A movie of a snake or, better yet, a live snake would help children see the difference. Describing the locomotion of an earthworm in writing is a useful exercise in observation for even grown students. I find that very young children (five to six years old) have difficulty comprehending it.

An inchworm (really the caterpillar of a *Geometer* moth) has a third type of movement of a very similar body shape. In some areas small green inchworms are very common and are found under oak trees. Look on outside walls or any structure off the ground under oak trees. Inchworms move by hitching up the rear to catch up with the front, but like snakes, they cannot change the length or circumference of their bodies.

Earthworm Gender — They're Hermaphrodites!

Each earthworm is both a male and a female; that is, each individual produces both egg and sperm. Being both sexes at once is called being a hermaphrodite and is not uncommon in the animal kingdom among animals without backbones. Hermaphroditism is an advantage to worms because they are solitary and burrowing and don't meet other worms very often. If the sexes were separate, as in humans, a female worm looking for a mate would have only a fifty-fifty chance that the next worm she encountered would be a male. To mate, the worms align their bodies and exchange sperm simultaneously. Then each forms a gelatinous ring with its clitellum, the smooth band around the body near the head end. As it slips this ring off the end of its body, the eggs are deposited in it and the ring closes to become an egg sac.

How to Get and Keep Worms

In North Carolina I can dig up worms outside even in the middle of the winter, but in areas where the ground freezes they're accessible only part of the year. Worms prefer rich, dark, loamy soil. I have my best success in a garden or under leaf litter in the woods when the soil is damp, although roots get in the way in the woods. If you dig with a shovel you will chop many of your worms in half, fatally. A pitchfork causes fewer injuries. Or you can dig up a big hunk of soil with the shovel and break it apart with your fingers.

If you live in an area where fishing is a possibility, someone will probably have worms for sale. In the phone book, I can find worm suppliers listed in the Yellow Pages under "fish bait" and "fisherman supplies." The local tackle shop sells three kinds of worms: redworms, Georgia wigglers and night crawlers. These are different species of earthworms, varying in size from 2 to about 7 inches (5–17.8 cm) for a fully extended night crawler. Children find the night crawlers most interesting, although any will do. Ask the supplier which type lives longest in captivity and for tips on how to maintain it.

To maintain worms, a container as small as a 2-quart (2 l) tub will do (see Figure 4.4), although the bigger the

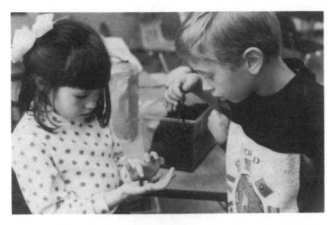

Figure 4.4 — Craig finds Jennifer's worm more interesting than his own. Note long-term worm storage container in background.

better. Get the lightest, fluffiest soil you can find. Ideally it should be black or dark brown and contain lots of organic matter. Potting soil, good garden soil or the top layer of forest soil is fine. Before you put the worms in, mix bits of decaying leaves (not oak) with the soil. Maple leaves are good. The leaves should be decayed enough to be in small pieces. The soil should be damp but not sodden. Add more leaf litter and spray well with a plant sprayer every few days. My worms seem to love used coffee grounds, which I feed them every few days by mixing the grounds slightly into the surface of the soil. You can add other foods as desired instead of or in addition to leaves (see Experiment 10 for suggestions).

Night crawlers kept in a small container will convert much of the soil to castings within a few weeks or less. Smaller worms will too, but not as quickly. The soil will look lumpy and compacted and less fluffy when it is all castings. Before this happens put in fresh soil and leaves. If any worms become injured by children, take them out. A dead and rotting worm smells awful.

Worms at School
Getting Ready

There are so many different things to do with worms — the simplest require no preparation other than clearing off a table or a desk for everyone to gather around.

Observations and Activities

The most fun thing I've done with worms has been taking about ten night crawlers to a kindergarten class. We put two tables together so that about thirteen children can gather around at once, and I take half the class at a time. I put three or four night crawlers on the table and ask the children to watch, not to touch. Night crawlers will leave castings on the table, so be sure to discuss them in advance.

Tell the children that the worms will be leaving little piles of "processed soil" behind them, which is one reason the worms are so good for gardens. Tell them the processed soil is called castings and contains nutrients that plants need. You may want to explain that some people think worms are "icky" because they just don't know much about them.

Here is a list of questions that will help the children observe the worms carefully, many of which are from Molly McLaughlin's excellent book *Earthworms, Dirt, and Rotten Leaves*. How does the worm move? Encourage the children to notice how it stretches its body out, then pulls it up. It gets long and thin, then short and fat. Does the worm have legs? eyes? ears? nose? mouth? stripes or rings? Is there a difference between head and tail (point out the clitellum toward the head end)? Is there a difference between top and bottom (it may be darker on top or may not)? How does its skin feel? Do you think the worm has a skeleton? What does the worm do when it comes to a block? To a pile of soil? What does it do when you hold it? Who has ever found a worm outside? Where was it? What shape is a worm? Why is this a good shape for it? Does it need legs or sense organs? Why not? Do we? Why?

Eventually, or maybe immediately, one or a few children will ask to hold a worm.

Figure 4.5 — Michael gives the night crawler the one-finger touch to start.

Figure 4.6—Jolyn's not squeamish in the least!

Those who are wary may be comfortable just touching at first (see Figure 4.5). My experience is that once one or two children have held the worms, almost everyone feels encouraged to try. They may soon be wrapping worms around their ears and draping worms over their noses with glee (see Figure 4.6)!

Experiments

Remember that the hypotheses I give are just examples. Most are written in the "if … then" format, but they don't have to be. Your hypotheses will be the predictions made by the class or a particular child. Your result for each experiment will be a statement of how your animals reacted to your experimental setup. Your conclusion is a statement of whether your prediction was confirmed or not. For each experiment, adding replicates increases your confidence in the validity of your conclusion, but they may be omitted if tedious for young children.

Experiments 1 to 4 explore the types of living conditions that worms prefer.

Experiment 1

Question: Do worms prefer damp or dry conditions?
Hypothesis: We think worms prefer dampness.
Methods: I use a 9-by-13-inch (22.9 x 33 cm) baking pan, but any sort of tray will do. Put a damp paper towel in one end of the tray and a dry paper towel in the other end, so that they almost meet in the middle. Put the worm into the middle. Wait until the worm has settled down on one side or the other and record the results. Repeat several times with the same worm or other worms. You can also do this experiment by setting the worms down between a pile of damp soil and a pile of dry soil in a box. You can record your results on a table (see Figure 4.7 for an example). Figure 4.8 provides a blank table on which to record your results. You can also record your results as a histogram in Figure 4.9. Figure 3.4 provides an example of a completed histogram. A final option is to create a line graph (see Figure 4.10 for an example). Figure 4.11 provides a blank graph on which to plot your data.

Result: Your result is a statement of your worms' choices.

Conclusion: The prediction is confirmed. In my experience, earthworms definitely prefer dampness. They will burrow under the damp paper towel if there are any blips along the edge of it. Worms breathe through their skin, and it must stay damp for them to breathe, so they are very vulnerable to dehydration.

Experiment 2

Question: Do worms prefer warmth or cold?
Hypothesis: We think worms prefer warmth.
Methods: I use a rectangular metal cookie sheet, about 16 inches (40.6 cm) long. I put a heating pad set on "high" (cloth cover removed) under one end of the cookie sheet and an ice tray full of ice cubes under the other end. Make the cookie sheet level. Put a layer of damp paper towels flat over the surface of the cookie sheet so the worms won't try to escape in search of moisture.

You need to allow a half-hour or more for the cookie sheet to change temperature before starting.

Have a child place one or more worms in the middle of the cookie sheet. Allow the worms a half-hour or more to settle down.

Result: Your result is a statement of your worms' choices. You can record your results on a table (see Figure 4.7 for an example). Figure 4.8 provides a blank table on which to record your results. You can also record your results as a histogram in Figure 4.9. Figure 3.4 provides an example of a completed histogram. A final option is to create a line graph (see Figure 4.10 for an example). Figure 4.11 provides a blank graph on which to plot your data.

Conclusion: The prediction is not accepted. In my experience, most worms come to rest toward the cooler end of the cookie sheet.

Experiment 3

Question: Do worms prefer darkness or light?

Hypothesis: We think the worms prefer light. (Children are usually anthropomorphic and predict "light" unless they've learned from other chapters to consider what it's like in the places the animal is found naturally.)

Methods: Any dish big enough for the worm to move around in will do for this experiment. For small worms I use petri dishes, which you can order (see Appendix). Line the dish with a damp paper towel. (If the worms insist on hiding under the paper towel, take it out.) Cover half the dish with black construction paper or anything opaque. If you're using a petri dish, the children can tape the edge of the paper to the midline of the lid. If you're using a kitchen dish, just lay the paper across to cover half of the dish. The paper must be low enough to make that side pretty dark. Put the worm in the middle of the dish. Wait until the worm has stopped investigating and has chosen a spot.

Result: Your result is a statement of your worms' choices and any relevant observations. You can record your results on a table (see Figure 4.7 for an example). Figure 4.8 provides a blank table on which to record your results. You can also record your results as a histogram in Figure 4.9. Figure 3.4 provides an example of a completed histogram. A final option is to create a line graph (see Figure 4.10 for an example). Figure 4.11 provides a blank graph on which to plot your data.

Conclusion: In my experience, most worms eventually settle in the darkness.

Help the children relate this to where the worms are found. This preference may be puzzling to the children if it occurs to anyone that worms have no eyes. How can a worm tell light from dark? Worms have light-sensitive cells in the skin on their heads. They are not able to form an image as our eyes do but they can detect light. It is to a worm's advantage to be able to detect light because they are nocturnal to avoid predators. They come out of their burrows only at night to get leaf fragments and other edibles, so they need to be able to tell when it's night. Why do worms need to be able to avoid predators? A worm out of its burrow is completely defenseless! It can't bite, can't sting, fly or jump. Their coloration doesn't disguise them, they're not spiny or tough or hard to eat and they don't taste bad. Many animals like to eat worms. Have the children name a few: moles, shrews, raccoons, opossums, toads, frogs and birds. Darkness is their only protection from predators when they're out of their burrows.

If you shine a flashlight on a worm halfway out of its burrow at night, it will retreat into the burrow. If you shine a flashlight on a worm crawling across a table, it will recoil from the beam of light, sometimes even when the room is already light.

Try shining the light on the worm's (1) head, (2) midsection and (3) tail. In which situation does the worm react the most strongly? You might have the children do this as part of a process for showing that worms detect light without eyes because the light-sensitive cells are on their "head."

Choice of Conditions Offered	Worms' Choice	Effect of Choice on Worms
Dampness or Dryness (Experiment 1)	Dampness	Keeps skin moist
Warmth or Cold (Experiment 2)	Cool	Keeps skin moist
Darkness or Light (Experiment 3)	Darkness	Keeps skin moist, avoids predators
Loamy Black Soil vs. Sand or Acid Soil or Alkaline Soil (Experiment 5)	Loamy black soil	Easy to tunnel in, not irritating to skin

Figure 4.7—Sample table summarizing results for Experiments 1, 2, 3 and 5.

Choice of Conditions Offered	Worms' Choice	Effect of Choice on Worms
Dampness or Dryness (Experiment 1)		
Warmth or Cold (Experiment 2)		
Darkness or Light (Experiment 3)		
Loamy Black Soil vs. Sand or Acid Soil or Alkaline Soil (Experiment 5)		

Figure 2.8 — Blank table on which to record your results for Experiments 1, 2, 3 and 5.

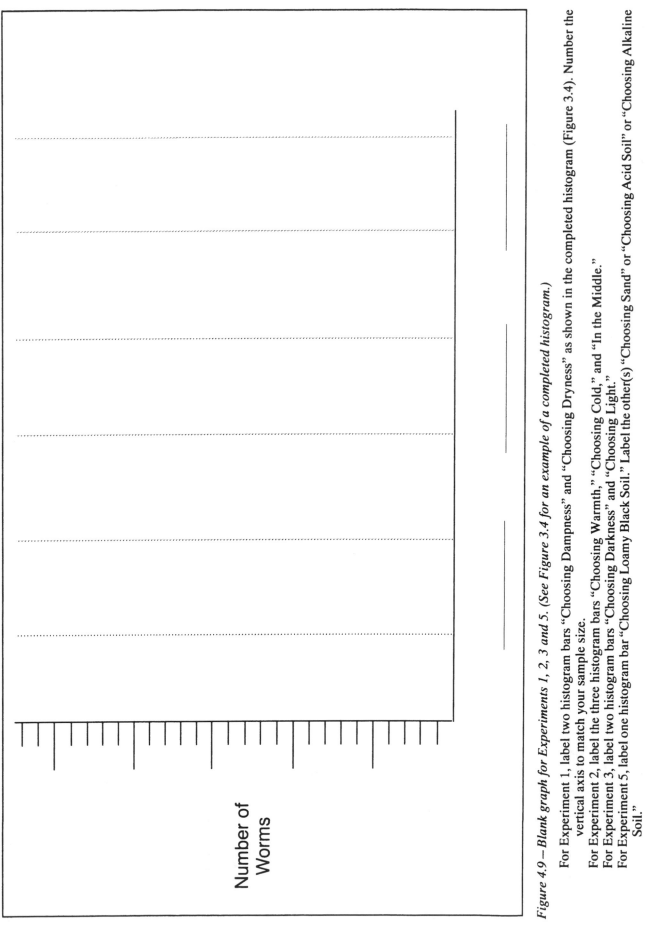

Figure 4.9 – Blank graph for Experiments 1, 2, 3 and 5. (See Figure 3.4 for an example of a completed histogram.)

For Experiment 1, label two histogram bars "Choosing Dampness" and "Choosing Dryness" as shown in the completed histogram (Figure 3.4). Number the vertical axis to match your sample size.

For Experiment 2, label the three histogram bars "Choosing Warmth," "Choosing Cold," and "In the Middle."

For Experiment 3, label two histogram bars "Choosing Darkness" and "Choosing Light."

For Experiment 5, label one histogram bar "Choosing Loamy Black Soil." Label the other(s) "Choosing Sand" or "Choosing Acid Soil" or "Choosing Alkaline Soil."

Experiment 4

Question: Do worms react equally to light beams of different colors?

Hypothesis: We think worms dislike all colors of lights.

Methods: Cover a flashlight with red cellophane, then blue cellophane. In a darkened room, illuminate a worm with white light, red light and then blue light. Does the worm react the same to all?

Result: Your result is a statement of your worm's reactions.

Conclusion: In my experience, worms react less or not at all to red light. Worms don't detect red light very well, so a red light would be best for hunting worms at night.

Experiment 5

Question: What type of soil do worms choose?

Hypothesis: We think worms prefer loamy black soil.

Methods: Put two or more different and separate types of soil in a flat container, such as a baking dish. For example you might have sand in one half of the dish and loamy, black garden soil in the other. You can also use clay or various mixtures of soil, sand and clay with or without leaf fragments. You can also alter the soil by mixing a little vinegar with the soil in one end to acidify it. Does the worm prefer the acid soil or the nonacid soil? Make one end alkaline by mixing a little baking soda solution with the soil, and offer that opposite the regular soil. Let the children choose what to compare. Can they offer different combinations and make a ranking of the worms' preference?

Result: Your result is a statement of your worms' choices. You can record your results on a table (see Figure 4.7 for an example). Figure 4.8 provides a blank table on which to record your results. You can also record your results as a histogram in Figure 4.9. Figure 3.4 provides an example of a completed histogram. A final option is to create a line graph (see Figure 4.10 for an example). Figure 4.11 provides a blank graph on which to plot your data.

Conclusion: The prediction is confirmed. In my experience, worms avoid sand, clay, acid and alkaline soil when given loamy black soil as an alternative. They also like humus and leaf fragments.

Experiment 6

Question: If we put a worm in a clear container filled with horizontal layers of different soil types, in which layer will the most tunnels appear?

Hypothesis: We think the worm will tunnel most in black loamy soil.

Methods: You need a clear, deep, flattened container for this, so that the worms will be forced to make their tunnels next to the wall where they will be visible. The homemade container in Figure 4.2 is made of two sheets of plexiglass or glass only 3/8 inch (1 cm) apart, mounted in a wood frame. Fill the container to about 8 inches (20.3 cm) from the top with each type of soil you want to test, in turn. I've used repeating layers of loamy black soil, sand and a soil–clay mixture. Put a healthy worm on top of the soil. Watch the worm for a few minutes, then put the cage in a dark place. After twenty-four hours, measure the total length of the tunnels it made. (You can have the students calculate the amount of tunneling that would occur in one week, one month or one year at that rate.) In which type of soil do they tunnel most?

Result: Your result is a statement of which layer had the most tunnels and any other relevant observations. You can record your results on the table in Figure 4.12.

Conclusion: In my experience, earthworms tunnel most in black loamy soil that they can easily push through. Is there evidence that the worm's tunneling mixes the layers?

Experiment 7

Question: Can worms convert food into soil?

Hypothesis: We think worms can make soil if we give them what they need to eat.

Methods (from Dorothy Hogner's book, *Earthworms*): Put a few rocks or pieces of broken flowerpot in the bottom of a jar. Fill the jar three-fourths full of damp sand or sandy soil. Add two to twelve worms. On top of the sand sprinkle food for the worms: 1 teaspoon (5 ml) coffee grounds, 1/4 teaspoon (1.25 ml) brown sugar, cabbage leaves, carrot tops, celery leaves or maple leaves. Wrap the jar with dark paper that you can remove to observe the worms or leave the jar in a dark room. If you use a red light to observe, you can see the worms moving in the burrows. Feed the worms and moisten the soil regularly for a month or two, then check your results.

To have an experimental control, you would need to set up a second jar simultaneously that is identical to the first one, but leave out either the food or the worms. This would provide evidence that the soil is a result of the worm and the food.

Result: Your result is a statement of your findings after a month or two. You can record your results on the table in Figure 4.12.

Conclusion: The prediction is confirmed. Earthworms will convert the food into a thin layer of soil on top of the sand.

Experiment 8

Question: Do earthworms in the soil improve the health of plants?

Hypothesis: We think earthworms in the soil won't affect the plants.

Methods: Get two plants of the same type and same size, equally healthy, and two flowerpots. Plant the two plants in separate pots in good quality garden soil or potting soil. Add two to four worms to one pot only (more for large plants and pots). Compare the condition and size of the two plants after a month or two.

Result: Your result is a statement of your observations of the two plants. You can record your results on the table in Figure 4.12.

Conclusion: The prediction is not confirmed. After a month or two, one plant should be taller and bushier than the other. Earthworms in the soil improve the health of plants by (1) tunneling and thereby aerating and loosening the soil so water can penetrate, and (2) improving the texture and nutrient content of the soil with their castings.

Experiment 9

Question: Can worms find their food in a maze?

Hypothesis: If we offer worms a forked path, only one fork of which leads to soil, we think they can find the soil.

Methods: You need a clear Y-shaped tube big enough for a worm to move through. You can buy one, but I made my own tube or maze by using two or three paper towel rolls, plastic wrap, foil and tape. Cut a lengthwise strip out of each roll so that you could watch a worm crawling through it. You'll have high-walled troughs now instead of rolls. Then trim one end of each roll so that you can fit them together to make a Y-shaped trough (see Figure 4.13). You may want to shorten them somewhat. Tape them together, then line the trough with foil so it will be smooth inside. Finally cover the top of the trough with plastic wrap, so you can see in, but the worms can't get out. You'll put the worms in at the base of the Y, so the two tips will be the exits. Plug one exit with cotton balls. Put the other exit hole into a pile of moist savory sand. Now put a worm into the entry hole and block the hole to keep it in. Watch where it goes.

I've used night crawlers with this experiment, but other worms will do.

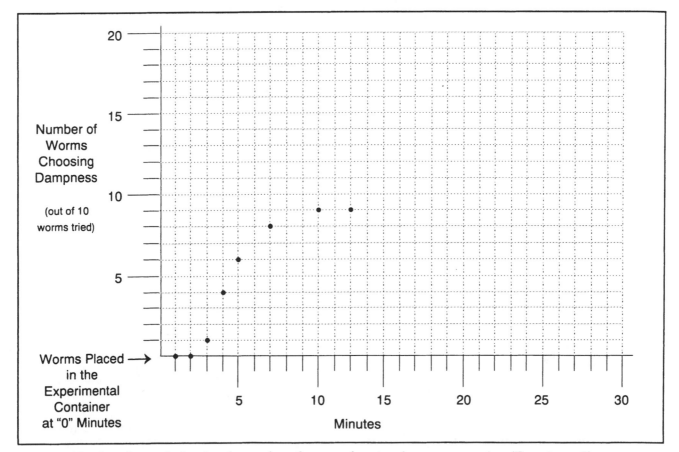

Figure 4.10 – Sample graph showing the number of worms choosing dampness over time (Experiment 1).

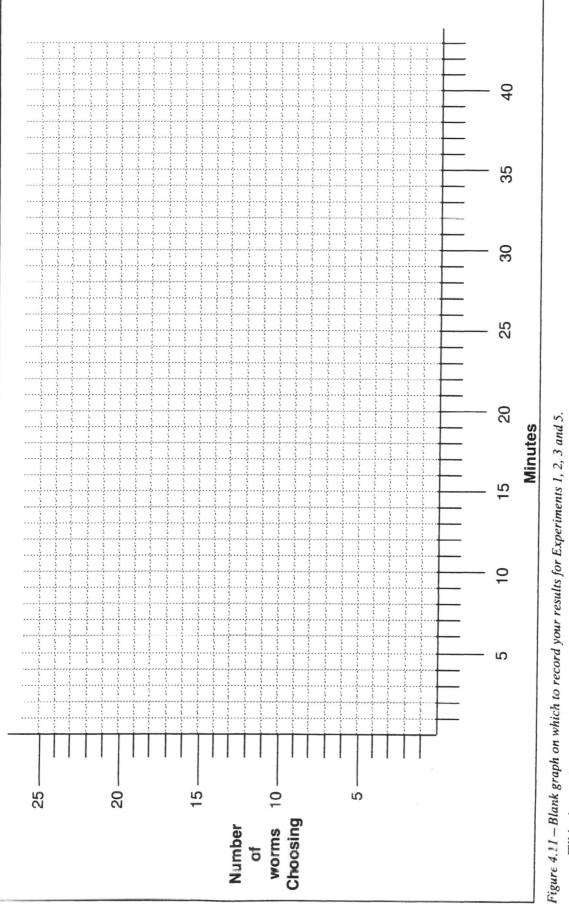

Figure 4.11 — Blank graph on which to record your results for Experiments 1, 2, 3 and 5.

Fill in the numbers on the vertical axis according to your sample size for each experiment.
For Experiment 1, put "Dampness" in the blank on the vertical axis label.
For Experiment 2, put "Cool" in the blank on the vertical axis label.
For Experiment 3, put "Darkness" in the blank on the vertical axis label.
For Experiment 5, put "Loamy Black Soil" in the blank on the vertical axis label.

THE EFFECT OF EARTHWORMS ON THE SOIL

Effect	Increased by Worms	Decreased by Worms
Number of Tunnels in the Soil (Experiment 6)		
Mixing of Layers of Soil (Experiment 6)		
Volume of Soil (Experiment 7)		
Health of Plants (Experiment 8)		

Figure 4.12 — Blank table on which to record your results for Experiments 6, 7 and 8.

Result: Your result is a statement of your observations of your worm's movements.

Conclusion: The prediction is confirmed, usually. Some worms will take off right away and go right to the soil. Some will just sit there and refuse to go anywhere, not responding to prodding, light or even tilting the tunnel. Replace them.

The most fun are those who take off and make the wrong choice. My son was worked into an absolute frenzy one day with a pair of night crawlers in the maze. "Mr. Worm" had made the wrong choice and was loitering in the wrong trough, unable to "decide" what to do. So we released "Ms. Worm" into the entry hole. She immediately joined Mr. Worm. They turned around and returned to the juncture of the three tunnels lying side by side. They then probed the intersection with their heads for several minutes, lying side by side, as though trying to "decide" which way to go. Alan was frantic. Finally Mr. and Ms. Worm took off down the "right" tunnel, side by side, and reached the tasty soil. Alan was jubilant. He couldn't refrain from probing the soil with his fat little fingers to congratulate the worms on their victory.

An individual worm can learn after fifty to one hundred trials to choose the correct tunnel.

Experiment 10

Question: Do earthworms prefer some foods over others?
Hypothesis: It depends on what is offered.
Methods: Place small amounts of different foods on top of the soil, such as cornmeal, green leafy vegetables,

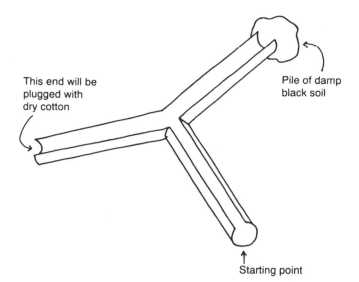

This end will be plugged with dry cotton

Pile of damp black soil

Starting point

Figure 4.13 — Y-shaped maze made from three paper towel rolls. Line the trough with foil and cover the open top with plastic wrap.

grass clippings, potato peelings, coffee grounds and small bits of other fruits and vegetables. Wait twenty-four hours or longer and note which ones have been taken.

Result: Your result is a statement of your worms' preferences. You can record your results on the table in Figure 4.14.

Conclusion: It depends upon the choices offered. Worms will eat almost any fruit or vegetable in small pieces and all of the things suggested here. Offerings like cornmeal or coffee grounds need to be spread out or worked into the soil a bit.

	Not Accepted	Accepted	Not Sure
Cornmeal			
Lettuce Bits			
Bits of Celery Greens			
Grass Clippings			
Bits of Potato Peel			
Bits of Apple			
Bits of Cucumber			

Figure 4.14 — Blank table on which to record your results for Experiment 10.

CHAPTER 5

Chirping Crickets

Introduction

Cricket studies range from the very simple to the rather complex. Herein are described several activities and experiments appropriate for children as young as four or five and others that will work better with somewhat older children. When I first began to learn about crickets, I was surprised at the intricacy of their aggressive behaviors. As I write this a pair of males sit on my desk head to head, alternating aggressive chirps. The children's interest in the chirps is by itself enough reason to keep a terrarium of crickets in your classroom. But there's more to it than that.

After you've done the experiments in this chapter and in Chapters 3, 4 and 6, refer to the table in Figure 1 in the Postscript, which provides a comparison of the results for the experiments in these chapters. Figure 2 in the Postscript is a blank table that can be filled out with the results of your experiments, for comparison.

Materials

1. Male and female crickets. Crickets are easy to catch, also easy to buy locally as fish bait (details provided later in the chapter).
2. One to several terraria, depending on how many activities and experiments you plan to do. Size of the terraria is flexible. I use some as small as 5 1/2 by 3 inches (14 x 7.6 cm) and others five times that size.
3. Sand for the floor of the terrarium.
4. Plastic dish, such as trimmed cottage cheese or yogurt containers, to hold wet sand for egg-laying.
5. Wet bread and lettuce for cricket food.
6. Small paintbrush with bristles 1/16 inch (1.6 mm) long and 1/16 inch (1.6 mm) across and model airplane paint for marking crickets.
7. Various materials like toilet paper rolls, film boxes or matchboxes to make houses for the crickets. One

experiment requires a piece of clear flexible plastic like the transparencies used for overhead projectors.

Background Information

Crickets have recently become a favorite around my house. My four-year-old son Alan sits by the cricket terrarium for a half-hour at a time handling them, using a pencil to make tunnels for them in the wet sand and moving their cardboard houses around. He and his sister have both demanded separate enclosures for their personal crickets. Sarah wants females only, please. They boast to one another, "My cricket is laying eggs." Alan watches his chirp, court and lay eggs while he eats his breakfast, filling me in on their every move.

Crickets are often used in college laboratories to demonstrate aggression and territoriality in insects, which is why I decided to investigate crickets as experimental subjects for children. I was well acquainted with crickets as food for praying mantises but had never kept them long enough to watch their behavior. Now after keeping two species of crickets on my kitchen table for a couple of months and sharing them with my own children, a class of kindergartners and two classes of older children, I see that their various aggressive behaviors are not the features that most attract children to them. The aggression—other than aggressive chirping—doesn't occur frequently enough to catch the children's attention. I learned what does interest them by watching the children watch the crickets.

Most of the simple experiments I describe here didn't occur to me until I saw the crickets through the children's eyes. Many of the questions they asked were anthropomorphic or simplistic ("Do crickets make friends with other animals?"), but many were not. The many that were not led to some interesting discoveries for us all.

I give much more information about the crickets themselves in the following sections as it relates to particular classroom setups for observation and to particular experiments.

How to Get and Keep Crickets

The easiest way to get crickets is to buy them at a fishing tackle store. Look under "fisherman's supplies" and "fishing bait" in the Yellow Pages. You can get fifty crickets for about the price of two soft drinks. If there is no tackle shop nearby, you can order crickets (see Appendix). Biological supply companies charge somewhat more than tackle shops.

Crickets are easy to catch too, especially if you set up an area they'll like in advance. Keep a pile of slightly damp grass clippings near a brushy area or on the edge of your yard. When I look through my neighbor's grass clipping pile, I can find ten crickets in ten or fifteen minutes every time. The crickets are quick — there's definitely a trick to catching them. I find that if I pull back a big hunk of grass clippings and just wait for a minute, a cricket or two will come out into the open space. I have a plastic peanut butter jar ready and slap it down over the cricket. Cover the opening with your hand while you turn the jar right side up. Have a second container with you as a holding jar. You'll miss the first few but then you'll get the hang of it. I find this technique much easier than trying to catch them by hand.

I also find crickets under the black plastic sheet that covers my compost pile, under my outdoor garbage can, in my children's damp sandbox under the toys, under the edge of the grass that abuts my wooden garden border and under the leafy plants in the flower garden. By far the most consistently successful place for cricket collecting for me, however, is the pile of damp grass clippings. This particular pile is on a slope above a ditch that sometimes has water in it. The ditch may contribute to its success.

All the crickets I've worked with have been field crickets or house crickets, which look similar and are very closely related. Much of what I've written here will apply to any crickets. The behavior of different species, however, is not identical, and you may find differences. I've never been bitten by a cricket, although some grasshoppers will bite.

Maintaining Crickets

I keep crickets in a terrarium with about 2 inches (5 cm) of sand on the floor (see Figure 5.1). Most of the books I've looked at on keeping crickets suggest sand, although it isn't essential. They do like to dig sometimes, and children may want to make tunnels for them in damp sand. If you want them to lay eggs you'll have to have at least a small area of damp sand. Otherwise dry sand or soil is okay. Adults may eat the hatchlings, so if you know you have eggs in an area, you many want to cover that area with a wire mesh cage or put the adults somewhere else. I've read that they're less likely to cannabalize if you give them

Figure 5.1 — Malcolm reaches for a subject in the terrarium.

plenty of other protein, like dog food, but my crickets won't eat dog food.

To provide water, you can simply spray the glass with water droplets once a day. Most insects drink from dew drops in their natural habitat. Or you can put a small dish of shallow water [1/8 inch (.3 cm) maximum depth] in the terrarium. Use something with short sides like a 35mm film can lid or a yogurt container lid.

Crickets will eat wet bread, moistened Cheerios and other cereal, lettuce, carrots and probably many other foods. Those are the items I feed mine. I keep food available at all times. You can remove it for a day or two to conduct an experiment, but you don't have to.

Field Hunt

If you want to take the children to look for crickets, any brushy area or area with leaves instead of lawn will do. Look under the leaves and under logs, in crevices in logs, under boards, under anything. You may find spiders and snakes in the same places, but don't let this stop you from looking. You probably won't. Still you should caution them about not picking up spiders and snakes, and you may want to turn logs and boards for them. It's never a good idea to stick fingers into dark places into which you can't see. Children enjoy going after the crickets with their hands as well as with jars.

Crickets at School
Getting Ready

The minimum you need to begin is a terrarium, sand for the terrarium floor, crickets and bread to feed them.

Observations and Activities

Before you give the students any information about the crickets, it's a good idea to let them watch the crickets at their leisure for a few days. Start with one male. Ask the children some questions to help them notice his behavior. What is he doing? He wanders around at first. Does he chirp? He may a little. Does he take cover? He will after he looks around, if cover is available. Does he show any courtship behavior (see description in the following paragraph)? Not if he is alone. Does he eat and drink?

After a day or two add a female. Does the male's behavior change? Does he chirp now? He probably will begin to court her. Courtship behavior consists of, for one thing, chirping softly by gently rubbing his wings together. (The wings have files on them that produce the chirping sound when rubbed together.) His wings will still be almost flat against his back during courtship chirping, not raised as they are in aggressive chirping. Courting males of the species I watched rock their bodies back and forth gently while chirping and claw at the sand gently with all legs continually. A courting male will eventually back up to the individual he is courting, to entice her onto his back. If she does get on his back, he will curl the tip of his abdomen up and transfer a sperm packet to an opening in the tip of her abdomen. The sperm packet is about half the size of a tomato seed and gray. Sometimes, if they are interrupted, the sperm packet will get stuck on one of them and be carried about.

Does the female accept his advances? Usually not. If he approaches her from behind, she may kick him in the face! Females you buy from a bait store have already mated and are full of eggs because they've had nowhere to lay them. In my experience they won't mate again until they find a place to deposit the eggs they already have. A female must have damp sand to lay her eggs. If she does have damp sand, she will almost certainly lay eggs in it unless she has been isolated from males previously for a good while. Eggs come out singly. She will continue to lay eggs intermittently and often throughout her lifetime.

After another day or two add another male. I like to mark my males with model airplane paint so that I can tell them apart. To mark one, I put the male in the bottom of a very small juice glass, with a bottom diameter of no more than 1 1/4 inch (3.2 cm) or so, so that he can't move around very much. Then I follow him around with the paintbrush until I can get a tiny spot on his thorax. It doesn't bother him, but don't get it on his abdomen because they breathe through pores in the abdomen.

You can also mark a male by clipping one of his antennae. If you get them from the bait store, some will probably already have broken antennae.

At least one of the two males will probably behave aggressively toward one another, but usually not right away. They may face off and chirp aggressively, or one may stalk the other while chirping, causing the other to retreat. The children may notice that an aggressive chirp is often louder than a courtship chirp. You can also see that the wings move higher to make the aggressive chirp. Males often court other males. A male is stimulated to begin courtship when he encounters another cricket and the other cricket does not respond to him aggressively, whether that cricket is male or female. In nature, a nonresponsive cricket is probably usually a female, so their behavior is usually appropriate. Write down all questions the children have during this initial period of observation.

After a couple of days of watching the terrarium with two males and a female in it, take an hour or so to gather the children around and talk to them about the crickets. Show them all the body parts (see below and Figure 5.2).

---

1. Big legs for jumping to escape from predators, like their relatives the grasshoppers.
2. Wings, which when rubbed together make a chirping sound.
3. Long antennae. All crickets feel one another with their antennae any time they meet. Males may lash one another with their antennae during low-level aggressive encounters. You can induce aggression in a male by lashing him with a fake antenna.
4. Cerci, which are the two prongs that project from the back of the abdomen. Stimulation of the cerci plays a part in courtship. It signals him that another cricket is behind him. He may back up, trying to back under her, to get her on his back. If I touch a male's cerci with my finger while he's courting, he kicks my finger repeatedly but doesn't run away! (The cerci are not genitals or reproductive organs, just feelers.)
5. Ovipositor (egg depositor). The female has a long sword-shaped projection from the back of her abdomen, between her cerci. She jabs it down into the wet sand and lays her eggs from the end of it. You can sometimes see the eggs come out when she pokes it between the sand and the side of the terrarium. The eggs are tiny and are laid singly. The male crickets will feel disturbed and won't court or chirp or show any aggressive behavior while the children are all gathered around the terrarium, but the females will still lay eggs.

I've found that what young children like best is holding the crickets and letting the crickets run up their arms (see Figure 5.3). The kindergartners and I had been watching the crickets for about a half-hour as a group when a little

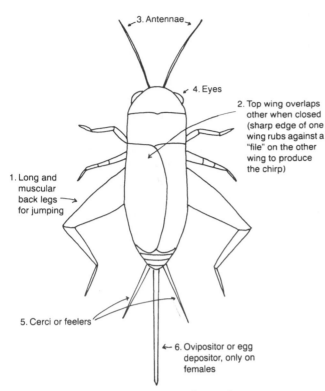

Figure 5.2 — External anatomy of a cricket.

3. Antennae

4. Eyes

2. Top wing overlaps other when closed (sharp edge of one wing rubs against a "file" on the other wing to produce the chirp)

1. Long and muscular back legs for jumping

5. Cerci or feelers

6. Ovipositor or egg depositor, only on females

boy asked if he could hold one. I told him to go ahead so he reached into the terrarium and caught one. Pretty soon half the class was asking to hold one. The first few bold souls simply held the crickets stiffly in their hands and then dropped them back into the terrarium. But a little red-head named Brian opened his fist and let his cricket wander up his arm, across his shoulders, across his back and on and on. He inspired the rest of them. Soon everyone was transferring or receiving crickets, amid squeals of eagerness. It was one of the most exhilarating experiences I've had with young children and creatures. They were enraptured.

As the time came to put away the crickets and get ready to go home, the children gathered in a circle to talk. Little red-haired Brian summed up the cricket experience aptly: "Something interesting happened today!"

Another thing children seem to enjoy particularly is being able to identify and name the individual males. I put a card on the wall by the terrarium showing several roughly drawn cricket shapes. On each shape was the pattern of paint spots for an individual cricket, labeled with the name of the particular cricket with that paint pattern. The children watch them and say, "Oh Larry is chirping at Thor again," or "Fred stays in that little house by himself almost all the time."

One of the first things children will notice about crickets is their tendency to burrow. If there is any wet sand in the terrarium, some of the crickets will probably dig into it. You can encourage burrowing by keeping a pile of loose wet sand in the corner of the terrarium. They'll be able to

burrow into the pile without hitting the bottom of the terrarium.

Crickets like already made burrows too. Poke a pencil horizontally through a pile of damp sand in the terrarium. With the pencil in place, pack the sand firmly over the pencil. Slowly withdraw the pencil, leaving a tunnel with two openings. The children can do this, but make sure they pack it well or the tunnel will collapse and smother the crickets.

If you have areas of wet sand as well as dry sand, the children will notice that the crickets prefer to rest on the wet sand. They'll also notice that the crickets take refuge whenever it (a film box, toilet paper roll, etc.) is available. Toilet paper rolls are real favorites.

The simple experiments I've done with very young children are derived from their own simple observations and questions, which is why I write down every question. Letting their questions be your guide is a good way to avoid getting too complex for their particular age.

Below are descriptions of the simple experiments I've done based on the observations of very young children. Following are some that are a bit more complex.

Experiments

In each experiment, unless otherwise specified, the terraria should all have a floor of damp sand or damp soil

Figure 5.3 — Alan grabs a cricket by the front legs, showing off its cerci.

— 44 —

with wet bread or other food available. Provide a water dish or spray the inside walls with water droplets once a day.

Remember that the hypotheses I give are just examples. Most are written in the "if ... then" format, but they don't have to be. Your hypotheses will be the predictions made by the class or a particular child. Your result for each experiment will be a statement of how your animals reacted to your experimental setup. Your conclusion is a statement of whether your prediction was confirmed or not. For each experiment, adding replicates increases your confidence in the validity of your conclusion, but they may be omitted if tedious for young children.

Experiment 1

Question: Do crickets prefer houses with two doors or one door?

Hypothesis: We think crickets will like two-door houses and one-door houses the same.

Methods: Make several houses out of camera film boxes or matchboxes or toilet paper rolls cut to about 2 inches (5 cm) in length. Put a corresponding number of crickets into the terrarium. Have only one opening in most of the houses, perhaps all but one house. In the remaining house make two openings on opposite ends. Which type of house do the crickets prefer?

Result: Your result is a statement of your crickets' choices. You can record your outcome on a table (see Figure 5.4). Figure 5.5 provides a blank table for your results. You can also make a histogram with Figure 5.6, using Figure 3.4 as an example of a completed histogram.

Conclusion: The prediction is not confirmed. My experience is that the crickets usually prefer two doors. The last time I did this experiment with field crickets, all six males stayed in the two-door house, ignoring the one-door houses. Apparently their preference for two doors outweighed their tendency to be solitary and aggressive toward other males. Two doors are obviously safer in terms of predators. An insect-eating shrew comes in the front door, the cricket goes out the back. Many animals are uncomfortable when they have no potential escape route.

Choice Offered to Crickets	Crickets' Choice	Effect of Choice on Crickets
1-Door House vs. 2-Door House (Experiment 1)	2-door house	Have escape route
Empty House vs. House with Company (Experiment 2)	Depend on crickets' recent experiences	Solitude reduces conflict between males
Damp Substrate vs. Dry Substrate (Experiment 3)	Damp	Reduces dehydration
Dark Tube vs. Clear Tube (Experiment 4)	Dark	Reduces dehydration
Dark End of Terrarium vs. Light End of Terrarium (Experiment 5)	Light end (always?)	Darkness reduces dehydration and predation
Damp Sand for Tunneling vs. Dry Sand for Tunneling (Experiment 6)	Damp sand for tunneling	Damp sand holds shape better
Moss vs. Damp Grass Clippings (Experiment 7)	Damp grass clippings	Reduces dehydration; easier to burrow into

Figure 5.4—Sample table summarizing the choices of the crickets in Experiments 1 to 7.

Choice Offered to Crickets	Crickets' Choice	Effect of Choice on Crickets
1-Door House vs. 2-Door House (Experiment 1)		
Empty House vs. House with Company (Experiment 2)		
Damp Substrate vs. Dry Substrate (Experiment 3)		
Dark Tube vs. Clear Tube (Experiment 4)		
Dark End of Terrarium vs. Light End of Terrarium (Experiment 5)		
Damp Sand for Tunneling vs. Dry Sand for Tunneling (Experiment 6)		
Moss vs. Damp Grass Clippings (Experiment 7)		

Figure 5.5 — Blank table on which to record your results for Experiments 1 to 7.

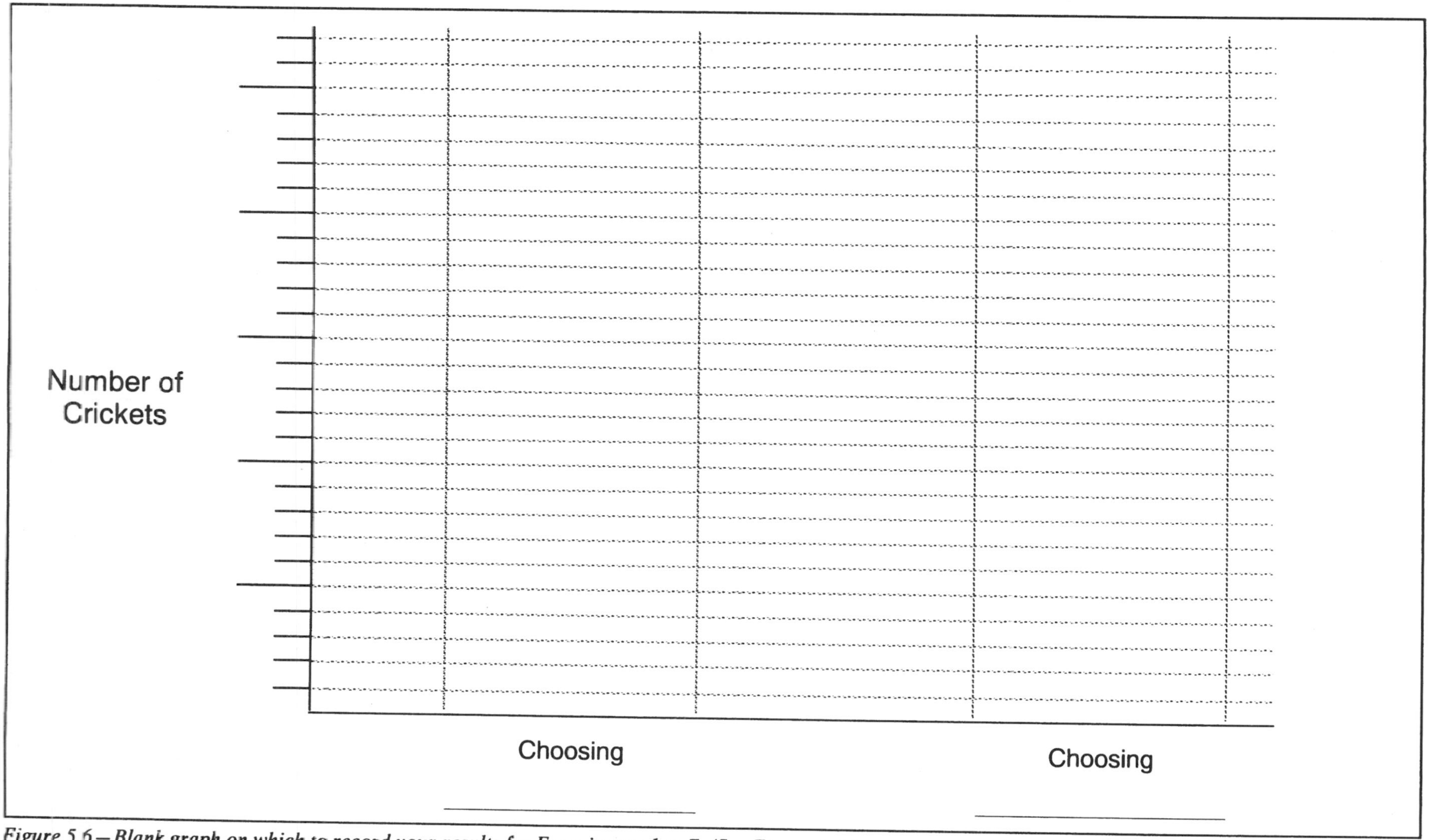

Number of Crickets

Choosing　　　　　　　　　　　Choosing

Figure 5.6 — Blank graph on which to record your results for Experiments 1 to 7. (See Figure 3.4 for an example of a completed histogram.)

　For Experiment 1, fill in blanks on horizontal axis with "1-Door House" and "2-Door House."
　For Experiment 2, fill in blanks with "Empty House" and "House with Company."
　For Experiment 3, fill in blanks with "Damp Substrate" and "Dry Substrate."
　For Experiment 4, fill in blanks with "Dark Tube" and "Clear Tube."
　For Experiment 5, fill in blanks with "Dark End of Terrarium" and "Light End of Terrarium."
　For Experiment 6, fill in blanks with "Damp Sand" and "Dry Sand."
　For Experiment 7, fill in blanks with "Grass Clippings" and "Moss" or "Damp Sand."

Experiment 2

Question: Will crickets choose houses with other crickets or will they house themselves singly?

Hypothesis: We think crickets will choose to have company.

Methods: Make several houses (see Experiment 1). Have two openings in each house. Put as many crickets in the terrarium as you have houses. Do they adopt separate houses or all inhabit the same one, or do they inhabit none?

Result: Your result is a statement of your crickets' choices and any relevant observations. You can record your outcome on a table (see Figure 5.4). Figure 5.5 provides a blank table for your results. You can also make a histogram with Figure 5.6, using Figure 3.4 as an example of a completed histogram.

Conclusion: It's hard to predict the outcome of this one, which makes it interesting. Crickets do prefer a refuge, and in nature they live singly and rather widely spaced, which is one reason the males chirp to help the females find them. But being crowded for long periods in captivity seems to affect their tendency to be solitary. In this situation, they probably will move into the houses separately, but they may not. You can try isolating the crickets for several days before the experiment or keeping them together. Does this affect the outcome?

Experiment 3

Question: Do crickets prefer a damp or a dry substrate?

Hypothesis: We think crickets will like damp sand and dry sand equally.

Methods: Pour water over the sand in one end of the terrarium. Leave the other end dry. Count the number of crickets in each location after the class has been absent from the room for a while. Activity outside the terrarium causes the crickets to mill around.

Result: Your result is a statement of your crickets' choices and any other relevant observations. You can record

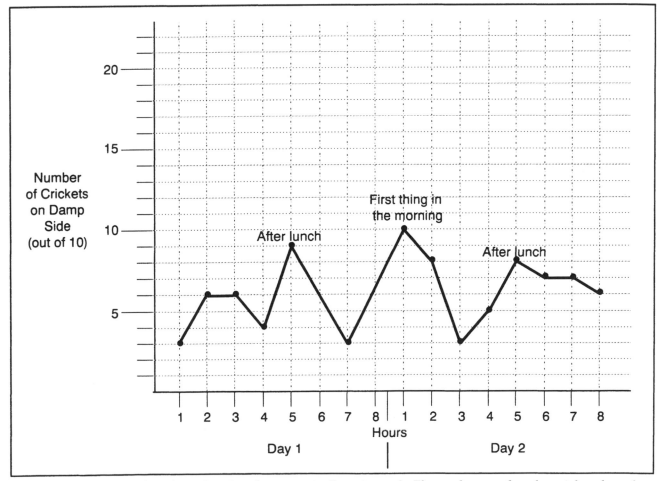

Figure 5.7 — Number of crickets choosing dampness in Experiment 3. The peaks are after the crickets have been undisturbed for a while.

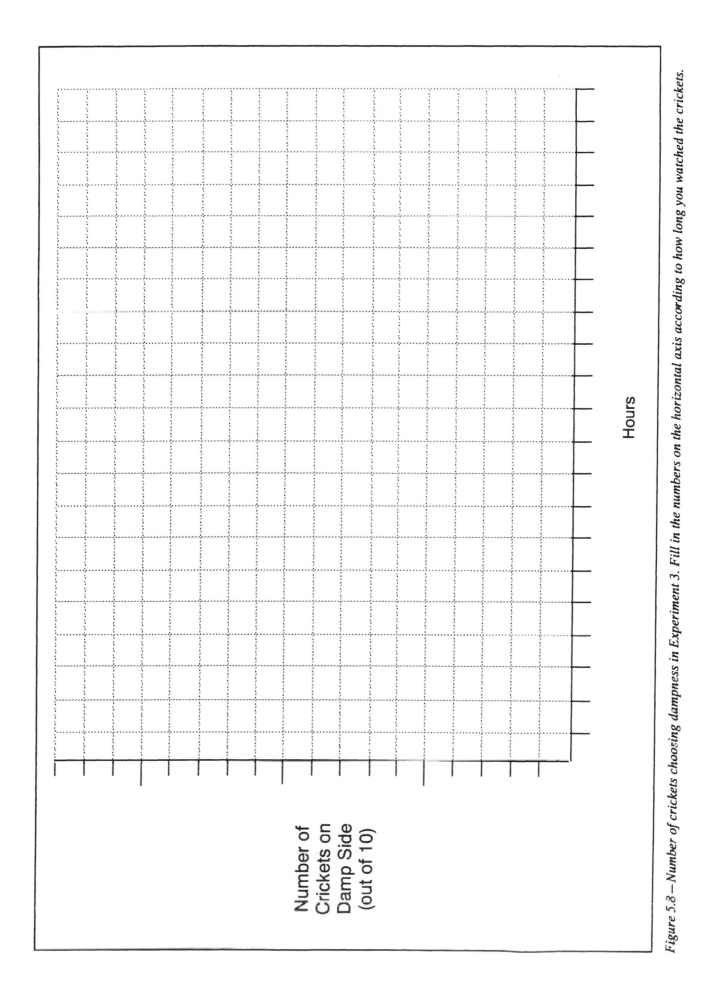

Number of
Crickets on
Damp Side
(out of 10)

Hours

Figure 5.8— Number of crickets choosing dampness in Experiment 3. Fill in the numbers on the horizontal axis according to how long you watched the crickets.

your outcome on a table (see Figure 5.4). Figure 5.5 provides a blank table for your results. You can also make a histogram with Figure 5.6, using Figure 3.4 as an example of a completed histogram. Finally, you can plot your count on a graph (see Figure 5.7). Figure 5.8 provides a blank graph for your results.

Conclusion: The prediction is not confirmed. Crickets have a definite preference for damp sand over dry sand. A damp environment helps them to avoid dehydration.

Experiment 4

Question: Do crickets stay in houses because they are attracted to darkness or because they like being enclosed?

Hypothesis: We think crickets are attracted to darkness.

Methods: Animals can be attracted to the feel of something around them, an urge that is called thigmotaxic. Roly-polies, for example, are thigmotaxic. They seek out crevices or other bodies to make contact with. When a cricket is inside a toilet paper roll, you can see that its antennae are making contact with the cardboard over and around it, so it is receiving physical signals that something is surrounding its body. Do crickets stay in the roll because of the darkness or because of the physical contact? To address this question you need to offer something that provides contact but not darkness. I made a clear tube open on both ends. As a control I offered at the same time a black tube open on both ends. You can make a clear tube out of a plastic transparency sheet for an overhead projector and a dark tube from black construction paper. As another option I have used *Drosophila* culture vials (see Chapter 14) from which I'd sawed the closed ends off. I covered one with black electrical tape. Lay the dark tube and the light tube horizontally on the terrarium floor. Put some sand in the floor of each tube to anchor it. If the instinct to be surrounded by something is responsible for the crickets' behavior, then they should like the clear tube just as well as the dark tube. Wait several hours or until most of the crickets have chosen one tube or the other.

Result: Your result is a statement of your crickets' choices and any relevant observations. You can record your outcome on a table (see Figure 5.4). Figure 5.5 provides a blank table for your results. You can also make a histogram with Figure 5.6, using Figure 3.4 as an example of a completed histogram.

Conclusion: The prediction was confirmed here. In my experience, most crickets prefer the dark tube. So, we

may extrapolate and assume that crickets stay in their houses a lot because, at least in part, they are attracted to darkness. They may also be thigmotactic.

The answer is not really that simple! See below.

Experiment 5

Question: Are crickets attracted to light?

Hypothesis: They prefer the dark tube in Experiment 4.

Methods: Put a lamp beside one end of the terrarium so that it shines down into that end only. Wait an hour or so and observe your crickets' positions.

Result: Your result is a statement of your observations. You can record your results on a table (see Figure 5.4). Figure 5.5 provides a blank table for your results. You can also make a histogram with Figure 5.6, using Figure 3.4 as an example of a completed histogram.

Conclusion: Within a few hours the crickets will all congregate at the illuminated end of the terrarium, obviously in response to the lamp light. I noticed this by accident when keeping a terrarium next to a lamp. I can think of only one explanation: The crickets are attracted to the warmth of the lamp instead of the light itself. You could test this by using alternately an incandescent bulb that gives off a lot of warmth and a florescent bulb that gives off little warmth. Or put a hot water bottle and a cold water bottle in the terrarium.

If this doesn't explain it, then there is obviously something else involved in their attraction to tubes and tunnels. Maybe your students will think of some other possibility.

Experiment 6

Question: Will crickets make more tunnels in dry sand or in wet sand?

Hypothesis: Crickets will make tunnels in either.

Methods: Wet the sand in part of the terrarium. Give the crickets twenty-four hours or so to make tunnels.

Result: Your result is a statement of your crickets' tunneling activities in each end of the terrarium. You can record your results on a table (see Figure 5.4). Figure 5.5 provides a blank table for your results. You can also make a histogram with Figure 5.6, using Figure 3.4 as an example of a completed histogram.

Conclusion: In my experience, crickets will tunnel in the wet sand only. Is this because it sticks together better?

Experiment 7

Question: Do crickets prefer moss, damp grass clippings or damp sand?

Hypothesis: We think they'll like moss because it's soft.

Methods: Cover one-third of the terrarium floor with moss, one-third with damp grass clippings and one-third with damp sand. Wait twenty-four hours. Where do the crickets hang out?

Result: Your result is a statement of where most of the crickets are located after twenty-four hours. You can record your results on a table (see Figure 5.4). Figure 5.5 provides a blank table for your results. You can also make a histogram with Figure 5.6, using Figure 3.4 as an example of a completed histogram.

Conclusion: In my experience crickets like substrates that are damp and easiest to burrow into, which means here the grass clippings.

Experiment 8

Question: Do crickets prefer food A or food B?

Hypothesis: Crickets prefer food A (or whatever the students predict).

Methods: Offer the crickets choices among these foods: carrot peelings, lettuce, dry dog food, wet dog food, apple peelings, wet bread, dry bread or anything else the children think of. The above items are those I've seen them eat or read that they will eat.

Result: Your result is a statement of your crickets' preferences. Crickets like food B better than food A, etc. You can record your results on the histogram in Figure 5.9. Figure 3.4 provides an example of a completed histogram.

Conclusion: Maybe the children can make some generalizations; for example, crickets like vegetables better than meat, or they like fresh vegetables better than rotting vegetables, or they like thinly sliced vegetables better than thick or raw or cooked, etc.

Male Aggression and Territoriality

The aggressive behavior of male crickets is complex and fascinating. It differs in one aspect from the aggressive and territorial behavior of any other animal I know. Usually when a male animal (other than a cricket) establishes dominance over other males, that dominance is based on his superior strength or size or daring or fierceness. He is consistently able to intimidate all of his rivals, which is what is meant by being "dominant." Other males know him and once they've been defeated by him, they generally don't challenge him again. He may be displaced eventually by a newcomer or by an animal that has just reached maturity.

A dominant male cricket is able to intimidate all other males. The dominance of a male has nothing to do with his size or strength. None of the other crickets recognize him or avoid fights with him. His dominance is not based on any innate quality that makes him a superior fighter. Rather, it is based on what has happened to him in the recent past. Certain transient events in the life of a cricket predispose him to feel more aggressive temporarily, to challenge other male crickets more and to fight harder. The outcome of any particular encounter depends on which cricket has experienced one or more of those predisposing factors most recently. The next encounter between the same two may have an opposite outcome.

The experiences that increase the level of aggression in male crickets are these: (1) having been isolated for twenty-four hours or more immediately prior to the encounter, (2) having just copulated with a female, (3) having just dominated another male cricket, and (4) having a refuge or territory of his own. Figure 5.10 provides a table on which to record how various factors affect aggressive behaviors in Experiments 10 to 13. Figure 5.11 provides a summation of how various factors affect the general level of aggression, for Experiments 10 to 13. Figure 5.12 is a blank summary table chart for the students to fill out.

The male that feels the most aggressive will probably dominate the others. We can manipulate the outcome of a particular encounter between two males by manipulating their circumstances prior to the encounter. Isolate one before the encounter but not the other. Allow one to establish a territory in a refuge (a matchbox house) and introduce a stranger. Children enjoy trying to predict the outcome of an encounter. I read about the influence of the four factors above before I saw it for myself, and it was fun to actually try each one and see them work.

Experiments 9 to 13 address questions about cricket aggression. Experiment 9 explores general aggressive behavior, while Experiments 10 to 13 explore specific types of aggressive behavior or the effect of one of the four conditions that affect aggression. Some experiments require the children to compare the level of aggressive behavior under these different conditions. Older children may want to assign numerical values to various aggressive behaviors and actually keep a tally in each situation, for comparison. Younger children can make a more subjective judgment about whether or not the crickets are more aggressive in one situation than another.

The following are aggressive behaviors in male crickets: (1) chirping, also called stridulation — the most common aggressive behavior, (2) kicking, (3) raising either head or tail end, (4) head-butting and (5) wrestling — the most intense of the aggressive behaviors, indicating that the crickets are extremely riled.

Aggressive encounters usually end when one cricket (the loser) retreats or turns around.

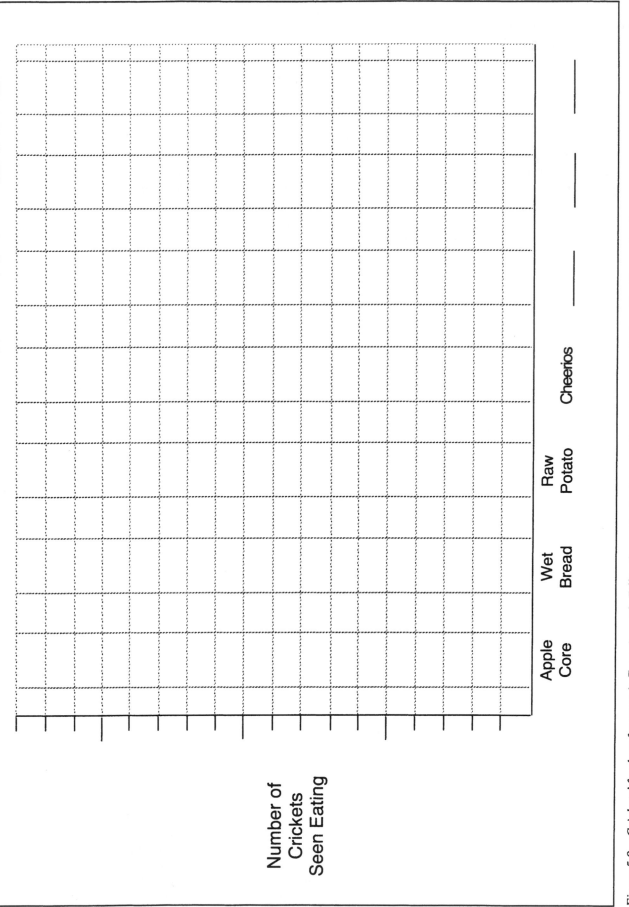

Number of Crickets Seen Eating

Apple Core   Wet Bread   Raw Potato   Cheerios

Figure 5.9 — Crickets' food preferences in Experiment 8. Fill in the vertical axis according to your sample size. (See Figure 3.4 for an example of a completed histogram.)

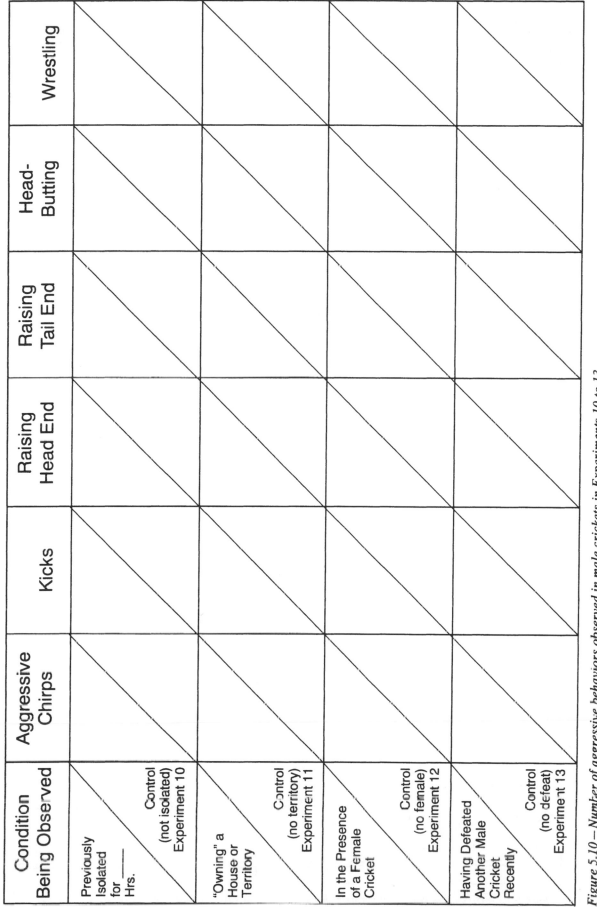

Figure 5.10 — Number of aggressive behaviors observed in male crickets in Experiments 10 to 13.

Experiment 9

Question: In a group, is one male consistently dominant over the other males, or does the dominance shift?

Hypothesis: We think one male cricket will be dominant over the others.

Methods: You need three to six male crickets. Mark each cricket's thorax with a different color of paint, different position of the paint or different number of dots, etc., so that you can tell them apart. (Don't put paint on the abdomen, as they breathe through pores in the abdominal wall.) Isolate the crickets in separate cups for a day or two. Keep a wet shred of bread and a crumpled piece of paper towel in each cup and cover with a cloth secured by a rubber band. Then put all the crickets in a terrarium together, with no refuges for any. Watch on and off for a few hours (say ten minutes per hour) and record who initiates aggressive encounters and who chirps. (Generally only the dominant cricket chirps.) Do this for two or three days.

Result: Your result is a statement of your observations of dominant behaviors in each cricket.

	More Aggressive, Less Aggressive or Neither	**What Aggression Did You See?** (chirps, kicks, raises head or tail end, head-butting, wrestling)
Previous Isolation Experiment 10	More aggressive	Chirps, kicks, raises head end
Owning a House or Territory Experiment 11	More aggressive	Chirps
Presence of a Female Cricket Experiment 12	Neither	None
Having Defeated Another Male Cricket Recently Experiment 13	More aggressive	Chirps and kicks

Figure 5.11 — How does each factor affect the aggressive behavior of a male cricket in Experiments 10 to 13? Your results might be different.

	More Aggressive Less Aggressive or Neither	What Aggression Did You See? (chirps, kicks, raises head or tail end, head-butting, wrestling)
Previous Isolation Experiment 10		
Owning a House or Territory Experiment 11		
Presence of a Female Cricket Experiment 12		
Having Defeated Another Male Cricket Recently Experiment 13		

Figure 5.12 — How does each factor affect the aggressive behavior of a male cricket in Experiments 10 to 13?

Conclusion: In most cases only one male is dominant in a group, unless more crickets are added or conditions are altered. This means that one male clearly will chirp more and initiate more encounters than the others. If a different cricket chirps the next day, then he has probably defeated the chirper of the day before. If more than one are chirping, then the dominance has probably not yet been established.

In Experiments 10, 11 and 12 the male crickets put in the terrarium first are called residents. The male crickets added later are called intruders.

Experiment 10

Question: Is a male that has been isolated more aggressive than a male that has not been isolated?

Hypothesis: A male that has been isolated will be more aggressive.

Methods: You need two terraria. Small terraria [5 by 3 inches (12.7 x 7.6 cm) or so] are best because the crickets are less able to avoid one another. To get ready, put two males into each terrarium. Give them a day or so to become familiar with the terraria. Meanwhile, keep a fifth male (cricket A), that is marked with paint or otherwise identifiable, isolated for a day or two. Keep a sixth male (cricket B) in a different container with other crickets.

To begin the experiment, add cricket A to the pair of males in one terrarium and add cricket B to the pair of males in the other terrarium. Is the previously isolated intruder (cricket A) more aggressive than the other one (cricket B)? Do the resident males react differently to the isolated intruder (cricket A) than they do to the nonisolated intruder (cricket B)?

Result: Your result is a statement of your observations of the behavior of cricket A and cricket B and any relevant observations of the other crickets. See page 51 for use of tables to record results of Experiments 10 to 13.

Conclusion: In my experience, a cricket that has been isolated is more aggressive. No two crickets will behave exactly alike, but here is an example from a recent experiment: Cricket B, the nonisolated intruder, behaved submissively. He ran immediately to a corner of the terrarium where there was a little dip in the sand. Both residents ran immediately to pin him in, leaning over him, trapping him in the corner for fifteen minutes or so. When he finally moved one of the residents chirped aggressively at him. Cricket B did not chirp at all.

In the other terrarium, the isolated intruder (cricket A) was ignored for about fifteen minutes. Then he chirped aggressively at one of the residents that did not chirp back.

To be confident that the results are generally applicable, do several replicates of each situation. You may find somewhat different results.

Experiment 11

Question: Does having a house make a male more aggressive toward an intruder?

Hypothesis: A male with a house will be more aggressive toward an intruder than a male without a house.

Methods: Set up two terraria with one pair of males in each, as described for Experiment 10. Put two houses in one terrarium. A house is anything about the size of a matchbox into which a cricket can crawl. I cut 35mm film boxes in half, or use a 2-inch (5 cm) segment of a toilet paper roll. Each house should be open at both ends. Give the males a day or two to get used to their houses. Don't start the experiment until at least one of the males is actually staying in a house. Then add a third marked male cricket to each terrarium. How do the residents react? How does the intruder act?

Result: Your result is a statement of your crickets' behavior in each situation. See page 51 for use of tables to record results of Experiments 10 to 13.

Conclusion: In my experience, the prediction is confirmed. Male crickets with houses tend to be more aggressive toward intruding crickets than are those without houses. In a recent test with several crickets in each group, the housed crickets began to chirp immediately when we put the intruder into the terrarium. Not all chirped but some did. No crickets in the terrarium without houses chirped for the half-hour we watched them. To be confident in generalizing the results to other crickets, you would need to repeat the experiment several times.

Experiment 12

Question: Does having a female present increase aggression in male crickets?

Hypothesis: Having a female cricket present does increase aggression.

Methods: Set up two terraria with one pair of male crickets in each, as described for Experiment 10. Add a female to one terrarium and give the males a day or two to get used to her and to court her or copulate with her or whatever they're going to do. Then add a third marked male to each terrarium. How do the residents react? How does the intruder act?

Result: Your result is a statement of your observations of the crickets' behavior. See page 51 for use of tables to record results of Experiments 10 to 13.

Conclusion: The prediction was rejected in my experience. I have found little aggression in this situation. In a recent test, no one chirped. A resident male kicked the intruder in the no-female terrarium, but that was all. Having recently copulated may increase the aggression of a male, but simply having a female present does not seem to.

Experiment 13

Question: How does a previous win or loss affect the level of aggression in a male?

Hypothesis: A cricket that has just won one encounter is in a fighting mood and will probably win his next encounter too. (By "win" I mean that he will dominate the other cricket, chirping more or showing more of the other aggressive behaviors listed earlier.)

Methods: Set up two pairs of males in two terraria and leave them until one member of each pair is clearly dominant. Put the dominant male from one terrarium (call this one cricket A) with the submissive cricket from the other terrarium (call this one cricket B). Who dominates who? (A recent win makes a male more aggressive, and a recent loss makes a male more submissive, so cricket A should dominate cricket B.)

Next match cricket A with other winners. Keep doing this until someone dominates cricket A. Meanwhile match cricket B with other losers until cricket B dominates someone. Now, rematch cricket A and cricket B.

Result: Your result is a statement of your observations of dominance in cricket A and cricket B. See page 51 for use of tables to record results of Experiments 10 to 13.

Conclusion: Cricket B should dominate cricket A in the end, since he is now the cricket with a recent win. A cricket with a recent win is likely to defeat a cricket with a recent loss.

CHAPTER 6

Many-Legged Millipedes

Introduction

Millipedes are homely, easily overlooked residents of the under-log world. Their most interesting aspects are the patterns of motion in their many legs and their modes of defense, both of which are unusual. They're a very low-maintenance creature for keeping in captivity. One minute of care every two weeks will keep them going, and they're easy and safe to handle. The experiments herein address habitat preference, food detection, response to predators and more.

After you've done the experiments in this chapter and in Chapters 3, 4 and 5, refer to the table in Figure 1 in the Postscript, which provides a comparison of the results for the experiments in these chapters. Figure 2 in the Postscript is a blank table that can be filled out with the results of your experiments, for comparison.

Materials

1. Millipedes, which can be collected under logs or under the bark of logs or ordered from a biological supply company (see Appendix).
2. A container of some sort for maintaining the millipedes. I use the largest size of plastic margarine tubs, with wax paper lids secured with rubber bands.
3. Soil for the maintenance container.
4. Rotting leaves, rotting wood and an occasional apple core to feed the millipedes.
5. Two terraria or dish pans or other containers for Experiment 1, one such container for Experiments 2 and 5.
6. A blender for Experiment 2.
7. Two containers at least as large as a petri dish [3 1/2 inches (9 cm) in diameter] for Experiment 3.
8. A cake pan or similar sized container [8 to 9 inches (20.3–22.9 cm) in diameter] for Experiments 4 and 7.
9. A variety of millipede foods (plant parts, fungi) for Experiment 5.
10. A cricket and a toad or a praying mantis for Experiment 6.
11. Several other under-log animals for Experiment 7.

Background Information

Millipedes are not to be confused with centipedes. Centipedes can be rather unattractive, especially the brown kind with long legs that you see scuttling around in houses. Millipedes really are not unattractive. They have short, tidy legs that stay more or less tucked under their bodies. And they move much more slowly than centipedes.

Neither millipedes nor centipedes are insects, although they're both Arthropods, which is the same phylum that includes insects, spiders and crustaceans. Millipedes are no more closely related to centipedes than they are to these other Arthropod groups, but they seem so because of the abundance of legs. Millipede means "thousand legs" and centipede means "hundred legs," although neither has that many.

I like millipedes. For several years I've kept a thriving population of them in a big margarine tub — several different kinds of millipedes. They are happy as larks, reproducing like crazy. My captives range in size from as small as the comma on this page to the length of my little finger. There is no larval stage; the hatchlings look like miniature adults except that they are all white and have only three pairs of legs. The adults have many more. As the young ones grow to adulthood, they shed their exoskeletons about seven times, get darker and acquire more legs.

The defensive behavior of millipedes is interesting. They have two unusual defenses: stinking and coiling. Most millipedes have rows of stink glands along both sides of the body. The glands secrete a foul-smelling and foul-tasting liquid when the millipede is upset. Predators generally avoid them. I once saw a film of an African monkey eating a big millipede during a shortage of other foods and making an awful grimace because of the taste. Most of the millipedes I find are brown to blend in with their background, but some are brightly colored. The colors warn predators. A predator that's tasted another similar millipede will remember the color and avoid it. A common millipede in summer in my area is black with bright yellow around the edge, called *Sigmoria*. It's pictured, along with others, in the Golden Field Guide, *Spiders and Their Kin*.

Some millipedes also coil when bothered. The head is in the center of the coil, protected. But not all millipedes do this. In my experience the ones that are most cylindrical are most likely to coil. Another millipede defense is running and hiding, although they run rather slowly.

How to Tell Millipedes from Centipedes

Anytime you see a long slim insectlike creature with dozens of legs running the entire length of its body, you know it's either a centipede or a millipede. The first things to look for in distinguishing between the two are the shape of its body and the length of its legs (see Figure 6.1). Millipedes are cylindrical, like a drinking straw. Centipedes are flattened cylinders, like you'd have if you laid a drinking straw on a table and flattened it with your hand. Some of the most common millipedes where I live have flattened shelflike projections sticking out from both sides along the entire length of their bodies. This makes them look somewhat like centipedes (which probably helps them avoid predators since centipedes bite). But there are

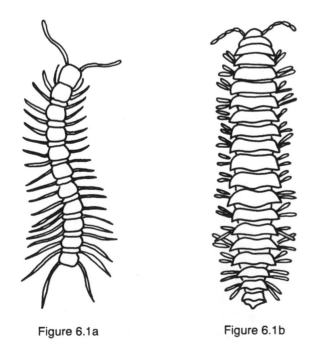

Figure 6.1a   Figure 6.1b

Figure 6.1a – Centipede. Some have much longer legs, like the common house centipede. This is one commonly found under bark on rotting logs. About 2 inches (5 cm) in length. Figure 6.1b – A flat-backed millipede, commonly found in leaf litter. About 1 inch (2.5 cm) in length.

other ways to tell the two apart. Most centipedes have longer legs than millipedes, and centipedes' legs tend to get longer toward the back ends of their bodies.

Millipedes have short legs, all the same length. Each body segment has two pairs of legs so when you look at a millipede from the side, you can see that the legs along that side look paired. Centipedes have only one pair of legs per body segment, so all legs on one side are equally spaced.

Centipedes move with an S-shaped motion. Legs on opposite sides of the body alternate movement. That is, if the first and third legs on the left are moving, then the first and third legs on the right are still. In contrast, most millipedes glide along without wiggling at all. They look as though they are flowing. This is because legs on opposite sides of the millipede's body move in synchrony instead of alternating. One of the activities in this chapter has to do with leg motion.

How to Get and Keep Millipedes

Centipedes (not millipedes) are hard to catch. I often see a beautiful orange type of centipede when I pull bark off dead logs. But centipedes run fast and they're gone in a flash. I'm afraid to grab them because they bite. Being predators, centipedes have strong jaws.

Because millipedes move more slowly, they are much easier to catch. They also don't (can't) bite. Millepedes are strictly vegetarians and lack the piercing jaws of centipedes, so you can pick them up.

The best place to look for millipedes is under rocks and under rotten logs, against the soil. They often burrow down into the soil if conditions are dry. They like damp places. The ones I find under logs are mostly brown and very slim, no longer than my little finger. Most are half that length. The brightly colored ones I'm more likely to see out in the open on the forest floor, unless it's very dry. Millipedes are almost as easy to find as roly-polies. If you turn over several logs and rocks in a damp place, it's almost guaranteed. Don't give up.

Millipedes are very easy to keep. The plastic margarine tub (the largest size) I keep them in is half full of soil. The lid is a piece of wax paper with holes cut into it, secured with a rubber band. A small piece of rotten log and a few damp rotting leaves lie on the surface of the soil, and I throw an apple core in there every couple of weeks. I drizzle some water over the contents of the tub every week or so. I originally set these tubs up for roly-polies, and the millipedes were in there only because a few were clinging to the piece of log I put in for the roly-polies. But the millipedes do as well as the roly-polies. Both have lots of tiny offspring that wander over the soil and fill the nooks and crannies of the log. You can also feed millipedes fungi, the roots of green plants and seedlings.

Field Hunt

You need an area shaded by trees, where the ground is covered with leaves. Flip logs, rocks, bricks and look under the leaves. They like damp places. Children can collect them in milk cartons or jars. (Remind them not to stick hands into dark places they can't see.)

If you're unsure about telling millipedes from centipedes, check out a book from the library and look at some pictures or check the encyclopedia. Some dictionaries may have pictures. After you've seen a few, it's quite easy to tell them apart, even when you see a new species. Be sure to provide some moisture for them as soon as you get back to the classroom. A damp crumpled paper towel will do, while you fix up a terrarium (or margarine tub) for them.

Millipedes at School
Observations and Activities

I first introduce children to the millipedes while they are sitting around a table, one group at a time. I put one to ten millipedes in the middle of the table (see Figure 6.2). All millipedes will start walking if completely exposed like that. The children enjoy watching them walk around, pushing them away from the edge, watching what the millipedes do if a child's finger becomes an obstacle. The next day I have the millipedes available in the margarine tubs, so the children can poke and prod and explore. I sometimes add to this other residents of the under-log world too: snails, worms, small slugs, ants, crickets, etc. The children can see in the tubs the natural habitat of these creatures in miniature and see the millipedes' natural neighbors. Children seem to especially like baby creatures. They get excited seeing the baby millipedes and baby roly-polies in the margarine tubs. Each child or group can make his or her own under-log world in a container. Children really enjoy fishing around in them (see Figure 6.3).

A good way to start observations of the animals' behavior is to have the children write down everything they notice about the millipedes. Following are some millipede behaviors that I find interesting.

Noticing Millipede Locomotion

The children may notice the wavelike motion of the legs on their own, although I never did before I read about it. If they look at a millipede from the side as it walks, they can see distinct waves of leg motion moving from one end of the millipede to the other. Do these waves of motion move from front to rear or from rear to front? (Rear to front.) How many waves can the children see at one time? On the millipedes I've watched I can see three to four waves moving at once.

If the children look carefully, they can see that what appears to be a wave are the legs that are raised off the

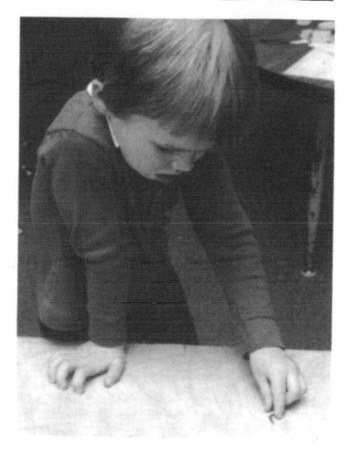

Figure 6.2 – Alan picking up a millipede.

surface. Most of the legs are in contact with the ground at any one time. Only a few are raised. At the beginning of the wave, legs at the back of the body are raised, then as they are put down, those just ahead of them are raised and so on. Thus, the raising and putting down of legs looks like a ripple or wave moving from the rear forward along the legs. Since millipede legs on opposite sides move in synchrony, the two sides look identical at any one time.

Try to figure out how this makes the millipede move forward. Why don't they instead move all the legs on the left, then all the legs on the right? That would be less efficient for one thing, because half of the legs would be in motion at any one time. It would also cause a lot of wiggling, which would make the millipede more conspicuous to predators. Centipedes do wiggle in an S-shape as they walk because legs on opposite sides of the body alternate movement.

Millipede Grooming

What will the millipede do if it gets something goopy on its legs? Put the millipede down on a surface that has been smeared with a thin layer of jelly, honey, petroleum jelly or oil. What does it do? Millipedes will clean and

Figure 6.3 — Alan getting millipedes out of his margarine container to put in a petri dish.

groom all their legs with their mouth parts when they get sticky or dirty. Millipedes are like cats and mantises in a way, using their mouths to clean their appendages.

Millipede Defenses

The students may notice on their own that the millipedes smell bad. The little brown ones usually smell less than the larger and brightly colored ones. Children may have to put the little brown ones up close to their noses to smell them or sniff their fingers after handling them. I can smell it at a distance, maybe because I know what it smells like. Larger ones can be smelled at arm's length. The brightly colored *Sigmoria* activates its stink glands at the slightest provocation, before the little brown ones do. What line of defense does your millipede use first: running, coiling or stinking? If you have more than one species, the children may notice that some coil and some don't. Put the millipede on a flat surface and watch it. After a minute or so, poke it with something soft, like a paintbrush, or touch it gently with your finger. Different types of millipedes may react differently. In my experience, the little brown ones that are so common in my area run first, stink if annoyed further and coil as a last resort. Those with projections on the sides, however, don't coil. Millipedes don't usually use all their defenses at once. Why not? If they discharged the contents of the stink gland every time they saw something moving, they'd spend an awful lot of energy synthesizing new fluid for the glands. It makes sense too that coiling should be a last resort, because it

doesn't protect them from large predators who might eat them whole, but only from smaller ones that might go for a piece of a millipede.

Experiments

Remember that the hypotheses I give are just examples. Most are written in the "if ... then" format, but they don't have to be. Your hypotheses will be the predictions made by the class or a particular child. Your result for each experiment will be a statement of how your animals reacted to your experimental setup. Your conclusion is a statement of whether your prediction was confirmed or not. For each experiment, adding replicates increases your confidence in the validity of your conclusion, but they may be omitted if tedious for young children.

Experiment 1

Question: Can millipedes find their food as quickly in the dark as in the light?

Hypothesis: Millipedes need light to find their food.

Methods: Catch several millipedes, preferably of the same type. Divide them into two groups of equal number. Ten millipedes in each group is optimum, but fewer is okay. Provide moisture but no food to each group for three or four days. Meanwhile, get empty containers of equal size, about 12 to 20 inches (.3–.5 m) in diameter, like plastic dish pans or shirt boxes. Put millipede food in a small pile in the center of each tub: plant rootlets, a seedling, a piece of fruit with mold on it and/or pieces of rotting leaves. After three or four days' starvation, put the millipedes in one corner of each box. Cover one box so that it's completely dark inside. Leave the other open. Wait three minutes, then count how many millipedes are on the food pile in each container. If none are, wait longer. Did more millipedes find the food in the light than in the dark?

Result: Your result is a statement of the number of millipedes on the food in each box. You can record your results on Figure 6.4, a histogram. Figure 3.4 provides an example of a completed histogram.

Conclusion: The prediction is not confirmed. The number of millipedes on the food should be about the same in the two containers. They locate their food by scent and have poor eyesight. Since millipedes are nocturnal, it makes sense that they would rely more on their sense of smell.

How else could you test this? See the next experiment.

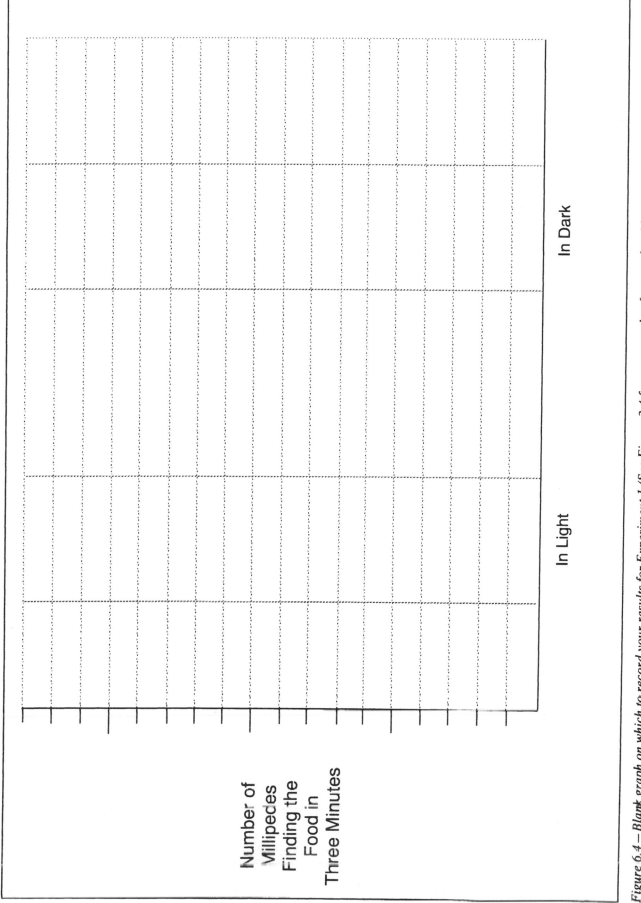

Figure 6.4 — Blank graph on which to record your results for Experiment 1 (See Figure 3.4 for an example of a completed histogram.)

Experiment 2

Question: Can millipedes find food by scent alone?

Hypothesis: Millipedes need to be able to see food to find it.

Methods: Put some seedlings, rotten leaves, fungus and plant roots in a blender with some water and grind it into a liquid. Soak a small piece of absorbent cloth with the liquid. Soak another piece of absorbent cloth with water. Put the two cloths on opposite sides of a container and place your millipede(s) in the middle of the container. Which cloth is chosen, if either?

Result: Your result is a statement of your observation.

Conclusion: The prediction is not confirmed. Millipedes are attracted to the blender liquid by scent, but not the water.

Experiment 3

Question: Does food availability affect the growth rate of millipedes, or their size at maturity?

Hypothesis: Those that eat more grow bigger and faster.

Methods: Put damp paper on the floor of two small containers, at least as large as a petri dish [3 1/2 inches (9 cm) in diameter]. Get two or several similar-sized young millipedes. Very young millipedes are white and 1/12 to 1/5 inches (2–5 mm) long. Those that have just hatched have only three pairs of legs. Put an equal number of young millipedes in the two containers. Spray the paper floor of the containers with water every day to keep them damp.

Keep food available for one group constantly. Make food available to the other group every other day, every third day or some other intermittent schedule. Measure the millipedes weekly and keep track of when they molt or shed their exoskeletons. You'll see the shed skin in the container. Millipedes molt when they've outgrown their exoskeletons, or outer "skins," so molting can be used as a measure of growth. Most millipedes molt seven times before reaching adulthood. (Adulthood is defined in animals by sexual maturity, not size.)

Result: Your result is a statement of your growth measurements for each group, or dates on which they molted. You can plot your measurements on a graph (see Figure 6.5). Figure 6.6 provides a blank graph for your measurements.

Conclusion: The prediction is confirmed. The millipedes fed intermittently will probably grow more slowly than those with food available constantly. They may have fewer molts and mature at a smaller size, depending on

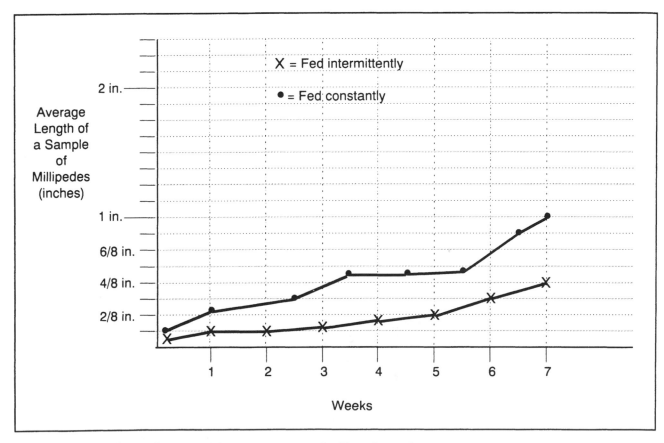

Figure 6.5 — Sample graph summarizing measurements for Experiment 3.

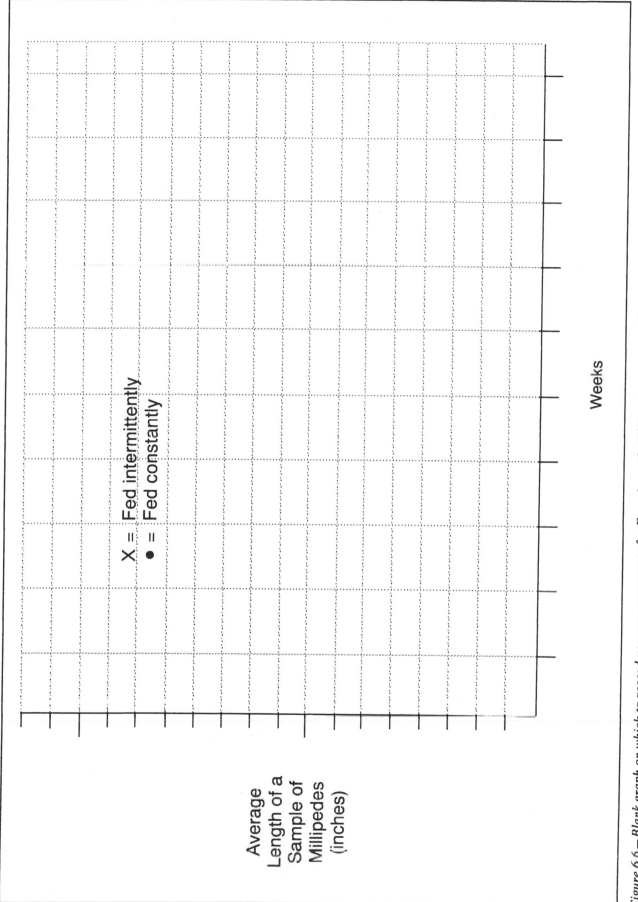

X = Fed intermittently
● = Fed constantly

Average Length of a Sample of Millipedes (inches)

Weeks

Figure 6.6 — Blank graph on which to record your measurements for Experiment 3. Fill in the numbers on both axes.

how much their feeding frequency is reduced. Making the millipedes "go hungry" may seem cruel to the children, but the feeding rate of cold-blooded animals is much more flexible than that of warm-blooded animals like ourselves. Most of our food goes to maintaining our body temperature.

Experiment 4

Question: What types of conditions do millipedes prefer?

Hypothesis: They like a bright, sunny place.

Methods: You can use one or several millipedes here. Offer the millipede(s) a series of choices. Just about any container big enough for the millipede to move around in will do, but it must have low sides. A cake pan is a good size [8 to 9 inches (20.3–22.9 cm) in diameter], with a plexiglass or tight plastic wrap lid. First make one side damp and one side dry by covering the bottom of the cake pan with two half-circles of construction paper, one damp and one dry. The two pieces of paper shouldn't be touching or the dry piece will soak up dampness. Put one or several millipedes in the center of the dish and leave them for a half-hour or so. Which side do they prefer?

Now make one side dark and one side light by covering the top on one side with something dark and opaque, like a piece of black construction paper. The bottom should be uniformly damp or uniformly dry. Put the millipede(s) in the center and come back in a half-hour or so. Which side do they prefer? Does the dampness of the substrate affect the outcome?

Make a little house in the dish with a small box or a film can cut in half lengthwise. Leave the house with the millipede(s) for a half-hour or so. Do they hide in it or stay out? Does the dampness of the substrate affect the outcome?

Get a long cookie pan with sides. Put a hot water bottle under one end of the pan. Put a tray of ice under the other end. After waiting a while for the respective ends of the tray to heat and cool, put the millipede(s) in the middle. Come back after a half-hour to an hour. Do they prefer the warm end or the cool end or the middle?

Result: Your result is a statement of your millipede's choices. You can record your results on Figure 6.7, a histogram. Figure 3.4 provides an example of a completed histogram. You can also record your results in the table provided in Figure 6.8. Figure 4.8 provides an example.

Conclusion: The outcome probably depends on the type of millipede. Those found under logs will tend to prefer darkness, dampness, cover and coolness. We see millipedes under logs because they find the conditions they like there.

Experiment 5

Question: What foods do your millipedes prefer?

Hypothesis: It depends on what you offer.

Methods: Use several millipedes for this one if you can. Put damp paper on the floor of a container about the size of a dishpan. Otherwise the millipedes may spend all their time trying to escape instead of looking for food. Offer your millipedes a choice between small seedlings (plants that have just sprouted from seeds), fungus (like the mold that grows on a rotten fruit or a mushroom), small rootlets of plants and rotting leaves. Put the four choices in different corners of a container and after a half-hour or longer, record which one your millipedes prefer.

Result: Your result is a statement of your millipedes' choice. You can record your results on the table in Figure 6.9.

Conclusion: The outcome depends on what species of millipede you have.

Experiment 6

Question: Does stinking deter predators?

Hypothesis: We think a predator will avoid a millipede that stinks.

Methods: Offer a praying mantis a millipede and a small cricket of comparable size. Make sure both are moving. Which does it take? Or offer a millipede and a worm of comparable size to a toad. Again, make sure both are moving. Which does it take?

Result: Your result is a statement of your mantis' or toad's choice.

Conclusion: The prediction is confirmed. Both predators will probably avoid the millipede. Can you think of a way to test the effectiveness of coiling in detering predators? (*Hint:* A chilled millipede will be unable to coil temporarily.)

Experiment 7

Question: Do other under-log inhabitants avoid millipedes?

Hypothesis: We think other under-log inhabitants will avoid millipedes, especially millipedes we can smell.

Methods: This experiment involves comparing (1) the distance between a millipede and another animal to (2) the distance between two things that we know to be indifferent to each other, like two peas. To do this you'll need a small container with steep sides, such as

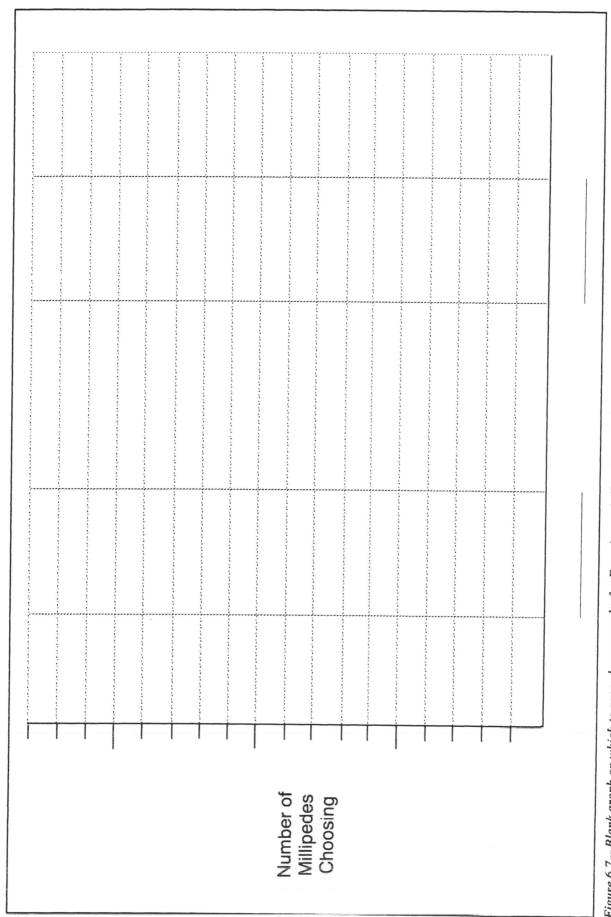

Figure 6.7 – Blank graph on which to record your results for Experiment 4. (See Figure 3.4 for an example of a completed histogram.) Fill in the blanks on the horizontal axis with these pairs of labels, for the four sets of conditions offered in Experiment 4: Dampness – Dryness, Darkness – Light, Cover – Open, Warmth – Cold.

Number of Millipedes Choosing

Choice of Conditions Offered to Millipedes	Millipedes' Choice	Effect of Choice on Millipedes
Dampness or Dryness		
Darkness or Light		
Cover or Open Space		
Warmth or Cold		

Figure 6.8 — Blank table on which to record your results for Experiment 4.

FOODS ACCEPTED BY MILLIPEDES

	Accepted	Not Accepted	Not Sure
Seedlings			
Fungus			
Rootlets			
Rotting Leaves			
Raw Potato			
Chunk of Apple			
_____			
_____			
_____			

Figure 6.9 — Blank table on which to record your results for Experiment 5.

Do other under-log inhabitants avoid millipedes?

Number of lines between peas (shake and count ten to twenty times). Record your counts here:

What was the average number of lines between peas?

Number of lines between millipede and worm (count ten to twenty times), allowing time for animals to move before counting again. Record your counts here:

What is the average number of lines between millipede and companion?

Repeat with millipede and roly-poly.

    Record counts here:

    Average number of lines:

Repeat with millipede and

    Record counts here:

    Average number of lines:

Were the pea pairs closer than the animal pairs?

Figure 6.10 — Blank table on which to record your results for Experiment 7.

a cake pan. Draw a grid on the floor of it with at least nine squares in the grid. Put two peas in the pan, shake it and put it down without looking. Then count the number of lines you'd have to cross to get from one pea to the other without curving. If the peas are in the same square, that counts as zero. If they are in adjacent squares, that counts as a one. If they are in squares that touch diagonally, that counts as a two, and so on. Do this ten to twenty times with a pair of peas and calculate an average. This is the number of lines you would expect to be between two animals if they were totally indifferent to one another.

Now do the same thing with pairs of animals, except there's no need to shake them. Put one millipede and one other animal at a time in the container and cover it with a clear lid like plastic wrap taped down tightly. (The animals will be able to breathe adequately for the short period of the trial.) Handle or prod the millipede first to try to get it to discharge its stink glands. Here are some suggestions for animals to pair with the millipede: a worm, a snail, a slug, a roly-poly, a beetle, a spider and a centipede. Check the pair after an hour. Record how many lines you'd have to cross to get from one animal to another without curving, as described for the peas. Do this ten times for each pair of animals. Then calculate an average number of lines for each pair, as you did for the pair of peas. Are the animals farther apart in general than the peas were? This is what you'd expect if the nonmillipedes are avoiding the millipedes. Here are some ways to vary the experiment.

1. Use a millipede and one pea instead of two peas to calculate your average for two things that are indifferent to each other.
2. Try pairs of animals where neither is a millipede and compare.
3. Try pairs of millipedes and compare.
4. Make your grid on a piece of brown paper towel and dampen it. Compare results on the damp substrate to results in a dry dish. Danger of dehydration may cause animals to seek out other bodies.

Result: Your result is a statement of your average line counts for pea pairs, for millipede-plus-other pairs and for pairs of nonmillipedes and pairs of millipedes, if you go that far. You can record your results on the table in Figure 6.10.

Conclusion: The prediction is confirmed generally. Other animals may avoid the millipede, especially a very stinky one. A millipede may seek out another millipede to mate, but otherwise are generally indifferent to each other. During mating, the male lies on top of the female, their bodies aligned. He also nibbles at her face.

Other animals are often indifferent to one another unless they are dehydrating. Huddling together or "bunching" reduces the amount of surface area in contact with drying air. I've never seen millipedes do this but they may in a dry dish. It would make sense for under-log residents to do it, because they are adapted to a damp environment and probably vulnerable to dehydration.

CHAPTER 7

The Fungus That Creeps

Introduction

A slime mold is a small, goopy fungus that stumped taxonomists for a long time because it has many animallike characteristics. It can creep slowly like an amoeba and pursue its food! Slime molds are easy to maintain and fascinate children because they are so peculiar. This chapter describes how to keep a slime mold in captivity and how to conduct experiments to answer questions about its feeding, its reproduction and its ability to regenerate.

Materials

1. Slime mold plasmodium. This can be cultured from dead wood, which may take a couple of months, or ordered from a biological supply company (see Appendix).
2. Petri dishes and lids, which can be bought at a science hobby shop or ordered from a biological supply company. One dish per child works well, or the children can work in groups. If you want to do all of the activities in this chapter, you'll need at least two dishes for each child or each group. Four-inch (10.2 cm) in diameter dishes are a good size.
3. Filter paper. You need at least one sheet per dish, the same diameter as the dish. You should have a few spares.
4. Tweezers or forceps.
5. Oatmeal or other food, if desired.

Background Information

A slime mold is not particularly charming at first glance. It looks rather like something you'd find in a jar of leftovers that's been in the back of the refrigerator for too long. But it's different from other molds, which digest and absorb the surface on which they're growing. The difference is that slime molds are able to move about freely and "capture" their food. This odd feature—the ability to creep—is what first attracted my attention to them.

A slime can be kept in captivity indefinitely as long as you feed it regularly, keep it damp and are careful not to introduce bacteria or other molds. When you feed your slime an oatmeal flake, it will creep slowly toward the flake to engulf it, which is wonderfully fun to watch! Slimes are like clocks in that you can't see them move, but you can easily see that they have moved over the span of a few minutes. Slime molds have a two-part life cycle. The two phases don't occur at the same time but alternate. The phase that creeps after its food is called a plasmodium (see Figure 7.1). The plasmodial phase of all slime molds prefers darkness and moisture. In nature they stay under or inside rotten logs and are rather hard to find. I have found

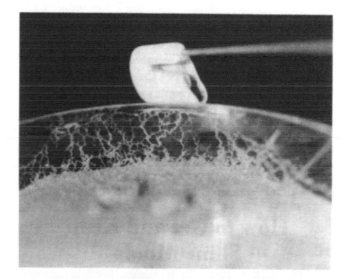

Figure 7.1—The plasmodium of a Many Headed Slime streaming or "creeping" up the side of the petri dish. Many have "escaped" onto my kitchen counter in this fashion. Diaper pin added for scale.

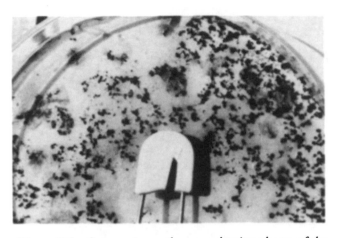

Figure 7.2 — Sporangia, or the reproductive phase, of the Many-Headed Slime in a 3-1/2-inch (9 cm) petri dish. Diaper pin added for scale.

active plasmodia in nature only once or twice, in very damp logs near streams.

The other phase of the slime life cycle, the reproductive phase, is much more conspicuous in nature than the plasmodium. During the reproductive phase all slimes make some kind of little capsule containing spores. (A spore is like a tiny seed except that it usually isn't produced by sexual union as a seed is, but instead by a single organism.) These reproductive capsules are easier to find than the plasmodium because they're often in the open, such as on top of a log. On top is a better place for the slime to disperse its spores. The reproductive capsules are called sporangia, and all fungi make sporangia (see Figure 7.2).

The slime species most often kept in captivity is the Many-Headed Slime, which has a bright yellow plasmodium. When pursuing a food item, the slime stretches itself out in long streams of yellow protoplasm (see Figure 7.1), but while eating an oatmeal flake, it looks like a yellow blob of goo. The slime mold doesn't actually creep; it really streams. It sends out a membrane in the shape of a channel, and then its protoplasm streams into the channel. We have protoplasm too! People can't stream from place to place because our protoplasm is all contained in cells bound by cell membranes. But the slime mold's protoplasm isn't packaged, so it flows along from one place to another. Slimes used to be considered animals because the plasmodial stage can move about, but now they're classified as fungi because of the way they reproduce.

How to Get and Keep Slime Molds

Growing Plasmodia from Spores

Any piece of rotting log will probably have spores on it that will often germinate if the wood is kept damp for a long time. I did it by keeping a wet washcloth over a piece

of rotting log in a terrarium for two to three months. I moistened the washcloth every day. After two and a half months, a Many-Headed Slime plasmodium appeared, followed by a cluster of Carnival Candy Slime sporangia.

For some reason plasmodia on logs are much more hardy and resistant to contamination by other molds or bacteria than are those in petri dishes. Perhaps the slimes have an advantage on the log because the log is their natural habitat to which they are finely adapted. I have a Many-Headed Slime plasmodium now that lives on a damp piece of rotting wood in a terrarium. It's one that I ordered and then released onto the log. I never feed it or tend to it in any way, other than keeping a damp cloth over the piece of log. I handle the log almost daily because I have to feed a salamander who lives under it. Yet I've had this slime for at least a year and it is perfectly healthy in spite of my handling.

A log is ideal for keeping one as a pet or as a "stock" slime for the long term. You can start one in a dish by taking a piece of the one on the log, although it may disappear into the log periodically and be inaccessible.

Ordering a Plasmodium

If you order a Many-Headed Slime mold from Carolina Biological Supply Company or Powell Laboratories, you can get active plasmodium in a tube or in a petri dish ("plate"). You can also get a dried, dormant plasmodium in a tube. This dormant form is called a sclerotium. The sclerotium can be reactivated by keeping it moist for several days. Instructions on how to do this come with it.

Propogating a Plasmodium

If you order an active plasmodium and want to propagate it for a class, the best thing to use is petri dishes. If you want to avoid the expense (which isn't much), kitchen bowls or saucers will do. You'll need to keep them tightly covered with plastic wrap to keep moisture in. Whether you use petri dishes or kitchen bowls you have to have absorbent paper in the bottom of the dish. Filter paper works well, as it holds water for about twenty-four hours. You can order a box of one hundred papers the same width as your petri dishes.

To get the slime from the plate or tube into a new dish, you can just scrape some up or cut into pieces the rubbery gel it comes on. Put a small glop of slime or a piece of the gel with slime on it into the new dish. Take the gel out when the slime creeps off of it. It's best to use more or less sterile tweezers and scissors.

If you scrape up the plasmodium to transfer it, it will take a day or two to recover and begin creeping again.

Maintaining a Plasmodium

To maintain a plasmodium in one dish, feed it no more than one oatmeal flake a day (see Figure 7.3). If you feed it more the food will rot. Add drops of water as needed to

Figure 7.3 — Pinching up one more oatmeal flake to feed the Many-Headed Slime. Someone has put in too many! The tweezers help minimize contaminating the slime with bacteria and the spores of other molds.

keep the filter paper barely moist. I use tap water that has been left standing uncovered twenty-four hours for the chlorine to vaporize.

The instructions that come with the slime say that everything that touches the slime must be sterile, including the water. (Boiling the water works.) I've had mixed experiences with this. Sometimes I can handle the filter paper or oatmeal and somehow not contaminate the culture. But if you let children add the oatmeal and touch the slimes with unwashed hands, you'll probably get a vast array of molds and other growths to keep the slime mold company. Once a particular plasmodium is contaminated, it's almost impossible to separate it from the other growths, and it usually dies.

Field Hunt

It's a lot of fun to find slime molds in nature, and they're quite common. It takes practice to be able to spot them because they are usually very small. Even the brightly colored sporangia are relatively inconspicuous because of their size. The first time I found a slime in nature I didn't know what it was. It looked like a reddish dusting of powder on a rotten log. Scattered throughout the fuzz were clusters of tiny black cups, each cup about the size of the head of a pin. I wondered if it might be a fungus because it was obviously something living, but it wasn't a plant or animal. I flipped through Audubon's field guide to the section on mushrooms when I got home and found it easily, because it looked exactly like the color photograph. It was Multigoblet Slime. What a name! That began my interest in slimes.

The sporangia of each slime species are distinctive. It isn't hard to tell them apart with the field guide. Chocolate Tube Slime sporangia look like little brown cigars on stalks; Carnival Candy Slime sporangia look like tiny pink puffs of cotton candy on stalks; Scrambled Egg Slime sporangia look like scrambled eggs; Yellow-Fuzz Cone

Figure 7.4 — Sporangia, or the reproductive phase, of the Yellow-Fuzz Cone Slime in nature.

Figure 7.5 — Sporangia, or the reproductive phase, of Tooth paste Slime (sometimes called Wolf's Milk Slime) in nature.

Slime sporangia look like tiny cones, some of which are full of yellow fuzz (see Figure 7.4). I've found all of the above in nature, most of them when I was just walking and not really looking.

Now that I have shown my children several in nature and the pictures too, they have become pretty good at finding sporangia by themselves. Their favorite is Toothpaste Slime, also called Wolf's Milk Slime. It looks like a cluster of round pink pillows, each about the size of a green pea (see Figure 7.5). My children like the Toothpaste Slime sporangia partly because we've found them several times and partly because if you squeeze one gently, it bulges and then ruptures with a satisfying pop. Out oozes a deep pink paste, somewhat like the consistency of toothpaste. Of course the kids find popping them irresistible, and race to get the next one, squealing, "Ooh, gross!" and "Aah." They love it. (Okay, I do too.) It's fortunate that they occur in clusters.

If left alone, the paste in Toothpaste Slime will dry out and turn into a packet of thickly packed dust. The dust is actually spores, encased in a little round sack with a pinhole at the top. Touch it and a cloud of pinkish "smoke" comes out.

Slimes at School
Getting Ready

After you've gotten as many slimes as you want growing in individual dishes, you're ready to take the dishes to school. Don't wait too long between getting the dishes ready and taking them to school, because if you have introduced molds or bacteria to the dish, they may overwhelm the slime in a week or so.

Observations and Activities

Feeding the slime molds is a good place to start, whether you want to do only that or go on to an experiment. After a few introductory remarks to the children describing what a slime is and what is interesting about it, pass out a dish of slime and a flake of oatmeal to each child. You should probably put each oatmeal flake on a small piece of paper so that the children can dump the oatmeal flakes into the dishes by picking up the papers without touching the flakes. They can use clean hands instead if you don't plan to keep the slimes more than a week or so. Tell them to put the oatmeal close to their slimes. Some of the oatmeal flakes will be engulfed by the slimes right away, but it may take a couple of hours before all are. The bright yellow color of the Many-Headed Slime makes it easy to tell when it has crawled onto the oatmeal. Help the children describe what they've seen.

You can extend these feeding observations and help the children begin to feel involved in decision-making by asking them what other kinds of things they think the slimes might eat. Encourage them to bring in their suggestions. They may bring food from home or things from nature that aren't food

for us but could be for the slime mold. You may want to encourage them to think about what the slime mold eats in its natural habitat of rotting logs. (Many eat microorganisms in the log, although they appear to be eating the log.) They eat a surprising variety of foods.

Food remnants in the dish seem to encourage the growth of bacteria and other molds that can be lethal to the slime mold. So you should probably set aside a couple of dishes for food testing and not plan to use them for anything else. Or the children can feed their own slimes the different foods if they do it after the other activities have been completed or if they all have extra slimes.

During their observations, the children will probably come up with questions. Here are some of the questions I've been asked by first-graders watching the slimes eat: You mean it's blind? Could it use glasses? Why doesn't it have any head? How does it know where to go? Does it have teeth? Does it have a tongue? Does it have a mouth? How does it eat? It doesn't have any senses? If they don't have a head, how do they know where their food is? If they don't have a head, how do they know anything?

Children seem to be fascinated by how something that possesses the ability to move independently can be so devoid of other similarities to ourselves. Slimes seem to get by just fine with only one sense—some sort of taste or chemical detection. Get the children to think about whether or not slimes really need any other senses. (This is a good opportunity to start the children thinking about how and why other animals are different from us. Does a tree need to be able to see or hear? How about a clam or an earthworm? No, because they are all either sedentary or burrowing.)

Another avenue of exploration is the ability of slimes to regenerate, which you've already seen yourself if you divided the one you ordered to make more for the children. If you have enough petri dishes you can let each child use a toothpick to scoop up the slime and transfer it to another dish. Feed the new one. How long does it take the new one to begin streaming toward its food? How small a portion of slime can they transfer to a new dish and still have a new slime develop?

Seeing the slimes survive and grow after being cut apart seems to intrigue children. They ask a lot of questions about this too: Why doesn't it kill them? How do you know it doesn't hurt? Why doesn't it hurt?

This is a good time to explain to them that the slime has no different body parts like we do. It has no organs inside, no heart, no stomach, no arms, no legs, no nerves. Every piece is, in a way, a whole body.

Experiments

Remember that the hypotheses I give are just examples. Most are written in the "if ... then" format, but they don't have to be. Your hypotheses will be the predictions made by the class or a particular child. Your result for each experiment will be a statement of how your fungi reacted to your experimental setup. Your conclusion is a statement of whether your prediction was confirmed or not. For each experiment, adding replicates increases your confidence in the validity of your conclusion, but they may be omitted if tedious for young children.

Experiment 1

It's a good idea if you can to derive your experiment from the children's questions. Sometimes the opportunity doesn't present itself, but for me it did with the slime molds. One child asked, "If they don't have a head, how do they know where the food is?" "How do they know" is not the type of question that lends itself to being answered by an experiment, but it can be modified slightly so that it is. The question, "Do they know where their food is?" is one that can easily be answered by an experiment. You can answer it the same way you would for any animal. Offer them food at a distance and see if they move toward it faster than they move toward a designated spot with no food. That's what we did.

Question: Do slime molds know where their food is or do they just stumble on it? Specifically, will they move faster toward their food than toward a designated spot with no food?

Hypothesis: We think the slimes just stumble on their food.

Methods: You'll need at least about ten individual slimes to participate. The children may volunteer theirs. The more you have, the more confidence you can have in your results. You'll need a fresh petri dish for each participant. (You can wash and reuse them. Let them air dry to help kill bacteria.) Before you put the filter paper in the dish, while the paper is still dry, draw two circles a little larger than an oatmeal flake on opposite edges of the filter paper. Then put the paper in the dish and moisten it. Put an oatmeal flake in only one of the circles, leave the other one empty. Place a wad of slime in the center of the paper (see Figure 7.6). Check it every half-hour or so and record which circle the slime enters first. If it enters the circle with the oatmeal-flake paper first in most of the dishes, then it probably "knows" where the oatmeal-flake paper is. If it enters the empty circle first in about half of the dishes, then you can conclude that its movements are random and it is not moving purposefully in one direction.

Result: Your result is a statement of how many slimes reached the food first, how many reached the empty circle first and any other relevant observations. You can record your results as a histogram in Figure 7.7. Figure 3.4 provides an example of a completed histogram.

Conclusion: In my experience, the slimes will start out moving randomly, sending out streams toward both circles. When one stream of protoplasm comes to within about 1/2 inch (1.3 cm) of the oatmeal-flake paper, then the rest of the plasmodium begins to stream toward it too. Apparently they somehow detect in the filter paper chemicals (carbohydrates, proteins) that have diffused into the paper around the oatmeal. My results have been that most of the slimes enter the circle with the oatmeal flake first, but not all of them do. But don't tell the children this until after the experiment is over or there'll be no suspense! Besides, you may get a different outcome. In my experience, this prediction has been rejected. Slime molds can move purposefully toward their food.

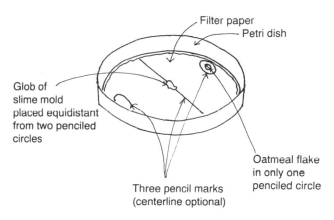

Figure 7.6 — Petri dish setup for Experiment 1.

Experiment 2

How would you determine more definitively the distance at which the slime can detect the oatmeal? You could vary the distance between slime and oatmeal in different dishes. You would record how soon the oatmeal ceases random movement and begins to stream purposefully toward the oatmeal in each dish.

Question: At what distance can the slime mold detect the oatmeal in the filter paper? In other words, at what distance will most of the slimes begin to move definitively toward the food right away?

Hypothesis: The slime mold will move all of its protoplasm toward the oatmeal right away when it is introduced at a distance of 1 inch (2.5 cm) (or whatever distance your students predict).

It will move in several different directions initially when deposited at a distance of 3 inches (7.6 cm) (or whatever the students predict) from the oatmeal.

Methods: Vary the initial distance between slime and oatmeal from 1/4 inch to 3 inches (.6–7.6 cm) in different dishes. At what initial distance do the slimes

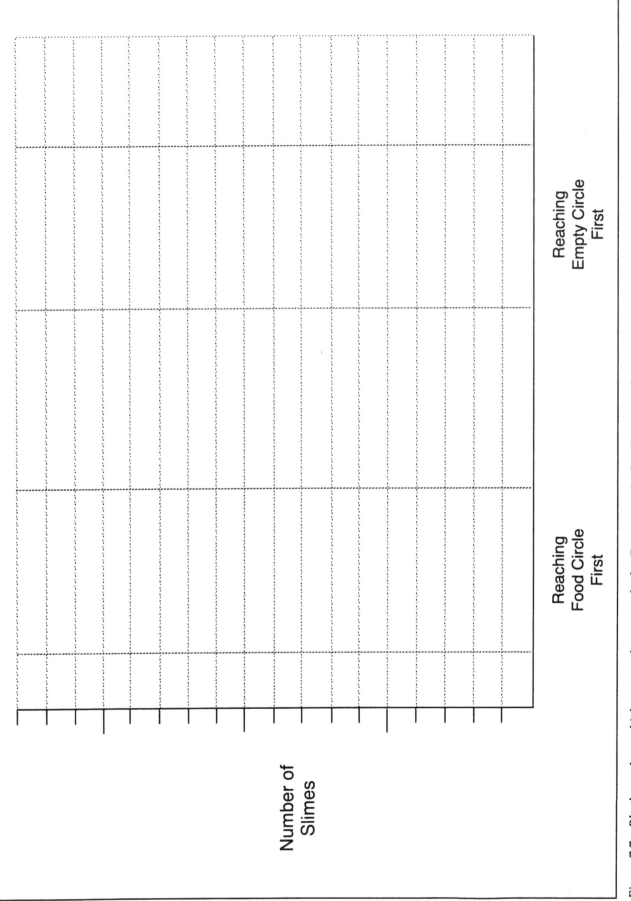

Figure 7.7 — Blank graph on which to record your results for Experiment 1. (See Figure 3.4 for an example of a completed histogram.)

Initial Distance	Did All of the Protoplasm Move Toward the Food and Not in the Other Direction?	
	Yes	No
¼ in.		
½ in.		
¾ in.		
1 in.		
1¼ in.		
1½ in.		
1¾ in.		
2 in.		
2½ in.		
3 in.		

Figure 7.8 — Blank table on which to record your results for Experiment 2.

	Drying	Light	Lack of Food
Which Conditions Caused Sporangia to Form? **Put a Check in the Appropriate Space.**			
Slime 1			
Slime 2			
Slime 3			
Slime 4			
Slime 5			
Slime 6			
Slime 7			
Slime 8			
Slime 9			
Slime 10			

Figure 7.9 — Blank table on which to record your results from Experiments 3 to 7.

begin to move all of their protoplasm toward the oatmeal right away?

Result: Your result is a statement of the slimes' behavior at different initial distances. You can record your results on the table in Figure 7.8.

Conclusion: In my experience the distance at which the slimes detect the oatmeal and begin to move all of their protoplasm toward it is between 1/2 and 1 inch (1.3–2.5 cm).

I'm not sure what causes the slime mold to shift from one stage of its life cycle to another. Scientific explanations include that exposure to light, lack of moisture or absence of food can cause sporangia to form from the plasmodium. At least one of these three conditions has been present every time I've seen sporangia form. It often happens when I stop taking care of them. If I throw a plasmodium in the trash while I'm cleaning some petri dishes, the next morning I'll probably see sporangia in the trash. Or, if a plasmodium escapes from its container, which often happens, the escaped portion often forms sporangia. This happens as a way of self-preservation and reproduction when conditions are not right for the plasmodium. Contact with plastic wrap seems to cause sporangia to form immediately, maybe because the plastic wrap is so completely nonabsorbent and devoid of moisture. I've put filter paper with slimes aboard on plastic wrap and found the next day that the edges that had crawled off the filter paper had formed sporangia, while the part remaining on the filter paper was still plasmodium.

Other times I've had slime molds dry up completely and not form sporangia. This uncertainty about what exactly causes it can lead to some interesting experiments. If the children know that plasmodia are normally found inside rotting logs, get them to talk about what it's like in there: dark and damp (and full of organic matter, although the children probably won't come up with this one). Sporangia form on top of the log. What's it like on top? Light and probably drier. Help the children to speculate about what conditions the plasmodium may need. Moisture and darkness and food. A table is provided in Figure 7.9 to record which factors cause sporangia formation. How can you test which of these factors will cause sporangia to form? Remove each factor one at a time. Let the children volunteer their slimes, although you may find that none want to volunteer, for fear of losing their plasmodium. If not, maybe you can use some spares for this experiment or give the children replacements.

Experiment 3

Question: Will drying induce sporangia to form?

Hypothesis: We think drying will induce sporangia to form.

Methods: Stop watering some of the slimes, while continuing to feed them moistened oatmeal flakes and keeping them in the dark. Continue to water some of the slimes, as a control.

Result: Your result is a statement of your observations. You can record your results on the table in Figure 7.9.

Conclusion: My experience is that some of the slimes that are not watered form sporangia but some don't. Some merely dry up. Thus, allowing the filter paper to dry may cause sporangia to form but not always.

Experiment 4

Question: Will light cause sporangia to form?

Hypothesis: We think light will cause sporangia to form.

Methods: Leave some in the light, some in the dark. Otherwise care for both groups with the usual feeding and watering.

Result: Your result is a statement of your observations. You can record your results on the table in Figure 7.9.

Conclusion: In my experience, light can but does not usually cause sporangia to form.

Experiment 5

Question: Will lack of food cause sporangia to form?

Hypothesis: We think lack of food will cause sporangia to form.

Methods: Stop feeding one group of slimes, while continuing to feed the other. Otherwise maintain both groups in the dark and with adequate moisture.

Result: Your result is a statement of your observations. You can record your results on the table in Figure 7.9.

Conclusion: In my experience, lack of food can but does not always cause sporangia to form.

Experiment 6

Question: Does placing or allowing the slime to crawl onto a completely nonabsorbent substrate like plastic wrap cause sporangia to form?

Hypothesis: We think being put on plastic wrap will cause the slime to form sporangia.

Methods: Put the slime on plastic wrap or allow a portion of it to crawl onto plastic wrap.

Result: Your result is a statement of your observations. You can record your results on the table in Figure 7.9.

Conclusion: In my experience, being on plastic wrap usually does cause sporangia to form.

Experiment 7

Remove any combination of food, darkness and moisture and see what happens.

CREATURES THAT LIVE OR START LIFE IN THE WATER

CHAPTER 8

Tadpoles to Toads

Introduction

This chapter describes experiments with both tadpoles and toads. Tadpoles are easy to maintain with a diet of lettuce (see Figure 2.9c for a drawing of a tadpole). A couple of tadpole experiments involve growth rates, another involves habitat preference. Toads are a classroom favorite (see Figure 8.1). Can a toad be hand-fed? Can it learn to come to a particular place to be fed? Will a toad stay in a "house" in its terrarium? Do they avoid or seek out one another? Does their behavior change as they grow? Do they prefer certain types of prey or just anything that moves, like mantises? Toads will eat readily, throwing out that long sticky tongue, even with a group of (quiet) children clustered right around them.

Figure 3 in the Postscript provides a range of questions and answers comparing behavior of the predators discussed in Chapters 8 to 13. A list of the questions represented in Figure 3 is provided in Figure 4, which can be photocopied and handed out for the children to answer.

Materials

For tadpoles:
1. A net [5 to 6 inches (12.7–15.2 cm)] to catch tadpoles.
2. A pond from which to catch tadpoles.
3. About ten tadpoles are ideal. You need a minimum of two same-sized tadpoles for Experiments 1 and 2. One tadpole will do for Experiment 3.
4. Two jars or aquaria to hold water and tadpoles.
5. Boiled lettuce or a steady supply of algae-covered leaves to feed tadpoles.
6. A refrigerator or cool outdoors for Experiment 2.
7. Aquatic plants that stay at least partly submerged to provide cover for a tadpole, either from a pond or a pet store that carries fish supplies.

For toads:
8. A walk in the country at night or a well-lit rural back porch at night for catching toads.
9. A box with high sides [20 inches (.5 m) or more] or a terrarium with a lid for keeping toads.
10. A large container with low sides (like a small wading pool) for a classroom demonstration of toad-feeding.
11. Toad food — living slugs, earthworms, caterpillars, roly-polies, crickets, beetles, etc. Toads have flexible diets, but the food item must be alive.
12. Two terraria, soil and earthworms for Experiment 6.

Background Information

A couple of small toads are current favorites in my household. We've had Pee-Wee and Reddy (both Fowler's Toads, one brown and one rusty red) for several months. They've both grown from 1/3 inch (.8 cm) to about 1 1/2 inches (3.8 cm) on a diet of fruitflies and small earthworms. Because Pee-Wee has learned to come to my hand for feeding, I've taken quite a shine to him. I didn't set out to train him, it just happened. At first he wouldn't eat a worm if my hand was visible. Then over a period of three to four weeks he went from eating it while my hand was still in the terrarium, to hopping toward my hand, to eating the worm right off my finger (see Figure 8.2). I always like animals that seem to like me. But I think it's been even more exciting to see Pee-Wee learn not only to come to my hand, but to seek out his own worms after I've plowed up an area of soil in his terrarium for him. He learned from experience that my hand in the soil means worms will appear for a moment or two. He knows he's got to be quick, and he's right there. I knew toads were smarter than insects, but I didn't know they were that smart.

Amphibians (like toads) and mammals (like humans) are all vertebrates, which means we all have backbones.

Figure 8.1 — Felicia finds delight in soothing her toad with a belly rub.

Birds, reptiles and fish are also vertebrates. In general, vertebrates have more developed brains and are smarter than other animals (invertebrates). Pee-Wee has certainly borne this out.

Most people don't think of vertebrates as having larvae, which are newly hatched insects. Actually a larva is any young animal that is substantially different in form from the adult. Larvae usually have a different habitat and a different diet from the adults of their species. Tadpoles qualify as larvae. They look very different from the adult frog or toad. They go through a period of metamorphosis just as an insect larva does. The tadpole absorbs its tail and sprouts legs and arms. Their habitat is different too. Tadpoles are aquatic, whereas most adult frogs and toads are terrestrial. The adults may live near water or even in the water, but they breathe air and can get around on land. The diet of a tadpole is also different from that of an adult. Most tadpoles are herbivorous (vegetarian), eating mostly or only algae, while adult frogs and toads are predators. This transformation from herbivore to predator is fun to watch.

Tadpoles are easier to keep than adults, since they thrive on a diet of briefly boiled lettuce. Toads, however, are much more dramatic. They'll eat almost anything that moves, and they'll do it while a crowd of children is watching. That long tongue flying out to nab a victim is a wonderful sight. Toads are not particularly timid, which makes them especially useful for the classroom.

The difference between a toad and a frog is that a toad has dry skin and can live in a drier environment. Most toads are brown and have warts and spots on their back. Frogs have moist skin and must live near water. They are often green, but not always, and they don't have warts. Tree frogs may or may not have dry skin, but they can be distinguished from frogs and toads by having disklike pads on the ends of their toes.

How to Get and Keep Tadpoles and Toads

You can order tadpoles (not necessarily toad tadpoles) and adult toads from a biological supply company (see Appendix).

Where to Look in Nature for Tadpoles

Most children come across tadpoles in nature sooner or later, but setting out to find one deliberately is another matter. Spring is the best time, about the only time, except for the tadpoles of bullfrogs and green frogs, which remain tadpoles a year or longer. Shallow, boggy areas are the best places to look. Many frogs and toads (and salamanders) lay their eggs in bodies of water that are so shallow that they dry up in mid- to late summer. The temporary nature of a pond like this excludes fish, many of which would love to eat tadpoles, so it's safer for the tadpoles. Since the tadpole stage of life is temporary anyway, the eventual drying of the pond is not a problem for them.

Many lakes have tadpoles from March through June, especially along the margins in the weeds. You may get some tadpoles with a net even if you don't see them in the water before you try (see Figure 8.3). Sweep the net through the weeds. Tadpoles of toads (genus *Bufo*) are usually black and very small. The body is about 1/8 to 1/4 inch (.3–.6 cm) long, excluding the tail. You may even find toad tadpoles in mud puddles, because they stay tadpoles such a short time. (This is not to say you have a very short time to find them, because the adults don't all lay their eggs at the same time.) The black color of toad tadpoles makes them relatively easy to recognize because most other types

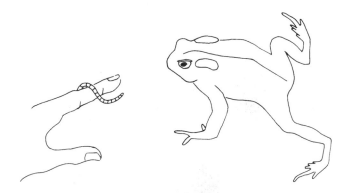

Figure 8.2 — Pee-Wee the toad goes after a worm on a finger.

of tadpoles are various shades of brown or gray. The tadpoles of the bullfrog and its relative the green frog are also easy to recognize because they are so large. If you find a tadpole with a body (not counting the tail) the size of an olive or grape or larger, it's probably a bullfrog or green frog or one of their relatives (genus *Rana*). Beyond this, identifying tadpoles is not easy and I won't attempt to tell you how here. An inexpensive paperback called *Amphibians of North America: A Guide to Field Identification*, in the Golden Field Guide series, has a key to tadpole identification. Since almost all tadpoles eat the same thing, there is really no need to identify them.

Keeping Tadpoles

Once you have tadpoles, all you need to keep them is a small aquarium or food storage container (a jar with no lid will do if you have nothing else) and water with no chlorine in it. I use pond water or bottled spring water. You can use tap water that has sat uncovered for at least twenty-four hours to allow the chlorine to vaporize.

Every other day feed the tadpoles a piece of lettuce (silver-dollar size) that's been boiled for a minute or less. Don't put in so much that it rots before the tadpoles can eat it. They'll also eat the living algae that coats dead leaves underwater.

Like all animals that are herbivorous, tadpoles must eat a lot to get enough nutrition. They consequently create a lot of feces. I usually keep tadpoles in a small container so that I can change the water easily, because they foul the water so quickly.

Metamorphosis and Keeping Young Toads or Frogs

Other than bullfrogs and some of their relatives, most species stay tadpoles for only a few weeks and metamorphose into miniature frogs when they're still tiny [1/4 to 1/3 inch (.6–.8 cm)]. The length of the tadpole period depends on the water temperature and food availability.

When your tadpole has fully developed arms and legs (and still has a long tadpole tail) you need to put a perch in its container or put it in a terrarium (soil floor) that includes a sunken bowl of pond water so that the toadlet can go back and forth between water and land. I use a plant sprayer to keep the terrarium damp. Young toads and tiny frogs will eat fruitflies. (See Chapter 14 for information on how to catch and maintain fruitflies.)

As they grow, toads and frogs will eat almost any little creature that is small enough and is moving enough to catch their attention: earthworms, caterpillars, crickets, etc. They may eat mealworms, which is convenient if you have a culture going (see Chapter 16). Some insects are toxic though and are avoided by predators, such as ants and some beetles. Most insects that have red on them are toxic or bad-tasting and are avoided. The red is a warning to predators.

Catching Adult Toads

Toads are abundant at night in the spring and summer. Being terrestrial, they are much easier to catch than most frogs. They are less timid than frogs because they are poisonous and hence need not be as cautious about avoiding predators. (Toads are not poisonous to the touch and will not cause warts, contrary to popular opinion.)

If you live in a rural area, a porch light left on at night will attract insects and probably toads, as a consequence of the insects. If you live in the city, you'll have to take an evening walk in the country or in a wooded park to find them.

I keep adult or near-adult toads in a cardboard box with sides at least 1 1/2 to 2 feet (45.7–61 cm) tall, depending on the size of the toad. They need a shallow water dish, which the toads will turn over frequently. I've never seen them drink, but I keep it there just in case. At least it keeps the humidity up and the cardboard damp. A frog must have both an out-of-water perch and enough water to submerge itself in. Toss in full-sized slugs, caterpillars, earthworms, crickets, beetles and roly-polies (pill bugs). Slugs can be captured at night by leaving some lettuce as bait on a sidewalk or the lawn. The toads may not eat right away but should within a week. If not, they may need a more secluded spot. Some individuals may not eat in captivity.

Figure 8.3 — Seth catches tadpoles from a pond.

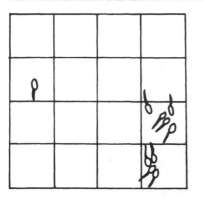

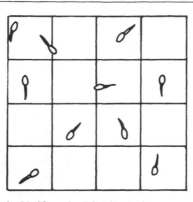

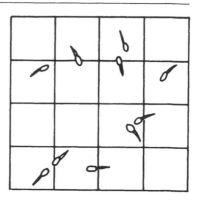

a. Clumped
(attracted to one another)

b. Uniformly Distributed
(avoiding one another)

c. Randomly Distributed
(indifferent to one another)

Figure 8.4 — Drawing of grids showing tadpoles (a) clumped, (b) uniformly distributed and (c) randomly distributed.

For long-term observation, a terrarium with a soil floor and a lid is a good home for toads. My friends Pee-Wee and Reddy live in a terrarium with damp soil, moss and a piece of rotting log.

Field Hunt

When taking a class to search for tadpoles, you need a body of water with vegetation in it, several nets and plastic jars.

Since toads are generally available at night, children will have to search on their own at home. Tell them to look in the garden, along the edge of wooded areas, on paths and in open areas that are near hiding places.

Tadpoles and Toads at School
Observations and Activities

In the beginning, let the students feed the tadpoles lettuce or algae-covered leaves and observe for a few days. Ask them to describe how the tadpole eats (it has mouth parts for scraping algae off surfaces, no teeth for chewing) and what it does when it isn't eating. What does the tadpole do when you take it out of the water? (It wiggles.) How might this behavior be beneficial to it?

Do tadpoles tend to cluster together, do they try to get away from each other or do they ignore each other? To answer this you can try the following activity. You need an aquarium or other container at least the size of a dinner plate. Draw a grid that divides the bottom of your container into about ten to twenty squares. Number each square. You can draw the grid on a piece of paper and put the paper under your container if the bottom is transparent. Or you can even put the grid on a piece of plastic wrap over your container if the students make sure to look directly down when recording tadpoles' positions. It's easier to have the grid under the container.

Put ten or so tadpoles into the container. Give them two hours or so to settle down. Then record the position of each tadpole on another piece of paper with a similar grid, numbered the same way. The students must be careful not to disturb the tadpoles.

Figure 8.5 — Kindergartners watch the toads eat and try to escape.

Figure 8.6 — Jolyn gets brave and grabs a toad, to Jessica's disgust.

Jessica watches Jolyn's delight at the toad's squirming.

Jessica decides to try it too, while Jolyn soothes her toad with a belly-rub.

Are the tadpoles clumped together (see Figure 8.4)? If so, most of them will be on one, two or three squares. Are they widely spaced, with a more or less uniform distance between them, as though all are trying to get away from each other? In this case most squares will be occupied by only one tadpole (or unoccupied). Or are they randomly distributed, the way ten beans would be if you dropped them from above? In this case a few might be clumped, while others are spread out. Maybe half the squares would be occupied.

My experience is that tadpoles either cluster or are randomly distributed, but this may vary according to species and age. What advantage would there be to clustering? Why do fish school? Clustering confuses predators and protects those in the middle of the cluster.

Why disperse from one another? Animals and plant seeds disperse to avoid competing with one another for food, for nest sites or other resources. Tadpoles are more likely to die from predation than from a shortage of food, so it makes more sense for them to cluster.

I often see toad tadpoles clustered in nature, but is this because they just haven't moved from where they hatched? Or is it because there's only a very small area of safe shallow water? The tadpoles in my homemade pond appear to be randomly distributed.

What about toads? Do toads aggregate, or do they repel one another? You need a big container, like a child's plastic wading pool, and at least two toads. Divide the pool or box visually into four numbered squares (use colored tape or a marker). For a couple of days, record each toad's position every hour, until you have at least ten observations. If they are positioning themselves totally independent of one another, they should be in the same quadrant approximately one out of every four observations. If they are together in one quadrant more than one out of four observations, then they may be attracted to each other. If they are together in one quadrant less than one out of four observations, then they may be avoiding one another. What do you find? Unless they are involved in courtship, two toads generally move about independently or avoid one another.

Tadpoles have reason to aggregate — protection from predators. They have no reason to disperse because there is plenty of algae to eat, and hence no competition for food. Adult toads, on the other hand, have more reason to disperse than to cluster or aggregate. Their poison glands largely protect them from predation. They are predators themselves and there may not be plenty of prey. They may compete for food. They may also compete for mates and for egg-laying sites. Competition is a reason to disperse from one another, to maximize the distance between oneself and the next toad.

It's fun, for me, to bring in a load of large toads (ten or so) and let the children feed and then handle them. A large container with low sides like a plastic sandbox or small

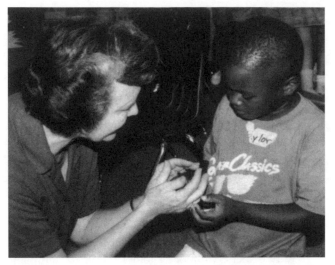

Figure 8.7 — Mrs. Stribling encourages a reluctant Taylor to hold a toad.

tongues unfurling to great lengths. To see it in the flesh is a treat. I was amazed at how cooperative the toads were when I first tried this with a class of first-graders. The children loved it.

After they've seen the toads eat, the children can handle or pet (not squeeze) them. (If they handle the toads before, then the toads probably won't eat.) Some children may be squeamish at first, but they'll come around when they see the glee on their classmates' faces (see Figure 8.6). This may be a good opportunity for a little one-on-one with someone who needs encouragement (see Figure 8.7).

Some of the toads may escape from the container, but with observers, they won't get far. It just adds to the fun.

Experiments

Remember that the hypotheses I give are just examples. Most are written in the "if … then" format, but they don't have to be. Your hypotheses will be the predictions made by the class or a particular child. Your result for each experiment will be a statement of how your animals reacted to your experimental setup. Your conclusion is a statement of whether your prediction was confirmed or not. For each experiment, adding replicates increases your confidence in the validity of your conclusion, but they may be omitted if tedious for young children.

wading pool works well for this (see Figure 8.5) Let the children toss slugs, roly-polies, crickets or worms into the container. If the children can sit or stand quietly, at least arm's length from the side of the container, many of the toads will eat. (The children in Figure 8.5 are too close.) The students may have seen drawings or cartoons of toad

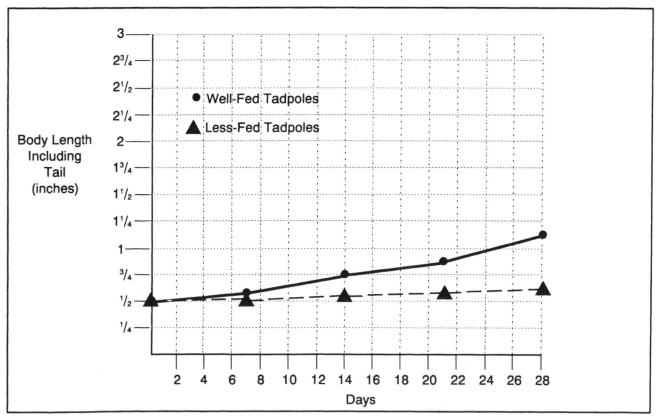

Figure 8.8 — Sample graph showing the effect of food availability on tadpole growth, measured weekly for four weeks for Experiment 1.

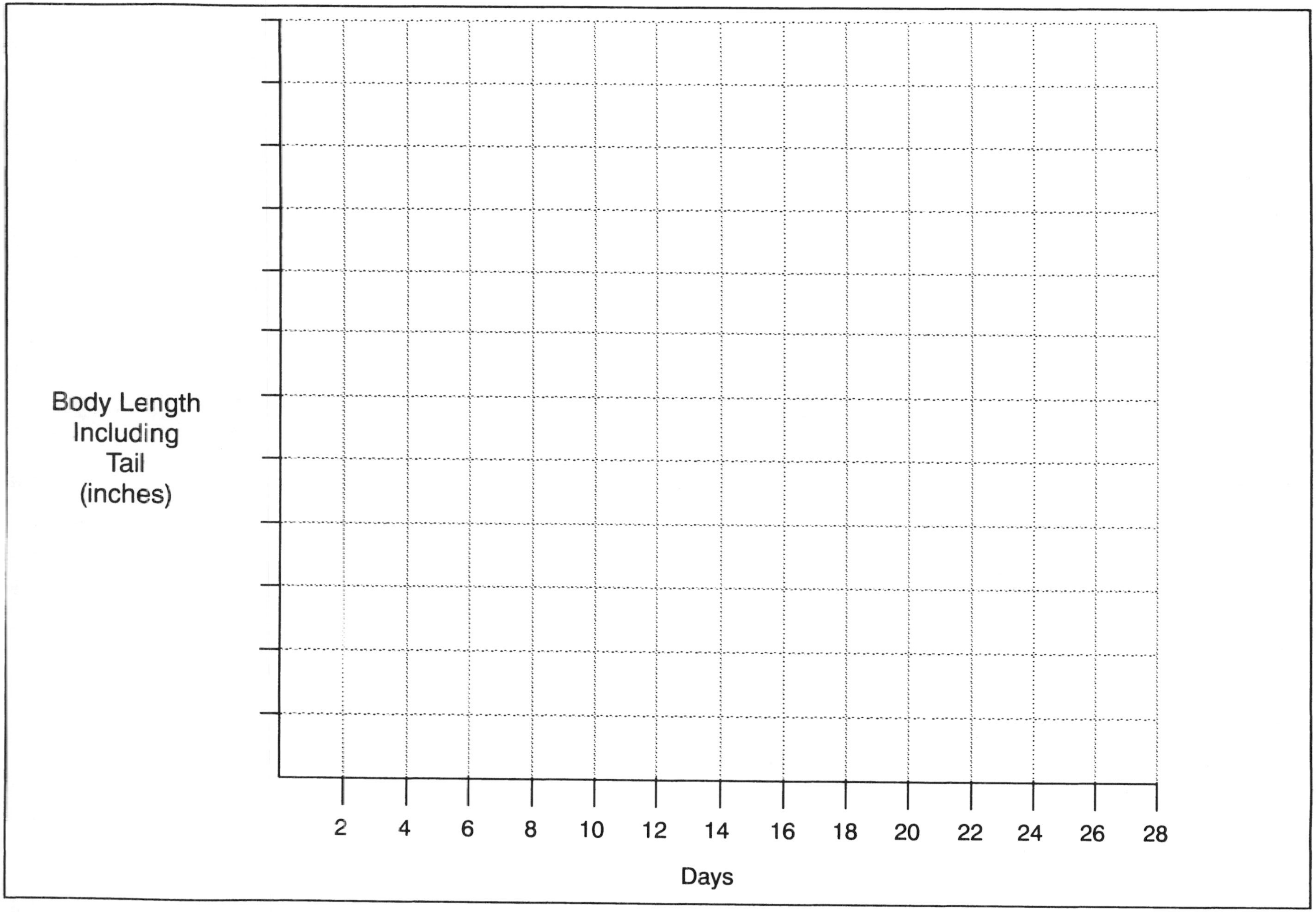

Figure 8.9 — Blank graph on which to record your measurements for Experiment 1.

Tadpoles

Experiment 1

Question: How does food availability affect the growth rate of tadpoles?

Hypothesis: If we feed one group of tadpoles more often than another group, the first group will grow faster.

Methods: Keep an equal number of same-sized tadpoles in two separate containers. Keep food (boiled lettuce) available for one group at all times. For the other group, have lettuce available only every other day or every third or fourth day. Measure the length of the tadpoles (excluding tails) at weekly (or other) intervals for a month or so. The students can calculate an average length for each group on each measurement day. You can plot your measurements on a graph (see Figure 8.8). Figure 8.9 provides a blank graph for your measurements.

Result: Your result is a statement of growth measurements on particular days and your graph.

Conclusion: Tadpoles that are fed more grow faster. The prediction is confirmed.

Growth rates of warm-blooded animals (mammals and birds) are more or less fixed. If food deprivation is severe enough to slow growth, then there is probably a loss of health as well. Food deprivation is cruel for warm-blooded animals. The growth rate of cold-blooded animals is much more flexible. If they have less to eat, their growth slows, but with no loss of health. One individual may take twice as long to reach adult size as another with no impairment whatsoever. So depriving tadpoles of food for a few days is not cruel.

What other factors might affect a tadpole's growth rate?

Experiment 2

Question: How does temperature affect the growth rate of tadpoles?

Hypothesis: If we keep one group of tadpoles cooler than another, the two groups will still grow at the same rate.

Methods: Keep an equal number of same-sized tadpoles in two separate containers. Keep one group in a cooler environment than the other, perhaps outdoors [20 degrees F (-6.5° C) difference is adequate]. The refrigerator (not freezer!) is okay. If this seems cruel, remind the children that tadpoles in nature often live in almost ice-cold water. Most hatch in early spring,

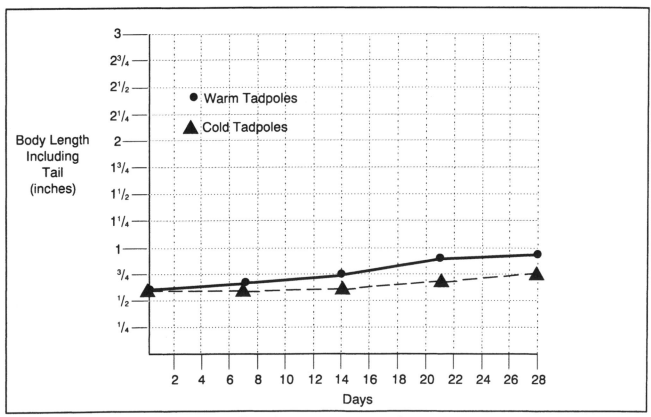

Figure 8.10 — Sample graph showing the effect of temperature on tadpole growth, measured weekly for four weeks for Experiment 2.

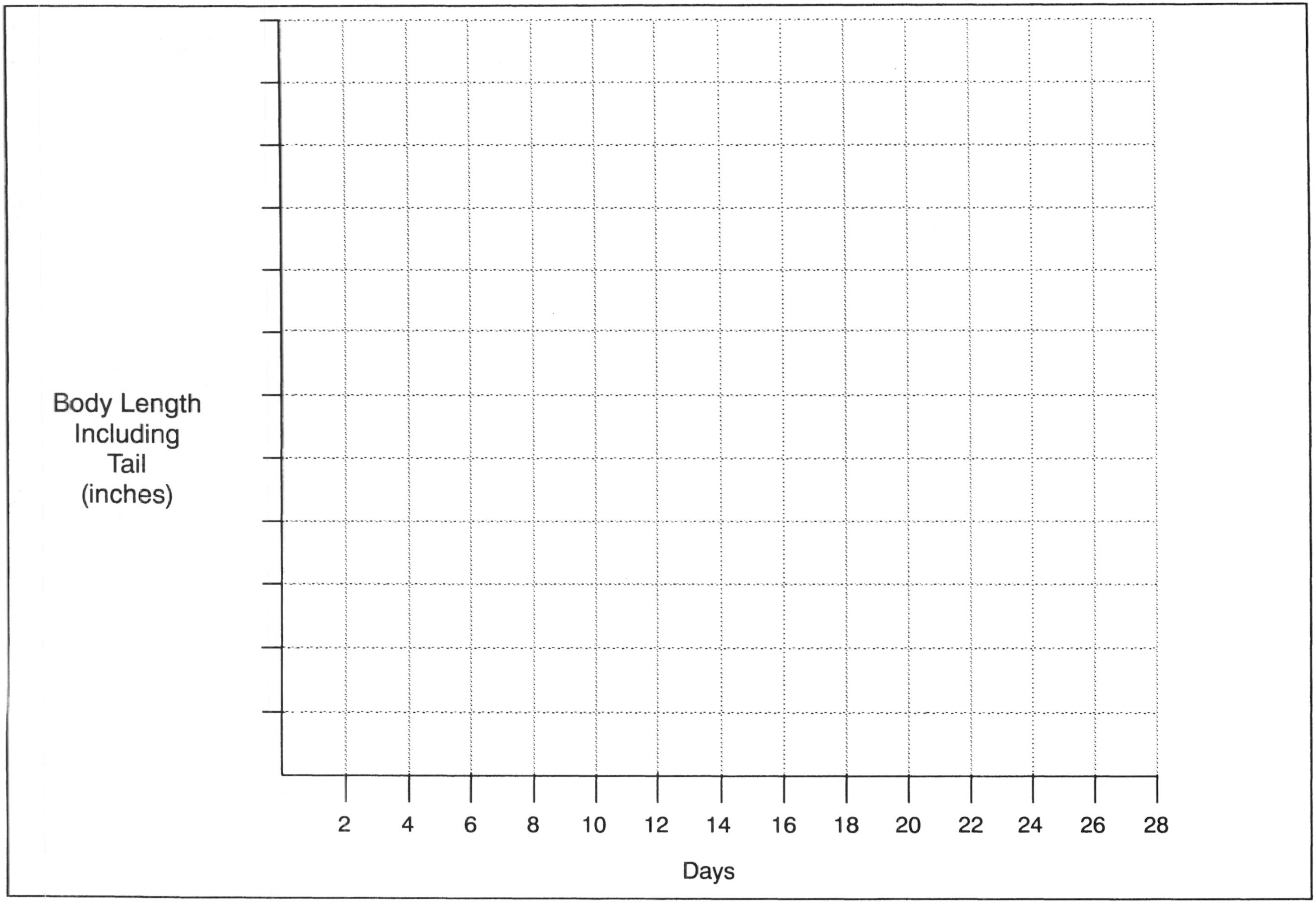

Body Length
Including
Tail
(inches)

Days

2   4   6   8   10   12   14   16   18   20   22   24   26   28

Figure 8.11 – Blank graph on which to record your measurements for Experiment 2.

and some even live over winter under the ice. Cold slows them down, but does not damage them in the slightest as long as it is above freezing.

Keep the other container at room temperature. Keep food available to both groups at all times. Measure the tadpoles (excluding tails) at weekly (or other) intervals. Are they different in size? The students can calculate an average length for each group on each measurement day. You can plot your measurements on a graph (see Figure 8.10). Figure 8.11 provides a blank graph for your measurements.

Result: Your result is a statement of your observations, measurements of each group made on particular days and your graph.

Conclusion: The refrigerated tadpoles grow more slowly. The prediction is not confirmed.

Cold slows down the growth rate of tadpoles. The body temperature of cold-blooded animals depends on the surrounding environment. Mammals shiver and cover themselves or huddle together to stay warm — tadpoles just cool off. A mammal's metabolism won't work if the body is too cool; a tadpole's metabolism just slows down.

What would happen if you crossed Experiments 1 and 2, so that you had four different groups of tadpoles: group 1 at a high temperature with lots of food, group 2 at a low temperature with lots of food, group 3 at a high temperature with little food and group 4 at a low temperature with little food? Would you have four distinct lines on the graph? Or would group 2 and group 3 be about the same and between group 1 and group 4? Or would groups 2, 3 and 4 all be about the same?

on Figure 8.12, a histogram. Figure 3.4 provides an example of a completed histogram.

Conclusion: When offered a choice between cover and no cover, most tadpoles prefer cover, as well they should! The prediction is confirmed. Experiments 3 and 8 in Chapter 9 show that pond creatures are more likely to avoid predation when they hide among plants.

What other habitat choices could you offer your tadpoles? Light and dark substrates is one possibility.

Toads

Like many predators, toads' response to prey has more than one component. When my toad Pee-Wee first notices a worm, he turns his head to look at the worm directly, and he may turn his body too, since his ability to turn his head is limited. He may hop a short distance to the prey, but won't pursue it very far as some predators do. He watches it for a moment, as though to make sure he really did see it move, and then strikes at it with his sticky tongue. After watching a toad eat just a few times, you'll learn to recognize easily when the toad has noticed the prey.

When toads strike, they often miss, especially small toads, and especially when the prey is wet like a worm or large. So you need to decide in advance for each of the next two experiments what you're going to measure: time until prey is noticed, time until it is struck at or time until it is in the toad's mouth.

Remember, toads may not eat during the first week of captivity, and they won't eat if children are loud and moving around them (arm's length or less). They'll learn to tolerate noise and movement, but at first need some space and/or privacy. They'll be fine on an out-of-the-way table in the classroom.

Experiment 3

Question: Do tadpoles prefer cover?

Hypothesis: If we offer tadpoles a choice between cover and no cover, they will choose cover.

Methods: Create a partition in the middle of the container that will hold plants on one side of the partition, but will allow the tadpoles to move freely back and forth from side to side. Chicken wire is ideal. You can bend the edges to hold it in place somewhat, but may have to tape it at the top. Fill one side of the container with aquatic plants that will stay submerged at least partly. You can collect them from a pond or buy them at a pet store. Have a small amount of boiled lettuce available on both sides. Put one to several tadpoles into the container. If you have more than one put some on the clear side and some in the plants. Wait a few hours or days, then count how many are on the clear side.

Result: Your result is a statement of your observations and counts at a particular time. You can record your results

---

Experiment 4

Question: Does prey have to be moving for a toad to eat it, as is true for the praying mantis?

Hypothesis: If we offer a toad moving prey and nonmoving prey, it will eat the moving prey first.

Methods: You can go about this systematically, offering a dead worm and a live worm, a dead cricket and a live cricket, etc. Or you can do it more subjectively by watching the toad while it has several prey available at one time. Decide what measure of preference you're going to use: time until noticed, time until struck at or time until eaten. Does it go for the one item that's moving the most? Does it ever eat one that has not moved at all?

Result: Your result is a statement of your observations. You can record your results on the table in Figure 8.13.

Conclusion: Toads do not notice prey that is not moving, so they eat only prey that is moving. The prediction is

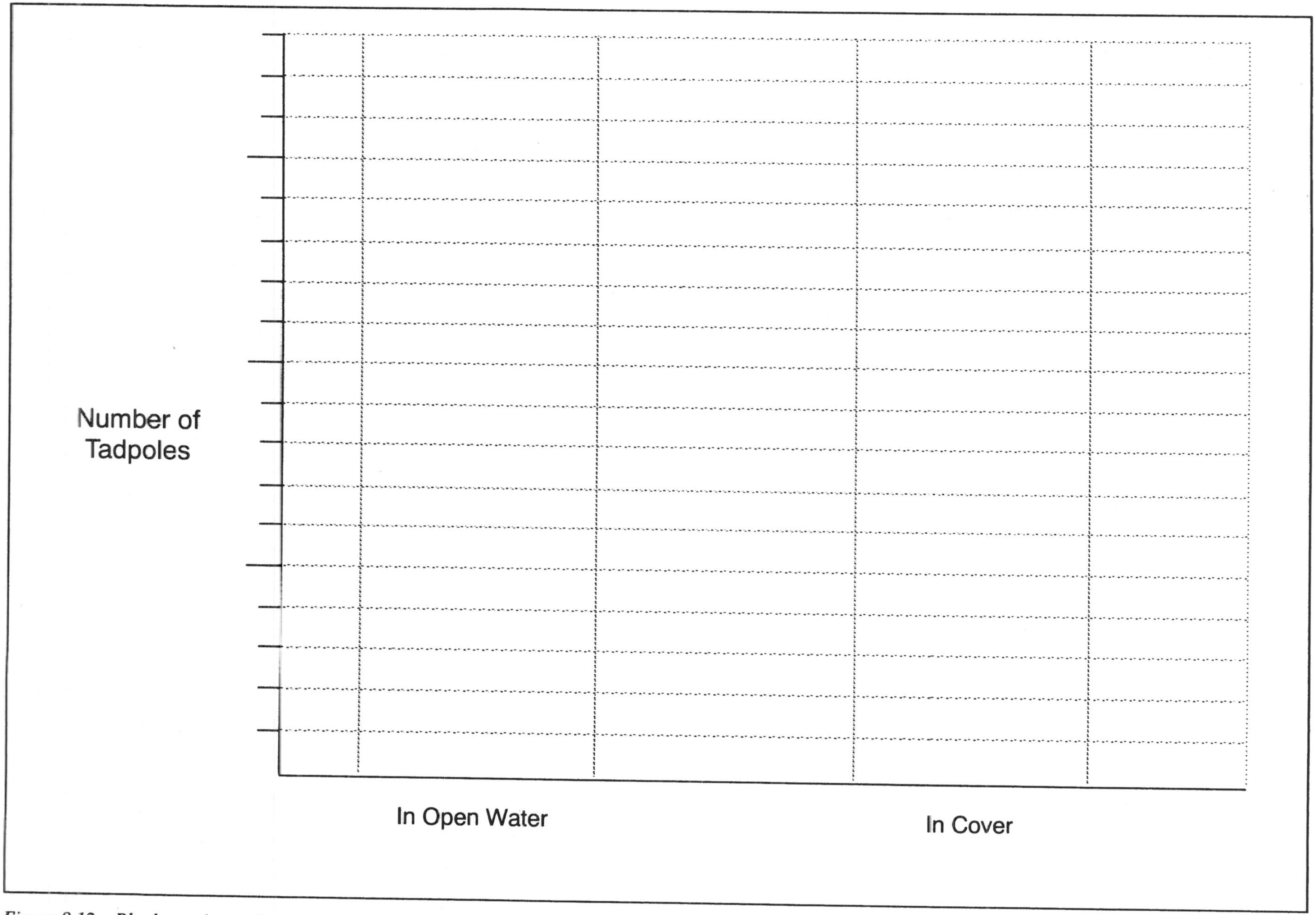

Number of Tadpoles

In Open Water   In Cover

Figure 8.12 – Blank graph on which to record your results for Experiment 3. (See Figure 3.4 for an example of a completed histogram.)

confirmed. Watching the toads' response to a variety of prey, the students will observe that the toads "notice" (turn their heads to watch) prey when the prey moves.

Experiment 5

Question: Do toads have preferences for certain foods?

Hypothesis: Toads prefer soft-bodied prey (worms, etc.) to hard-bodied prey (grasshoppers, etc.) Or toads prefer flying prey to crawling prey. Or toads prefer slugs to caterpillars. And so on.

Methods: Decide what measure of preference you're going to use: time until noticed, time until struck at or time until eaten. Offer your toad(s) various pairs of prey and record its preference.

Result: Your result is a statement of your observations and time measurements. You can record your results on the table in Figure 8.14.

Conclusion: Depends on what was offered. Toads have a very broad diet. My impression is that a toad's selection of prey is affected by prey movement and size more than by the particular type of prey.

Experiment 6

Question: Can a toad be trained like a dog or cat to look for food in a particular place or at a particular time?

Hypothesis: A toad can learn to look for food in response to a particular signal.

Methods: Anyone who's had a cat and dog knows that a cat will come running into the kitchen to get its food when it hears the electric can opener running, or a dog will sit under the table when the family eats, to pick up the children's dropped items. A toad can learn the same sort of thing and you can prove it experimentally. There are lots of different ways to do this, as many different ways as there are of training a dog or cat. What follows is just one suggestion, based on what I've done.

Keep two toads in separate but identical terraria. Each terrarium should contain about 5 inches (12.7 cm) of rich loose soil the consistency of potting soil containing many earthworms. (Dig the worms up outside or look in the Yellow Pages for a fishing supply store.) You can keep the worms reproducing in the soil by adding a couple of handfuls of used coffee grounds every week or two and keeping the soil moist.

Feed one toad (toad A) crickets or beetles or anything else it will eat except earthworms. Drop them in from above. Never dig into toad A's soil when he is present, because you don't want him to see the worms. You also don't want him to become accustomed to your hand. Feed the other toad (toad B) only earthworms. To feed it, scoop up some soil in his terrarium, where he can watch you and pull out a worm or two. In the beginning just lay the worm in front of the toad and take your hand out. As time goes on, leave the worm closer and closer to the scooped-out place where you got it, instead of laying it right in front of the toad. Leave your hand in longer and longer too so that the toad gets used to it. He will learn to hop over to the worm and to your hand if you lay the worm across your finger. Do this gradually enough that he continues to always eat the worm. Eventually, it may take a month or two, he will come right over to your hand as soon as you scoop into the soil. At that point, if you move your hand and the soil is loose enough, he will learn to hop into the hole and pull out his own worm. Now you are ready for your test.

At the same time (if you have two people) put both toads in a back corner of their respective terraria. Scoop out a divot in the soil in the front of each terrarium to expose several worms and leave your hand in the terrarium. Record what happens.

Result: This is my result: Toad B will hop right into the depression and grab a worm. Toad A will just sit there, afraid of your hand, having no reason to expect anything to eat from the scooped-out place.

For me toad B is Pee-Wee of course, and toad A is many other toads I've had that I've fed in other ways. Pee-Wee has learned from experience that my hand in the soil leaves a wake of worms, and he has learned to get them, either from me or for himself.

Conclusion: The prediction is confirmed. Toads can learn to look for prey in response to a particular signal, in this case a human hand in the soil. Toads have opportunities for this type of learning in the wild too. The nightly gathering of toads on rural porches under a porch light is probably the result of their learning that insects are abundant there, because toads have no innate attraction to light, as you can determine yourself. Can the children think of other opportunities toads might have for learning in nature? How about worms on a sidewalk after a rain? Can other predators, like praying mantises or jumping spiders, be trained similarly?

Following this experiment, offer both toad A and toad B a small cricket with no human hands present. Has toad B's steady diet of earthworms made it less likely to notice other foods than toad A? What do the children predict?

Foods Accepted by Toads. Put a Check in the Appropriate Blanks.

Food Item	Struck at by Toad	Eaten by Toad
Cricket		
Roly-Poly		
Slug		
Caterpillar		
Earthworm		
Others:		

Figure 8.13 — Blank table on which to record your results for Experiment 4.

Prey Offered in Pairs		How Many Times Prey 1 Chosen	How Many Times Prey 2 Chosen	Which One Preferred?
Prey 1	Prey 2			
Worms	Grasshopper			
Moth	Cricket			
Slug	Caterpillar			
Others:				

Figure 8.14 — Blank table on which to record your results for Experiment 5.

Experiment 7

Question: Will a toad stay in a "house"?

Hypothesis: If we bury half of a plastic cup on its side, the toad will use the resulting three-sided room as a refuge.

Methods: You need a terrarium with soil on the floor, and a toad. Get a milk carton from lunch or a yogurt cup, or something similar, and bury it on its side so that the protruding half makes a room, open at one end. Does the toad stay in the room?

Result: Your result is a statement of your toad's reaction. You can record your results on a table (see Figure 8.15). Figure 8.16 provides a blank table for your results.

Conclusion: My toads will stay in their rooms all day long, facing the opening. The prediction is confirmed. A hungry toad will come out sometime during the night to forage, but a satiated toad may not. What happens if you have only one house but more than one toad?

Experiment 8

Question: If offered a choice between a jumble of plants and a bare space, which will the toad prefer?

Hypothesis: If offered a choice between a jumble of plants and a bare space, the toad will stay in the plants.

Methods: Fill half the toad's container with a jumble of plants, like honeysuckle, so that the toad can get inside the tangle. Leave it for a few hours and check the toad's position. Repeat several times or with several toads.

Result: Your result is a statement of your observations. You can record your results on a table (see Figure 8.15). Figure 8.16 provides a blank table for your results.

Conclusion: Toads do prefer the jumble of plants, the prediction is confirmed. This tendency is especially pronounced with young toads. Hiding among plants reduces the likelihood of predation and also reduces the danger of dehydration, which is a real threat to newly metamorphosed toads. Since toads generally come out in the open at night to forage, your result may be different if you leave your terrarium in a dark room.

Choice of Conditions Offered to Toad	Toad's Choice	Effect of Choice on Toad
House or Open Experiment 7	House (may choose open at night)	Protects against predators
Jumble of Plants or Bare Space Experiment 8	Plants (especially very young toads)	Protects against predators, provides humidity
Dry Sandy Soil or Wet Leaves Experiment 9	No preference in older toads, wet leaves in very young toads	Provides humidity for very young
Dark Substrate or Light Substrate Experiment 10	No preference in older toads, dark substrate in very young toads	Protects against predators, in nature may provide humidity

Figure 8.15 — Sample table for Experiments 7 to 10.

Choice of Conditions Offered to Toad	Toad's Choice	Effect of Choice on Toad
House or Open Experiment 7		
Jumble of Plants or Bare Space Experiment 8		
Dry Sandy Soil or Wet Leaves Experiment 9		
Dark Substrate or Light Substrate Experiment 10		

Figure 8.16 – Blank table on which to record your results for Experiments 7 to 10.

Experiment 9

Question: Do toads prefer dry sandy soil or wet leaves and moss?

Hypothesis: If offered a choice between dry, sandy soil or wet leaves and moss, toads will choose wet leaves and moss.

Methods: Set up a terrarium or box with dry sand or sandy soil on one side, and very wet matted leaves on the other. Make both sides flat, so there are no hiding places. We're testing substrates here, not attraction to refuge. Wait a few hours. Which side does the toad prefer?

Result: Your result is a statement of your observations. You can record your results on a table (see Figure 8.15). Figure 8.16 provides a blank table for your results.

Conclusion: Adult toads generally show no preference, unlike many of the smaller animals we've tested. The prediction is not confirmed. But some toads may, depending on the species. Newly metamorphosed toads will prefer the wet side.

With their dry skin, adult toads are not particularly vulnerable to water loss and hence have no preference for damp areas.

Experiment 10

Question: If offered a choice between a dark substrate and a light substrate, will the toads have a preference?

Hypothesis: If offered a choice between a dark and light substrate, the toads will have no preference.

Methods: On one half of the floor of a container put moist white construction paper. On the other half of the floor put moist black construction paper. Put a toad or toads in, and after a few hours record their response.

Result: Your result is a statement of your observations. You can record your results on a table (see Figure 8.15). Figure 8.16 provides a blank table for your results.

Conclusion: Adult toads show no preference, although this may vary with species. The prediction is confirmed here. Newly metamorphosed toads, however, show a strong preference for the dark side. This is probably predator avoidance for one thing, because the toadlets are dark themselves. It's probably also because dark places tend to be more humid and the toadlets are extremely vulnerable to dehydration in their first few days following metamorphosis. The attraction to dark is so strong in the tiny ones that, in a white container, they will hop on top of one another until they are just a little black pile of toadlets. Drying enhances this tendency. If you try it, don't leave them in a completely dry container for long because the tiny ones (with tail stubs left) will dehydrate and die in a matter of hours.

CHAPTER 9

Pond Ecology in the Classroom

Introduction

This chapter involves many of the tiny animals that are found in almost any fresh-water pond and sometimes in ditches. Just watching the animals move around the containers is interesting. Some are plant eaters, some are scavengers, many are predators. Several of the experiments in this chapter involve predation. Some involve habitat choices; one addresses the role of sunlight in supporting plant-eating animals. Although all of the animals in this chapter are quite common, most are seldom seen. Pond life is an intricate world in itself. Familiarity with some of its inhabitants will encourage students to explore this world on their own.

Figure 3 in the Postscript provides a range of questions and answers comparing behavior of the predators discussed in Chapters 8 to 13. A list of the questions represented in Figure 3 is provided in Figure 4, which can be photocopied and handed out for the children to answer.

Materials

1. Two or three aquaria or other containers for maintaining animals.
2. For all of the experiments and activities, an assortment of pond critters, listed here and described in Chapter 2. All but two of the animals, which are not essential, can be ordered from a biological supply company (see Appendix).
3. A plankton net or cloth fixed to some sort of rim for collecting plankton, unless you order them. A plankton net can be ordered from a biological supply company.
4. An aquatic dip net for catching creatures at a pond, or at least a pet store fish net, unless you order all the animals. A dip net can be ordered from a biological supply company.

5. For Experiment 1, one aquarium with a chicken-wire partition across the middle.
6. For Experiments 1 and 2, and for long-term aquaria, aquatic plants from a pet store, a pond or a biological supply company. Any leafy plants that live submerged, like elodea or hornwort, will do.
7. For Experiments 2, 3, 5 and 6, two aquaria or two large bowls, buckets, etc.
8. For Experiments 2, 3 and 5, at least one type of predatory pond creature: fish or aquatic insects.
9. For Experiment 6, a dark room.

Background Information

Most, if not all, of the creatures in this chapter will be foreign to the students and for that reason alone will be interesting. Watching them eat one another is riveting. The first time I saw a backswimmer (a beetlelike aquatic insect) attack and eat a small fish in one of my kitchen bowls, I was revolted and mesmerized at the same time. The fish was paralyzed and killed by the backswimmer's stinging mouth parts. The backswimmer then took its time sucking out the body fluids of the fish. Backswimmers hold an air pocket around them, which gives them a silvery sheen and made the whole incident look rather eerie. The backswimmer alone is odd enough — an insect with long oarlike legs that swims on its keeled back. But an insect eating a fish — it's enough to give anyone a shiver! Kids will find it thrilling.

Before ordering any predators or prey, check the diet of the predators to be sure you're getting appropriate prey. (See the beginning of the Experiments section of this chapter.) If the predation seems too grisly, you can stick with herbivores and scavengers, which eat algae and decaying plant matter, respectively.

Descriptions and drawings of each animal and how to catch them are given in Chapter 2 (Figures 7 to 10), in the section on how to make a small pond.

How to Get and Keep Pond Organisms

All the animals described here can be caught with persistence at a well-established pond. See the How to Stock Your Pond section in Chapter 2 for guidance on how to look for them. Ordering the animals from a biological supply company (see Appendix) is easier. Whirligig beetles and water striders are the only animals described here that can't be ordered, to my knowledge. These two are suggested only for observation and not required for the experiments. If you do decide to order, you'll save on shipping charges by ordering all at once. The animals will come in separate small plastic jars. Let the children examine them before putting them all together in an aquarium (see the Observations and Activities section).

All of the herbivores and scavengers, as listed below, can be kept in a terrarium together. None of them are any longer than a child's fingernail, with the exception of large tadpoles, and none of them can bite. You'll probably want to keep your predators separate except during specific periods of observation or while conducting experiments. Otherwise your predators will deplete your supply of other animals and will eat each other as well.

Use pond water, at least in part, to fill your aquarium. It contains the microorganisms plankton eat. Any tap water you plan to add to the aquarium should be left uncovered for twenty-four hours first to allow the chlorine to vaporize. Before transferring animals from a temporary container to an aquarium, water temperatures should be more or less equal (to the touch) to avoid temperature shock to the animals.

You can put in a small volume of aquatic plants, like elodea, to see how the animals react to it. Too much will obscure the animals. The herbivores may scrape the algae off of it, but none will eat the plant itself. Do they hide in it or rest on it? Do they ignore it?

For the herbivores to eat, add to the aquarium a few dead leaves covered with algae (they'll feel slick) from a pond or ditch. For the scavengers add a small amount (the volume of two fingers) of rotting plant material from a pond. Large amounts will make the water smell bad. Avoid putting soil on the bottom of your aquarium, which will obscure bottom dwellers, like planarians, amphipods and isopods.

Mosquito fish (*Gambusia*) can be maintained on a diet of mosquito larvae or plankton or commercial fish food. They have to learn to eat fish food, and won't try it until they've not had any other food for a week or so. They should be kept alone unless you want them eating smaller animals. *Gambusia* cannot bite people. A large number of *Gambusia* will quickly deplete the plankton supply in an aquarium.

Diving beetles can be maintained on a diet of other animals or small pieces of raw or cooked meat. They have

biting mouth parts, but to my knowledge will not bite people, or at least not painfully so.

Backswimmers and giant water bugs have piercing and sucking mouth parts and suck up body fluids, hence they must have live prey. Both inject poison into their prey through the piercing mouth part and can do the same to human hands, with the effect of a bee sting.

Dragonfly nymphs have biting mouth parts and may eat meat or may require live prey (there are many different species of dragonflies and their relatives, the damselflies). Their bite is a pinch, which may be painful if the nymph is large. (Immature insects that look very much like the adult and do not go through a pupal stage are called nymphs instead of larvae.)

Herbivores and scavengers include the following (some of these are both): amphipods and isopods (crustaceans), mosquito larvae (will turn into mosquitos), planaria (flat worms), plankton (plants and animals no bigger than a comma), snails, tadpoles, water boatmen (insects) and whirligig beetles.

Predators that can be maintained on nonliving food include diving beetles, dragonfly nymphs (may eat nonliving food) and mosquito fish.

Predators that must have live prey include backswimmers (insects), giant water bugs and water striders (insects).

In the next section, I'll tell you what to feed the predators for action.

Pond Creatures at School
Observations and Activities

A good way to get the children acquainted with the animals is to put each type of animal into a separate white bowl so the children can examine them closely. Label each bowl with the name of the animal. Remember that backswimmers and giant water bugs bite with a stinging effect and large dragonfly nymphs may bite with a pinch.

Who Eats What?

You may want to get older children to write down what they know (what you tell them) about each animal's lifestyle. Is it a predator or scavenger or herbivore? On the basis of this information, the children can make predictions about how the animals may interact when they get together. Who will eat whom? In general, of course, predators will eat herbivores (plant-eaters), but will one predator eat another? (The insect predators will eat one another and will eat fish, depending on their relative sizes. Some will eat prey larger than themselves! The fish will probably not eat the insect predators, because they swallow prey whole and have small mouths.) Can the children say which animals will share food but won't bother each other? (Tadpoles and snails, both being algae-eaters. Also, amphipods and isopods and to some extent planaria, water boatmen and whirligig beetles, all being at least partly scavengers.)

All the organisms that live together in one community, like a pond, can be arranged into a food web. This is simply an illustration of the species' feeding relationships and consists of a diagram with lines that connect the species' names on the basis of who eats whom. Can the students construct a food web like the one given (see Figure 9.1), or fill in the blanks of a partially constructed one (see Figure 9.2)?

Organisms can be labeled or categorized in terms of how they obtain their food. Plants, being photosynthetic, provide their own food and are called producers. Herbivores eat plants and are called primary consumers. Predators or carnivores eat other animals and are called secondary consumers. They may be eaten by other predators or by parasites, or after they're dead by scavengers or decomposers.

Where Do They Hang Out?

After the children have examined the animals separately in bowls, I've suggested putting herbivores and scavengers into an aquarium with leaves and algae and a small amount of decaying plant matter. The predators will be going into individual containers. Have the children observe for a while and record the location of various animals: surface, bottom or in the water column. Do their observations agree with the information in Figure 9.3?

Have the children fill in a chart (see Figure 9.4) indicating where various animals spend most of their time. Many of the animals move around, especially the insects, which come to the surface to breathe or to entrap a fresh air supply to take down with them. Thus, the children's charts may vary.

You may want to let the children observe some predation before you do any experiments. Do they see any interactions other than predation? Do any of the animals tend to aggregate? Do they avoid one another or behave aggressively? Do they seem indifferent to one another?

Experiments

Remember that the hypotheses I give in the book are just examples. Most are written in the "if ... then" format, but they don't have to be. Your hypotheses will be the predictions made by the class or by a particular child. Your result for each experiment will be a statement of how your animals reacted to your experimental setup. Your conclusion is a statement of whether your prediction was confirmed or not. For each experiment, adding replicates increases your confidence in the validity of your conclusion, but they may be omitted if tedious for young children.

For the predation experiments (Experiments 2, 3 and 5), here are the main prey that each particular predator will eat. You will probably find some deviation from these lists.

Predators and Their Respective Prey

Mosquito fish (*Gambusia*) will eat mosquito larvae and plankton.

The next four are all aquatic insects: Dragonfly nymphs will eat fish, other aquatic insects and tadpoles.

Backswimmers will eat fish, other aquatic insects and small tadpoles.

Diving beetles will eat fish, other aquatic insects, snails and tadpoles.

Giant water bugs will eat fish, other aquatic insects, tadpoles and small frogs.

Although water striders are predators in that they eat live insects that fall onto the surface of the water, I have not intended to include them in the experiments. They are interesting to have for observation because of the way they move around on the surface tension as though ice skating.

Reminder: For each experiment use either pond water or tap water that has been standing uncovered for twenty-four hours to allow the chlorine to vaporize.

Experiment 1

Question: If given a choice between open water and water filled with submerged plants, which animals choose the open water?

Hypothesis: The children will probably need guidance to come up with this prediction, but it makes sense that prey would stay around the plants more for protection, while predators would show less preference. What about animals that are both predator and prey?

Methods: Make a partition in the center of an aquarium that will confine plants to one side of the aquarium, but will allow animals to pass freely from side to side. Chicken-wire mesh works well because it has large spaces between the wires. Put white paper under the terrarium so you'll be able to see the animals. After you have the partition in place, submerge aquatic plants on one side of the partition only. Then introduce about ten individuals of one type of animal at a time, such as ten amphipods. Give them an hour or so to settle, then count how many are on the plantless side. (You may need to give slow movers like snails or planaria more time to settle.) Which side is preferred? After your tally remove all the amphipods or whatever as well as you can (some may cling to the plants) and start over with a different animal.

Result: Your result is a statement of your animals' choices and other relevant observations. You can record your results on the table in Figure 9.5.

Conclusion: Some will show a definite preference, while others won't. Consider each animal type individually. Do the children think it has chosen the plant side to hide itself or because it is eating the plants? Since herbivores and scavengers may scrape the algae off the leaves or eat dead plant parts, what could you do to rule out the influence of diet? What about replacing the plants with a tangle of plastic rope, or a plastic plant that has not previously been in water to accumulate algae?

After trying several different types of animals, do the children see any trends? For example, are prey species more likely to choose the plant side than predators? Just about all of the animals in this chapter are prey to another organism, so you may find that few stay in open water.

Experiment 2

Question: Do more prey survive when plants are present in the container?

Hypothesis: If we have one container with plants and one without plants, we think prey will survive longer in the container with plants.

Methods: Have two containers of the same size, somewhere between the size of a casserole dish and a medium-sized terrarium. The containers should be big enough that the animals have plenty of room to move around, but not so big that the animals will never encounter one another. In one dish have plants submerged in the water; in the other have no plants. Put one predator in each dish. Choose from the list of predators preceding Experiment 1. The predators should be the same type and more or less the same size. Give the predators a day or so to get used to the containers. Then put about ten individuals of your selected prey animal in each dish, making sure your prey is on the list of appropriate prey for the particular predator you chose. Leave the predators in the dish until all or almost all of the prey are gone from the dish with no plants (but no longer). Then remove the predators and count how many prey remain in the dish with plants. Are there any left?

The experiment needn't take longer than about twenty-four hours. If it does, adjust your starting numbers so that it takes a shorter time. If you know that you want the experiment to last no more than four hours or so, then start with an observation period to see

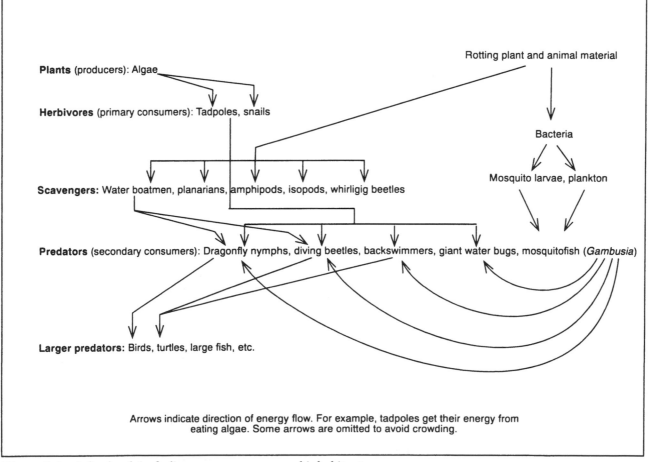

Figure 9.1 — A food web including some common pond inhabitants.

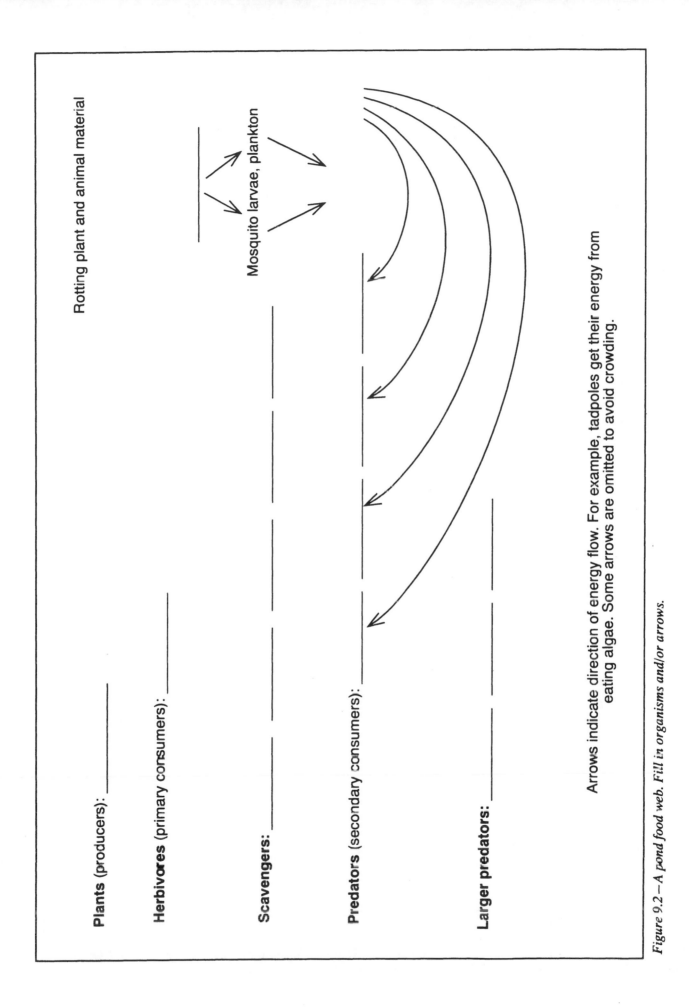

Rotting plant and animal material

Mosquito larvae, plankton

Plants (producers): _____

Herbivores (primary consumers): _____

Scavengers: _____

Predators (secondary consumers): _____

Larger predators: _____

Arrows indicate direction of energy flow. For example, tadpoles get their energy from eating algae. Some arrows are omitted to avoid crowding.

Figure 9.2 — A pond food web. Fill in organisms and/or arrows.

how long it takes the predator to eat a certain number of prey and set your starting numbers accordingly. Many predators will not eat at all with children watching them. If you find that your predator won't eat, move the containers or try a different type of prey.

Result: Your result is a statement of the number of survivors in each dish and other relevant observations. You can record your results on the histogram in Figure 9.6. Figure 3.4 provides an example of a completed histogram.

Conclusion: The prediction is confirmed. There probably will be several surviving prey in the dish with plants after the other prey are all gone. Plants serve as hiding places and help prey survive, in nature as well as in aquaria. You can repeat this experiment with different combinations of predator and prey, and different plants or other types of hiding places.

Are the prey that are more attracted to plant cover (as discovered in Experiment 1) more likely to survive with the predators?

Experiment 3

Question: Will predators eat less of one particular type of prey if other types of prey are present as well?

Hypothesis: We think predators will eat less of one particular type of prey in a container that has other types of prey available as well.

Methods: You need two containers or you can do the two trials in sequence if you have only one container. It has more impact if you do them simultaneously. Have no plants in either container. In container A, put ten individuals of each of two different prey types, for example, ten fish and ten tadpoles. In container B, put ten individuals of one prey type only, for example, ten tadpoles. Then put one predator from the list of predators given earlier into each container. Make sure your prey are appropriate for your predators, as listed before Experiment 1. Your prey should be close in size and smaller than the predators. When all or almost all of the tadpoles are gone from container B, remove the predators from both containers and count the surviving tadpoles in container A. Did more tadpoles survive in container A, where fish were present as an alternative prey?

Result: Your result is a statement of the numbers of survivors in each container and other relevant observations. You can record your results on the histogram in Figure 9.6. Figure 3.4 provides an example.

Conclusion: The outcome depends on which prey and predator you use. Some predators may have a definite preference for certain prey, and the alternative prey won't affect the number consumed. For other combinations, the alternative prey may make a difference. In some situations, the alternative prey may actually increase the number of the other prey eaten. For

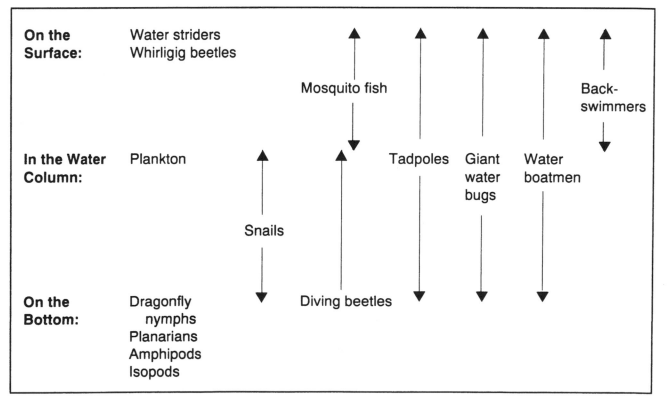

Figure 9.3 — The location of organisms within the aquarium. Arrows indicate movement. These are not rigid, but they are usual locations.

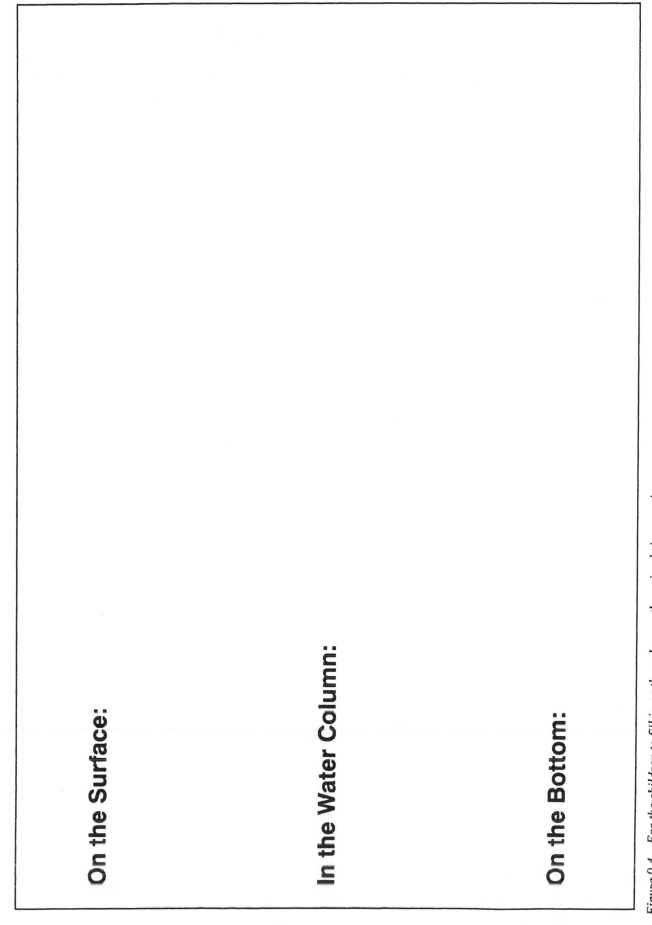

On the Surface:

In the Water Column:

On the Bottom:

Figure 9.4 — For the children to fill in as they observe the animals in aquaria.

Do the Animals Prefer Open Water or Cover?

Animal	Number of Animals in Open Water at Time of Observation	Number of Animals in Plant Cover at Time of Observation (by deduction)
Diving beetles		
Giant water bugs		
Whirligig beetles		

How many types of animals were found primarily in plant cover?

Were any types of animals equally distributed between plant cover and open water?

Figure 9.5 — Blank table on which to record your results for Experiment 1.

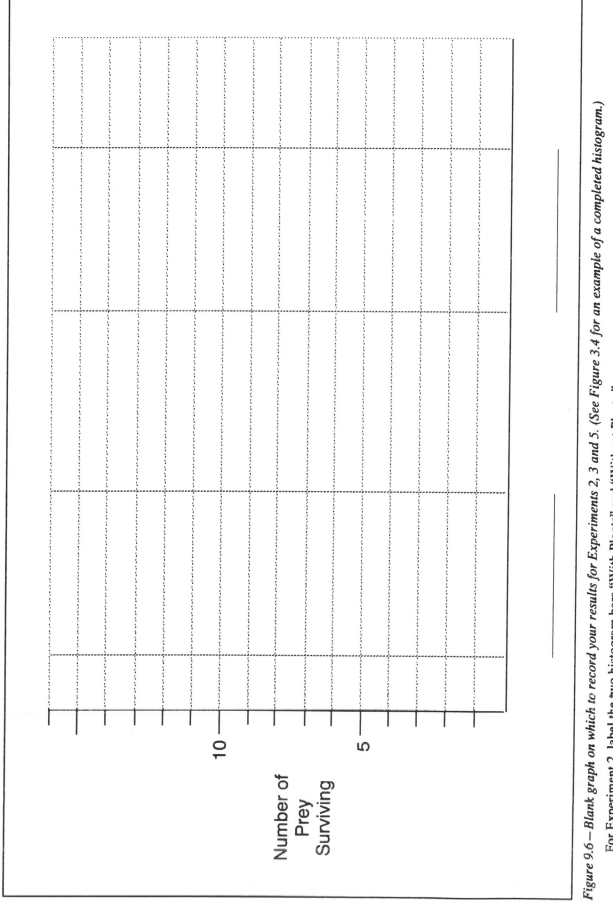

Figure 9.6 — Blank graph on which to record your results for Experiments 2, 3 and 5. (See Figure 3.4 for an example of a completed histogram.)

For Experiment 2, label the two histogram bars "With Plants" and "Without Plants."
For Experiment 3, label the two histogram bars "With Alternative Prey" and "Without Alternative Prey."
For Experiment 5, label the two histogram bars "In Darkness" and "In Light."

example, many predators are more likely to eat prey that moves and attracts their attention, and many tadpoles will sit still unless bumped. An amphipod scuttling around the dish may bump the tadpoles and send them swimming into the jaws of the predator.

This is a good opportunity to talk about the complexity of nature—the fact that all the animals in a particular habitat affect one another. Can the children think of examples of how one prey species might affect the survival of another prey species in nature?

This experiment is also a good illustration of how difficult it is to make general rules in the field of ecology, because the outcome of an experimental setup depends on which species are involved.

Because alternative prey can affect the survival of a particular prey species, this issue is important in managing populations of wild animals. Almost all wild animals are either predators or prey or both.

Experiment 4

Question: Do pond animals have any preference between light and dark?

Hypothesis: If we offer the pond animals a choice between light and dark, they'll all choose light.

Methods: Use a low-sided container like a cake pan for large animals. A petri dish will work well for small ones. Cover half of it with something dark and completely opaque, like black plastic or black paper. Put enough water in the dish to cover the animals and allow them to swim. Introduce animals one at a time to the dish, give each a half-hour to an hour to settle down (or at least wait until there has been no movement for several minutes), then record the animals' choices. Is there any pattern? Do scavengers stay in the dark more than predators?

Result: Your result is a statement of the choices you recorded for each animal.

Conclusion: The outcome varies depending on species. Since all of the animals are prey to other organisms, they may have reason to seek darkness. Some predators, however, may have reason to seek light.

Experiment 5

Question: Does darkness affect the ability of the predators to catch the prey?

Hypothesis: Predators will catch fewer prey in the dark than in the light.

Methods: Set up two containers identically, choosing one predator for each and about five individuals of one prey type appropriate for that predator, as in the lists preceding Experiment 1. For example, choose five small *Gambusia* (be consistent between dishes) and one giant water bug for each dish. Put one dish in a room that stays dark and leave one in a well-lit area secluded from classroom activity. For the dark treatment, turn off the light immediately after adding the predator before it has a chance to grab the prey. When only one or two prey remain in the well-lit container, check the container in the dark. How many prey are left?

Result: Your result is a statement of your prey counts for the two dishes and any other relevant observations. You can record your results on the histogram in Figure 9.6. Figure 3.4 provides an example of a completed histogram.

Conclusion: The prediction is confirmed. The predators used in this chapter should have less success in locating prey in darkness. All have good vision and rely at least in part on vision to locate prey. So fewer prey should be eaten in the dark. You can try different pairs and compare results. Is prey location simply delayed or completely prevented by darkness?

Experiment 6

Question: If we put one container of algae and snails in the dark for a month, will it have fewer snails than a similar container left in the light?

Hypothesis: We think the dark container will have fewer snails than the container in the light after one month.

Methods: Put an equal amount of algae and an equal number of same-sized snails (about ten each) into two dishes. Put one in a dark closet and leave one out in the classroom. After one month compare the size and number of snails in the two dishes. Are they different? Is the algae different?

Result: Your result is a statement of your snail counts and observations of their sizes in the two dishes.

Conclusion: The prediction is confirmed, although it may take more than a month, depending on the type of algae, type of snail, etc.

Snails eat living algae. Algae is photosynthetic, that is, it requires sunlight to live and make food so the algae will certainly suffer from light deprivation, as will the snails, eventually.

TERRESTRIAL PREDATORS

CHAPTER 10

Ant Lions—Terrors of the Sand

Introduction

Most of the children I've worked with have never seen or heard of an ant lion, but they are soon fascinated by these peculiar creatures. In this chapter I describe where to find ant lions (sandy playgrounds mostly) and how to set them up in the classroom so that they'll build their spectacular prey traps, which are pits in sand. Ant lions are insects, but they're similar to spiders in their feeding methods. I also describe several experiments regarding the ant lions' pit-building behavior. Ant lions require very little maintenance—an ant or other small insect for dinner every other day or so.

Figure 3 in the Postscript provides a range of questions and answers comparing behavior of the predators discussed in Chapters 8 to 13. A list of the questions represented in Figure 3 is provided in Figure 4, which can be photocopied and handed out for the children to answer.

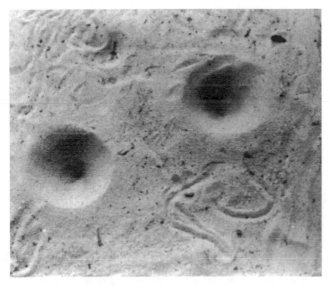

Figure 10.1—Ant lion pits and trails.

Materials

1. At least one ant lion.
2. One 8-ounce (.25 l) yogurt cup or similar container per ant lion.
3. Sand to fill two-thirds of each cup.
4. Larger containers for Experiments 1 to 5.
5. Ants, fruitflies (see Chapter 14) or other small insects to feed the ant lions.
6. About 1 cup (.25 l) of sugar, salt, soil, coffee grounds, etc., per ant lion as additional building substances for Experiment 1.
7. Shelf paper that's sticky on one side for Experiment 6 (optional).

Background Information
Building the Pit

My husband once said that every time he goes into the study where I keep my thirty ant lions he hears the sound of sand flying. He's hearing sand grains hit the sides of sand-filled yogurt cups as the ant lions work to repair their pits, or prey traps. I love that sound. My ant lions are telling me that they're happy and healthy and busy doing the peculiar things they were born to do.

I try to imagine how a newcomer would perceive this scene. What meets the eye is a low-cut cardboard box holding thirty cups filled with sand and otherwise apparently empty. But if you follow the sound, you see in a few of the cups something tiny moving along just under the surface. A tiny head snaps back every few seconds, flinging sand. If you focus on one for as long as fifteen or twenty minutes you'll see the circular path of this mysterious creature spiral inward and downward as sand is tossed away. When the creature reaches the center of the spiral, the result is a conical pit (see Figure 10.1). The pit is

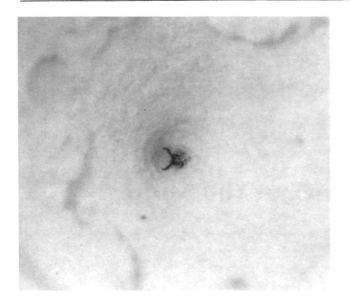

Figure 10.2 — Ant lion larva in sugar pit, with jaws open waiting for prey.

Figure 10.3 — Ant lion larva in sugar pit, grasping fruitfly with jaws.

smooth-sided and tapers down to a perfect point. If your gaze wanders to the cups where there is no activity — those where the pit has been completed — you wonder what became of the architect. You have to look very carefully to see that it's still there. Its body is buried at the bottom point of the pit, hidden from its prey. But its jaws, its piercing caliperlike jaws, jut upward to receive its victims (see Figure 10.2). This is a unique kind of insect certainly; you can't relate it to any bug you've seen before.

Catching Prey

After you've watched an ant lion build its pit, the next thing to do is to feed it. Children love the drama. (I left an ant lion and some prey with a class of hearing-impaired second-graders once. They took turns feeding the ant lion for several days with delight, their teacher said.) When you drop an ant or a fruitfly into the cup, the prey slides down the side of the pit toward the waiting jaws. If the victim tries to scramble up, the sand slides out from under its feet. When it reaches the bottom, you'll see the ant lion's jaws slam shut, piercing the prey between them (see Figure 10.3). Or you may just see a flurry of activity if sand dislodged by the prey's slide has obscured your view. The ant lion may slam the ant back and forth against the sides of the pit, trying to get a better grip with its jaws. If the ant lion misses on its first grab, you may see sand grains flung precisely against the escaping ant, knocking it back down toward the waiting jaws again.

When the ant lion gets a good grip on the ant or other bug, it draws the prey partially down into the sand and the jaws inject a paralyzing fluid into the ant's body. The struggle soon stops. Then digestive juices, which dissolve the prey's internal organs, are injected through the jaws.

The resulting fluid is sucked up through the jaws. (This is very similar to the way a spider eats, except that the spider uses a web instead of a pit to trap its prey. Both predators leave an empty husk of the prey behind.) The ant lion flips the empty carcass out of its pit with a quick flick of the back of the head. This head flick is its all-purpose manner of moving things, sand or finished prey. If you take an ant lion out of the sand, you'll see a plump oval body, a distinct flat head and larger jaws, altogether no bigger than your little fingernail (see Figure 10.4). The largest are about 3/8 inch (1 cm), the smallest 1/16 to 2/16 inch (1.6–3.2 mm). Their looks are not impressive but their behavior is something else.

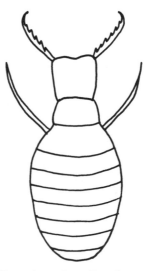

Figure 10.4 — Drawing of ant lion larva with jaws wide open. It has six legs but the back four are not usually visible from above. From 1/16 to 3/8 inch (1.6 mm–1 cm) in length, depending on age.

The Life Cycle

The ant lions that I keep for experiments are actually not mature insects, but larvae. They molt and shed their skins three times before they're ready to pupate. The larval period may last three years or more, depending on food supply. When an ant lion is ready to pupate, it spins a round cocoon about 1/3 inch (.8 cm) in diameter. The cocoon is sticky and picks up sand grains (see Figure 10.5). I can tell when one of my ant lions has pupated because its pit will vanish or look in disrepair. If I start pouring the sand onto a newspaper I'll find the spherical cocoon close to the surface. I found four or five while looking for missing larvae before I realized that they weren't lumps of sand but sand-covered cocoons. The pupa stays in the cocoon for about a month, then the winged adult emerges. An adult is beautiful. It has a long skinny abdomen like a dragonfly and two pairs of long transparent wings (see Figure 10.5). The wings and body are both about 1 inch (2.5 cm) long. The adults are attracted to light and will fly to a window when they emerge, which is how I've caught the only living ones I've had. If you keep the pupa in an enclosure to capture the adult, check it every day because the adult will die if neglected. Some species eat fruit. I've kept one in captivity for several days, with two pieces of paper towel soaked with water and sugar water. After mating, the female lays her sand-grain-sized eggs in sand.

Figure 10.5 — Ant lion pupa, larva and adult.

How to Get and Keep Ant Lion Larvae

I don't know of anywhere to order living ant lions, so you'll have to find your own. They are abundant in naturally sandy areas like sand dunes at the beach. There are very few naturally sandy areas where I live, but I am able to find ant lions pretty regularly in artificially sandy places like playgrounds. Many schools and city playgrounds now have sand. You'll find the ant lion pits only in places that are protected from trampling feet. For example, many wooden play structures have horizontal beams 2 to 12 inches (5–30.4 cm) above the ground. My children's school has a low balance beam, a wooden jungle gym and a picnic table all in areas that have had sand added. They all have ant lion pits under them in the places where feet never go. I also occasionally find pits in areas with very loose, fine soil.

An intact pit is easy to recognize. It is a very symmetrical cone-shaped hole in the sand, from 1/2 to 3 inches (1.3–7.6 cm) across at the top and up to 1 1/2 inches (3.8 cm) deep, depending on the age and size of the ant lion. A small pit looks something like the small hollows in the sand that form under an edge from dripping water. But the pit has a point at the bottom, while a drip mark is more bowl-shaped. Once you've located a pit, you must have a spoon to get the ant lion out. Scoop down at least 1/2 inch (1.3 cm) under the lowest part of the pit and bring up the sand. Then hold the spoon over a bowl or cup and gently shake the sand out of the spoon until the ant lion appears. Being somewhat buried in the spoon momentarily won't hurt it. Then put the ant lion in an empty cup to transport it. You can put them all in the same cup — in my experience they will not eat each other or anything else unless they're in their customary position at the bottom of a pit.

If you want the ant lion to live, it needs a pit. So set them up as soon as you get home. I keep my ant lions separated at home, so they won't interfere with one another and there's no chance of cannibalism. Each ant lion needs a cup to itself, about two-thirds full of relatively fine sand, in order to make a pit. The sand must be dry and relatively free of lumps and leaf fragments. If you need to retrieve one from a cup of sand and it has not dug a pit, dump the cup of sand out slowly on a piece of newspaper, spreading the sand out as you go.

Put the cups in a place where they won't be disturbed until it's time to take them to school. A bump may cause the sand to slide down the pit and cover the ant lion. Moving the cup almost certainly will.

After their pits are complete, feed them at least twice a week. Any nonflying insect will do. I prefer wingless fruitflies because they're easier to keep and easier to control than ants. (See Chapter 14 for information on how to get and keep wingless fruitflies.) You can find ants by looking under logs or boards or putting some fruit out in your yard. I toss two or three apple cores in different parts of the yard, and I usually get ants on at least one. Ants are often found in loose soil, like that in gardens or flower beds, because it's easy to tunnel through. Use ants that are no more than half the length of the ant lion.

Field Hunt

If you take children on an ant lion field hunt, you may want to spoon them up yourself unless your kids can be very careful. Children can enjoy themselves just learning where to look for the pits and watching you catch the ant lions.

Ant Lions at School

Getting Ready

One ant lion per student is nice if you can find that many. I've used as few as one ant lion per class, though. Many of the experiments can be done with only one.

When it's time to go to school, I spoon each one out of its cup and put all the ant lions into one container, without sand. I take the cups to school empty, so the children can have the experience of setting up their own cups.

Observations and Activities

I start by explaining to the children that the ant lions we have are larvae, not adult insects. I draw a rough picture of the ant lion on the board, explaining that they are predators, describing the jaws and the pit and how they capture their prey. If I have enough ant lions, I tell them that everyone is going to get a cup of sand and an ant lion that they will put into the cup themselves. After everyone has

Figure 10.6—Mandasa watching an ant lion burrow under the sand.

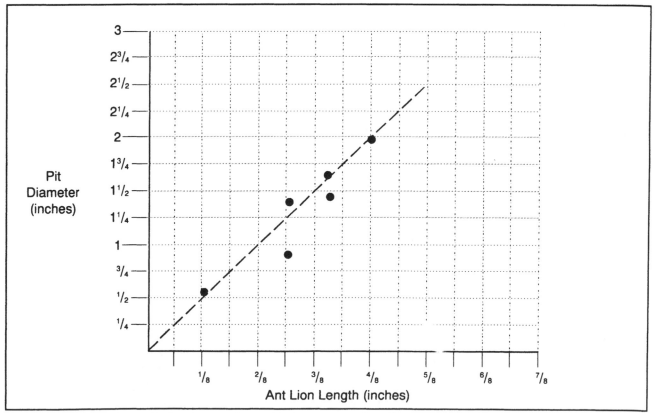

Figure 10.7—Sample graph showing a relationship between ant lion length and pit diameter. If the points lie along a straight or curved line (roughly), as these do, then there is a correlation between ant lion length and pit diameter.

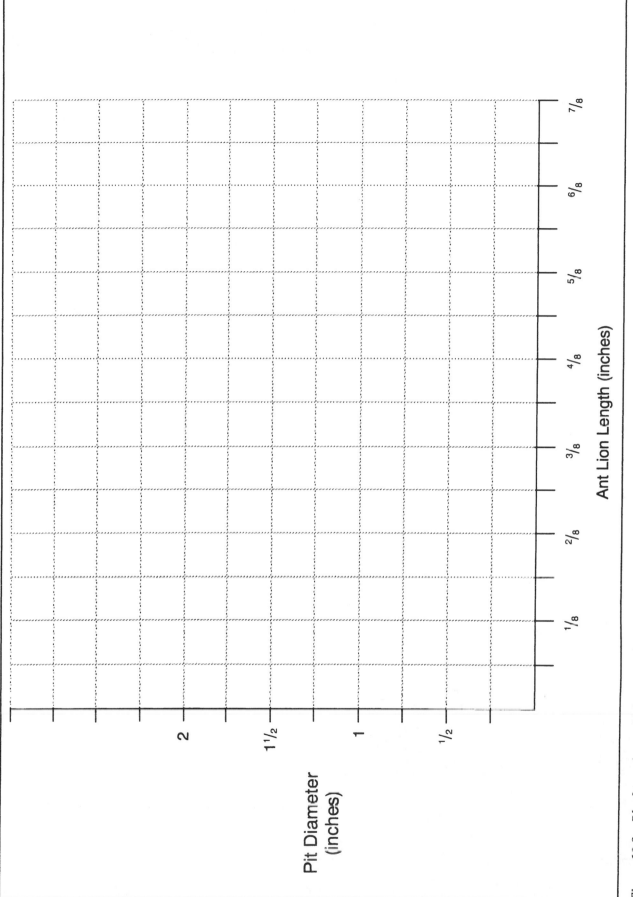

Figure 10.8 — Blank graph on which to plot your measurements of ant lion length and pit diameter.

a cup of sand, I give each child an ant lion in the palm of his or her hand with a small amount of sand [1/4 teaspoon (1.25 ml) or less]. Very few children decline holding the ant lion, but those who do can receive it in the cup. As the child holds the ant lion, point out the jaws, which will usually be wide open. (Ant lions never bite or try to bite people. Their jaws are for feeding only, not defense.) The children will see the very fine tip on each jaw that pierces the victim. Closed jaws are harder to see. The ant lion will waggle its rear end up and down while walking backward trying to burrow under the sand. The small amount of sand in the child's hand allows the child to see how the waggling rear end works in the sand. Children find this delightful. The first time I took ant lions to a class, I did all the handling myself, thinking the ant lions would get dropped or mashed. But I found with later classes that handling the ant lions was probably their favorite part, and none were damaged.

At this stage, while the ant lions are uncovered, have each child measure his or her ant lion to the nearest millimeter. You can use this information later to see if there is a correlation between animal size and pit size. The class may also find a correlation between animal size and time to pupation.

I tell the students to put the ant lions in the cup after a minute or two of watching. Then they'll see the ant lion quickly bury itself, as it tried to in their hands (see Figure 10.6). In a few seconds it will be out of sight. One child asked, "How do ant lions protect themselves?" I answered his question with another question: "Why do ant lions bury themselves immediately?"

It would be nice to leave the ant lions on the children's desks all day so that they can watch the ant lions digging their new pits. But in order to see this the children must be able to keep their hands completely off the cup all day and refrain from bumping their desks at all. In my experience,

Figure 10.10 — Sammy and classmates watch an ant lion in a yogurt cup grab at a fruitfly after Sammy dumps a fly from the vial into his ant lion's pit.

most children can't do this, so I have them put their names on the cups and put them somewhere else.

The next morning most of the ant lions will have made new pits. Have each child measure the diameter of his or her pit at the top rim. You can make a graph for the whole class, plotting pit size against animal length (see Figure 10.7). Figure 10.8 provides a blank graph for your measurements. Is there a correlation? That is, do bigger ant lions make bigger pits? Yes — you will be able to see the relationship on the graph.

The next thing to do is feed the ant lions. I let each child put one prey insect, a fruitfly or an ant, into an empty fruitfly vial (or any small container) and feed his or her own ant lion. Even first-graders can get a single fly out of a vial of reproducing fruitflies (a culture vial, see Chapter 14). Tell them to knock the bottom of the culture vial hard on the palm of the hand to shake the flies down from the top. Then remove the sponge from the top, shake one or two flies out into an empty vial and put the sponge plugs back in both vials (see Figure 10.9). Then invert the vial with one or two flies over the ant lion's pit and rap the bottom of it until the prey falls into the pit (see Figure 10.10). I find that I have to tell children constantly not to rap the container against the cup, not to touch the cup in any way and not to touch the sand. All these actions will cause sand to slide down the sides of the pit and cover the ant lion. Still, some children do it. I prefer to have the children feed their ant lions in groups of three or four, at least the first time, so I can watch closely and make sure they understand about not touching the cup. After that they can do it on their own, usually first thing in the morning.

Pits in Sugar

A favorite activity of mine with ant lions is getting them to build pits in substances other than sand. Sugar works great. The white pits are beautiful, and you can see

Figure 10.9 — Stephanie shaking one fly from a fruitfly culture vial into an empty vial, preparing to feed her ant lion.

the ant lion's jaws so much better against the white background. You can also see ejected carcasses clearly around the rim of the pit. (They're very hard to see on sand.) Do the carcasses pile up all around the pit or only behind the ant lion? Have the children measure the distance between the ant lion and the fly and ant carcasses. Which carcasses are flung further? You can make another graph here, showing carcass size on the horizontal axis and distance from ant lion on the vertical axis.

Humidity causes a sort of crust to form on the sugar eventually, which helps would-be victims escape from the pit.

Spacing

If you have extra ant lions or not enough for everyone, put several together in a large box. I use one about 12 by 12 inches (30.4 x 30.4 cm), containing dry sand 2 to 3 inches (5–7.6 cm) deep. You can observe the spacing between the pits and the trails that the ant lions leave in the sand. Does spacing seem to be uniform (equal distances between neighboring pits) or random? What is the minimum distance between two pits?

Cannibalism

An interesting activity with ant lions in a box of sand is to try to push one ant lion into the pit of another. It's not easy to push one — they're well equipped for walking in sand and don't slide easily. After doing this, do the children think that ant lions often stumble into one another's pits while looking for new pit sites? What if you actually drop an ant lion into another pit from above? Does the resident ant lion kill the intruder? Sometimes. Can the intruder get out? Yes, if it escapes the jaws of the resident, it can easily burrow through the side of the pit to escape. Let the children discover this on their own.

Keep your ant lions until some of them pupate. Those that are 1/3 to 1/2 inch (.8–1.3 cm) are good candidates. All the pupations I've recorded have been in late spring and have followed a period of daily feeding. If you have body-length measurements for the organisms, you can create a graph to plot body length against the length of time to pupation (see Figure 10.11). Figure 10.12 provides a blank graph for your measurements. Larger ant lions can be expected to pupate sooner.

Experiments

Remember that the hypotheses I give are just examples. Most are written in the "if … then" format, but they don't have to be. Your hypotheses will be the predictions made by the class or by a particular child. Your result for each experiment will be a statement of how your animals reacted to your experimental setup. Your conclusion is a statement of whether your prediction was confirmed or not confirmed. For each experiment, adding several replicates increases your confidence in the validity of your conclusion, but they may be omitted if tedious for young children.

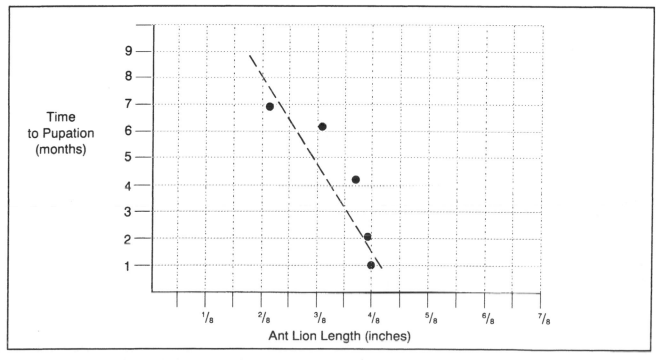

Figure 10.11 — Sample graph showing a relationship between ant lion length and time to pupation. If the points lie along a straight or curved line (roughly), as these do, then there is a correlation between ant lion length and pit diameter. Your numbers may be different from these, depending on the animals' diet.

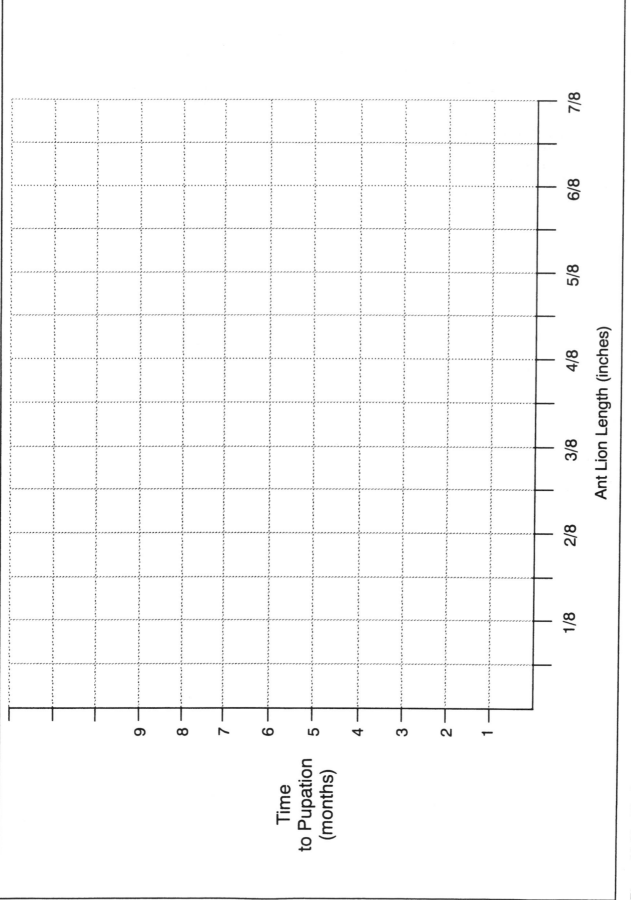

Figure 10.12 — Blank graph on which to record your measurements of ant lion length and time to pupation.

Experiment 1

Question: If offered a choice between sand and some other building material, will the ant lion always choose sand?

Hypothesis: Ant lions will always choose sand over other materials.

Methods: Get a container at least 7 inches (17.8 cm) long, 4 inches (10.2 cm) wide and 3 inches (7.6 cm) deep. The shape of the container is not important. Make a vertical partition dividing the container into two halves, each of which is big enough to accommodate a pit. Fill one side with fine dry sand up to the top of the partition. Fill the other side with sugar, coffee grounds or soil — whatever material is being tested. Put an ant lion in the middle and record where it builds its pit. Repeat several times if desired.

Result: Your result is a description of the ant lions' choices. You can record the results on the table in Figure 10.13.

Conclusion: Ant lions will build in many materials and don't always prefer sand. Texture seems more important than substance.

Experiment 2

Children hunting for ant lions on a playground will notice that pits are always under something. If they don't go with you on a field hunt, tell them you've noticed it. Why are the ant lions always under something? Is it because the ones who build in the open get stepped on, so we never see them? Or is it because they all choose to build under something? If they do choose to build under something, is it because they are attracted to darkness or dryness?

Question: When given a choice, will ant lions build out in the open or under a cover (in shadow)?

Hypothesis: If we give an ant lion a choice between cover and no cover, it will choose to build under cover.

Methods: Put fine, dry sand at least 2 to 3 inches (5–7.6 cm) deep in a container at least 7 by 4 inches (17.8–10.2 cm) or big enough for two pits. Cover half of the container with opaque cardboard, about 1 inch (2.5 cm) or so above the surface of the sand. Leave the other side exposed. Put an ant lion in the center of the container and record where it builds its pit. Repeat several times if desired. Do more build under cover or out in the open?

Result: Your result is a description of the ant lions' choice. You can record the results on the table in Figure 10.14.

Conclusion: In my experience, ant lions choose to build under cover somewhat more often than in the open, but the difference is not pronounced. Their prevalence under play structures can't be explained solely by a preference for darkness or cover.

Experiment 3

Question: Do ant lions prefer dry sand to wet sand? (This could partly account for their prevalence under shelters.)

Hypothesis: Ant lions like dry sand better than wet sand.

Methods: Get a container at least the size of that described in Experiment 1. Shoe-box size is fine. Add sand to a depth of 2 to 3 inches (5–7.6 cm). Put a foil or plastic partition into the sand in the middle of the box to divide the sand into two separate halves, then wet the sand on one side. The partition is to keep the dry side dry. It must not protrude above the surface of the sand. Put an ant lion in the center right over the partition, leave it a while and record where it builds its pit. Repeat several times if desired.

Result: Your result is a description of the ant lions' choice. You can record your results on the table in Figure 10.14.

Conclusion: When offered a choice between wet sand and dry sand, ant lions build pits in dry sand. This preference for dry sand may partially account for their prevalence under structures. I often find them under structures like balance beams, though, which probably offer little protection from rain. I also see them out in the open in protected areas. On the coast of North Carolina, walking is forbidden on some sand dunes in state parks to protect the sea oats that anchor the dunes. Ant lion pits abound in some open areas like this. So it appears that human feet account at least in part for their absence in open areas of sandy playgrounds.

Ant lions often change the location of their pits. An ant lion traveling just under the surface of the sand leaves a shallow but easily traceable furrow in the sand. I've followed furrows through twists and turns for at least 10 feet (3 m) across the dunes on the North Carolina coast. Why do ant lions move their pits?

Experiment 4

Question: Will rain cause the ant lion to change the location of its pit?

Hypothesis: If we spray an ant lion with water regularly, it may move its pit.

Methods: Put sand 2 to 3 inches (5–7.6 cm) deep in two boxes big enough to give the ant lions room to move

Building Material	Chosen for Pit Site (when offered another option)	Chosen for Pit Site (without another option)	No Pit Built
Sugar			
Salt			
Coffee Grounds			
Fine Soil			
Lumpy Soil			
Fine Sand			
Coarse Sand			
Any of the Above, Wet			

Figure 10.13 – Blank table on which to record your results for Experiment 1.

Choice of Conditions Offered	Ant Lion's Choice	Effect of Choice on Ant Lion*
Under Cover or Out in the Open Experiment 2		
Dry Sand or Wet Sand Experiment 3		*Cover protects from feet and rain *Wet sand is not flingable

Figure 10.14 — Blank table on which to record your results for Experiments 2 and 3.

Why Do Ant Lions Change the Location of Their Pits? Does Rain Cause Movement?

	Example:
a. Number of ant lions sprayed in pits _____	a. 2
b. Number of sprayed ant lions that change pit site _____	b. 2
c. Proportion of sprayed ant lions that change pit site (b/a) _____	c. 2/2
d. Number of ant lions not sprayed in pits _____	d. 2
e. Number of unsprayed ant lions that change pit site _____	e. 1
f. Proportion of unsprayed ant lions that change pit site (e/d) _____	f. 1/2

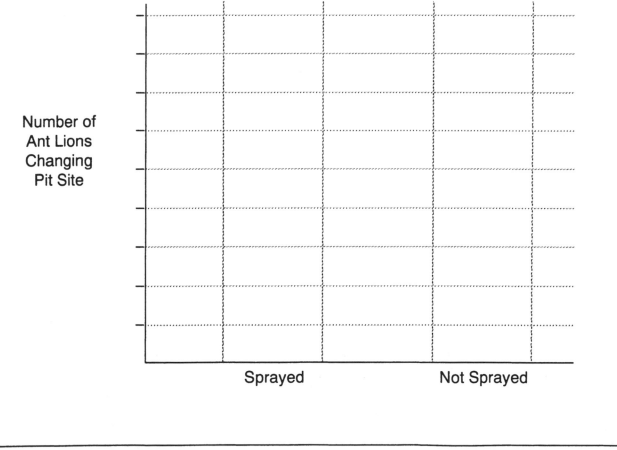

Figure 10.15a — Table and blank bar graph for recording the number of sprayed ant lions that move pit site versus the number of unsprayed ant lions that move pit site.

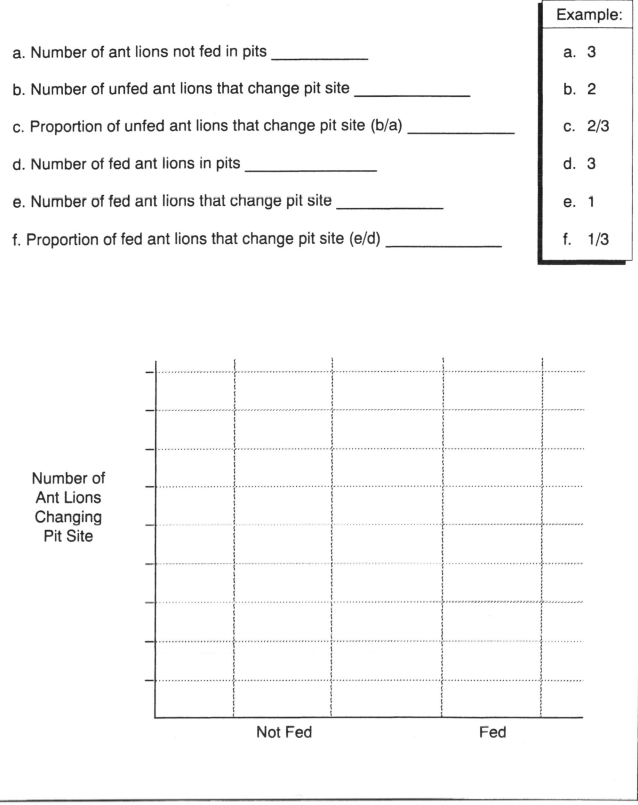

Why Do Ant Lions Change the Location of Their Pits? Does Hunger Cause Movement?

	Example:
a. Number of ant lions not fed in pits _____	a. 3
b. Number of unfed ant lions that change pit site _____	b. 2
c. Proportion of unfed ant lions that change pit site (b/a) _____	c. 2/3
d. Number of fed ant lions in pits _____	d. 3
e. Number of fed ant lions that change pit site _____	e. 1
f. Proportion of fed ant lions that change pit site (e/d) _____	f. 1/3

Number of
Ant Lions
Changing
Pit Site

Not Fed   Fed

Figure 10.15b — Table and bar graph for recording the number of well-fed ant lions that move pit sites versus the number of unfed ant lions that move pit site.

Measure the Diameter of the "Circle" of Scattered Sugar and Scattered Sand around Your Cups.

If you had several cups of each type of substrate, calculate an average diameter for each type.

a. Diameter of circle of scattered sugar _____

(single measurement or average)

b. Diameter of circle of scattered sand _____

(single measurement or average)

Which substance was flung the farthest? _____

Was your prediction confirmed? _____

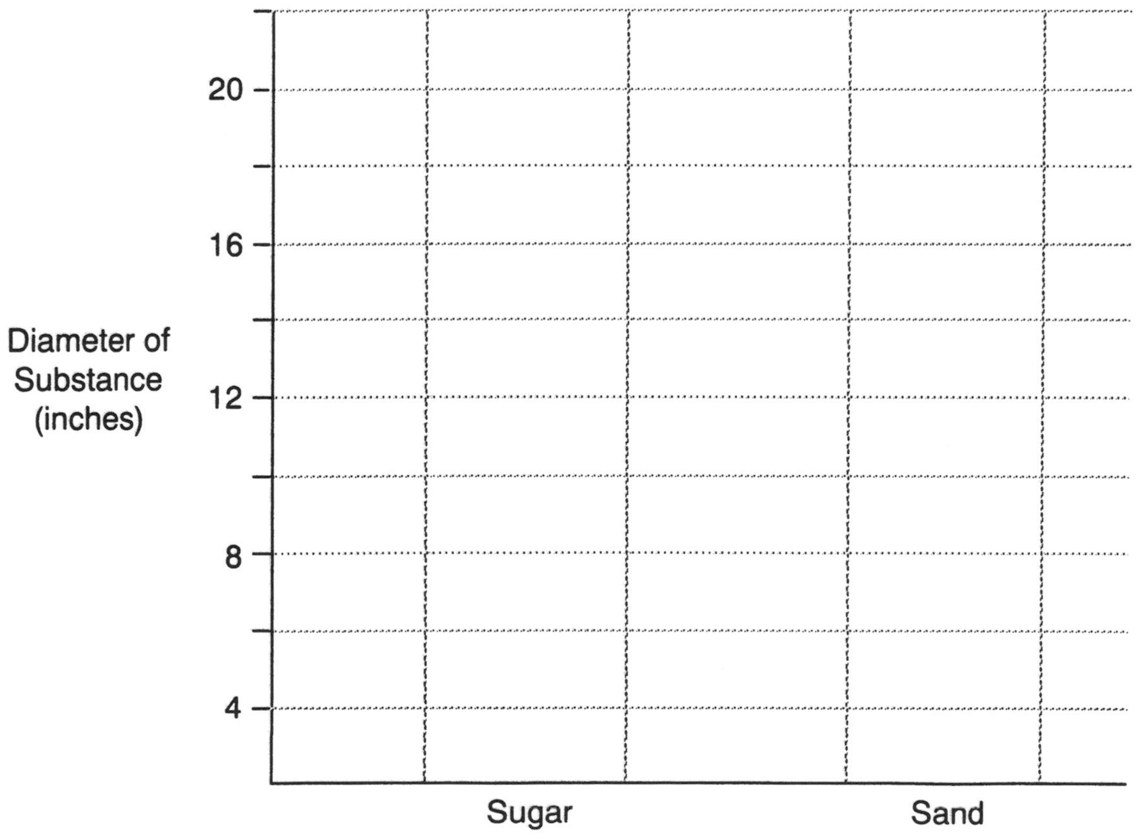

Diameter of Substance (inches)

```
20 ┤
16 ┤
12 ┤
 8 ┤
 4 ┤
   └──────────────────────────
      Sugar           Sand
```

Figure 10.16 — Blank graph on which to record your results for Experiment 6. (See Figure 3.4 for an example of a completed histogram.)

around. I use boxes that are 12 by 18 inches (30.4 x 45.7 cm). Put at least one, preferably two or three, ant lions in each box. After they've dug their pits, thoroughly spray the pits in one box several times a day for a week or so. Don't spray those in the other box as a control (for comparison). Feed ant lions in both boxes normally. You can mark the location of each pit by sticking a toothpick in the sand next to it. Do more of the sprayed ant lions move their pits?

Result: Your result is a description of the ant lions' movements during the week. Record your results on the table and histogram in Figure 10.15a. Figure 3.4 provides an example of a completed histogram.

Conclusion: In my experience ant lions that are sprayed are more likely to move. Apparently, rain may cause ant lions to move their pits.

Experiment 5

Question: Is a hungry ant lion more likely to change the location of its pit?

Hypothesis: An ant lion that's not catching prey will move more than a well-fed one.

Methods: Set up two boxes as in Experiment 4. Introduce one ant lion (two or three is better) into each box and allow it to dig pits. Feed the ant lion in one box daily for a week or two. Withhold food from those in the other box for the same period. Mark the location of each pit with a toothpick stuck in the sand beside it. Are the hungry ant lions more likely to move their pits?

Result: Your result is a description of the ant lions' movements during the week. Record your results on

the table and histogram in Figure 10.15b. Figure 3.4 provides an example of a completed histogram.

Conclusion: In my experience, a hungry ant lion is more likely to move than a well-fed one.

Experiment 6

Question: How far do ant lions fling sand, and how far do they fling sugar when making pits? Are the distances the same?

Hypothesis: Ant lions fling sand and sugar the same distance.

Methods: Put shelf paper down on the table, sticky side up so the sand and sugar will stick to it and not slide. Put one ant lion in sugar and one in sand 2 to 3 inches (5–7.6 cm) deep in cups on the shelf paper. (Shelf paper is not essential if the cups are in an area that won't be disturbed or swept.) Give them a day to make pits, then measure the diameter of the circle of scattered sugar and sand around the respective cups.

Result: Your result will be a description of exactly what happened and a statement of your distance measurements. Record your results on the table and histogram in Figure 10.16. Figure 3.4 provides an example of a completed histogram.

Conclusion: Was your prediction confirmed or not? In my experience, ant lions fling sugar farther than sand. Ant lions on my desk in cups with sugar fling sugar all over my papers, but the ones in sand are much neater. Sugar must be lighter than sand. You can confirm this by weighing equal volumes of sugar and sand in equal containers.

CHAPTER 11

Spooky Spiders

Introduction

In this chapter, children will discover through experimentation that some spiders need webs to catch their prey but some do not. They'll see how inflexible each type of spider is in its method of prey recognition and capture. Each type of spider must have a specific signal, or stimulus, to recognize an insect as a meal. Without the signal the spider won't attack. Most children are unable to predict the outcome of the experiments, and the surprise element makes a big impression.

Figure 3 in the Postscript provides a range of questions and answers comparing behavior of the predators discussed in Chapters 8 to 13. A list of the questions represented in Figure 3 is provided in Figure 4, which can be photocopied and handed out for the children to answer.

Materials

1. Funnel weaver, orb weaver, cobweb weaver or other web-building spider.
2. Jumping spider or nursery web spider or wolf spider or other "wandering" (non-web-building) spider.
3. Plastic jar or other enclosure for each spider. I often use plastic peanut butter jars, approximately 1 quart (1 l) size.
4. Lids with air holes or cloth lids and rubber bands for the jars.
5. Plastic petri dishes as alternative enclosures for jumpers and other small non-web-builders. These allow excellent visibility. These are available at science hobby shops or biological supply companies (see Appendix).
6. Fruitfly culture vials are also good alternative enclosures for small non-web-builders. (See Chapter 14 for information on how to get vials.)
7. A terrarium for Experiments 4 and 5.
8. Prey for spiders (suggestions below).

Background Information

Categorizing Spiders

There are thousands of species of spiders. There is no need to identify any of them to species, and I don't try. It's easy to recognize a few broad categories of spiders. I use an inexpensive paperback from the Golden Field Guide series, called *Spiders and Their Kin*. The most obvious major categories of spiders are these: web-building spiders and wandering spiders. Web-builders rely on their webs for prey capture and usually stay on the webs at all times, which makes them easy to recognize. I use the term "wandering spiders" to mean any spiders that don't build webs for prey capture, but either ambush prey or actively pursue it. (There is a family of tropical spiders that are sometimes called "wandering spiders," not to be confused with my much broader use of the term.) The wanderers can be recognized by the fact that they are not found on webs, but rather hiding or walking, across a sofa or a sidewalk or through the grass, etc.

Children generally think that all spiders build webs and that they all build the circular webs with spokes that we see in storybooks. But the circular web with spokes, or orb web, is only one of many different styles of webs. There are platform webs, cobwebs, funnel webs and so on. Closely related spiders build similar webs, so an easy way to categorize web-builders is by type of web: cobweb weavers, funnel weavers, orb weavers, etc. There are only a few common web types, and they're easy to recognize. *Spiders and Their Kin* helps by having spiders grouped by web-type. The non-web-builders are grouped according to behavior or body shape, and the most common groups are not hard to recognize or remember. Jumping spiders jump and have short, strong, stocky legs; crab spiders have legs that project sideways and then curve forward like crabs' legs; wolf spiders are big and hairy, etc.

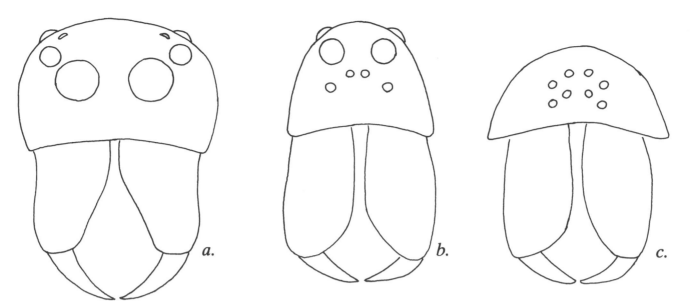

Figure 11.1 — Three spider faces. Compare eye size of (a) jumping spider, (b) wolf spider and (c) funnel weaver. Also note fangs on tip of jaws.

Spider Anatomy and Basic Behavior

All spiders have eight legs and two main body parts: a cephalothorax and an abdomen. This distinguishes them from insects, which have six legs and three main body parts: head, thorax and abdomen. The cephalothorax of the spider is equivalent to the head and thorax of the insect. Like insects, spiders molt or shed their exoskeletons several times as they grow to adulthood.

Most spiders have eight eyes (see Figure 11.1). The size of the eyes is related to the quality of vision. Jumping spiders have much better vision than other spiders. They have two eyes in front that are much bigger than the other six and can form images as well as detect motion. Jumpers are active hunters and rely on their acute vision to detect prey. Many other wandering spiders, like the wolf spider, rely on vision to detect prey, but can detect motion only. For a sit-and-wait predator like the wolf spider, this type of vision is adequate. Most web-builders, like the funnel weaver, have very small eyes and poor vision. They generally rely on vibrations in the web to locate prey.

Because all spiders are predators (which means they eat live prey), they almost all have the same body parts for holding and eating prey. Each spider has a pair of mouth appendages called pedipalps that grasp the prey. Some pedipalps are quite large. (The pedipalps on a trap-door spider are so large that on my first encounter I mistook them for a fifth pair of legs.) Between the pedipalps, on the front of the head, are the jaws or chelicerae (see Figure 11.2). At the tip of each of the two jaws are the fangs. The spider injects poison into its prey through the hollow fangs. After the poison has killed or paralyzed the prey, the spider injects digestive juices, which liquify the insides of the prey. (Some spiders spit digestive juices.) The spider then sucks up the insides and leaves a hollow shell of the insect. Some spiders have spines on the inner edges of the jaws and crunch the hollow body into a wad.

All spiders secrete silk from a cluster of glands on the tip of the abdomen, called spinnerets (see Figure 11.3). The non-web-builders use the silk only for wrapping up prey or making egg sacs or as a safety line (dragline) when moving around. I poked a webless spider under the eave of my house one morning, and it dropped halfway to the ground

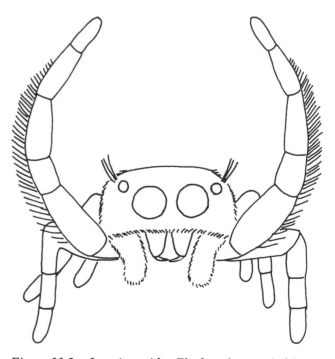

Figure 11.2 — Jumping spider. The front legs are held up as in courtship, to display the hairy ornamentations.

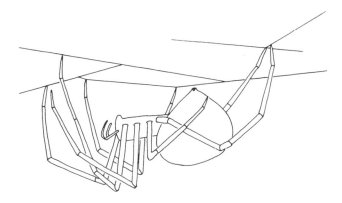

Figure 11.3—American house spider in usual upside-down posture. Points on tip of abdomen are spinnerets.

on a dragline in half a second by affixing some silk to the eave and secreting a line as it dropped. I was amazed at how fast it secreted that line when it perceived itself to be in danger and jerked to a stop right in front of my face.

Spiders are not my favorite creature to handle but their behavior is interesting. There's a lot of action with a captive spider. Some predators won't eat out in the open, like the centipedes I've kept, but spiders don't care who's watching. My four-year-old, Alan, has a "pet" nursery web spider (very similar to a wolf spider but less hairy) that he found in the living room and caught with a plastic peanut butter jar by himself. It's been in the jar for about a month. He feeds it a housefly every other day or so, which he catches bare-handed against the living room windows. His spider is about 1 1/2 inches (3.8 cm) long, including the legs. He unscrews the lid, throws the usually wounded fly in, then puts the lid back on and watches. The spider is on the fly as soon as it moves. Nursery web spiders spit digestive juices on their prey and crunch the outer skeleton of the prey as they extract the insides. When the spider is through, the fly is just a tiny mass.

Alan has a pet jumping spider too that he caught outside on a water fountain at the park. It ate small fruitflies at first, but has now grown and molted and can handle Alan's houseflies. It doesn't crunch its prey but merely sucks them dry, so its jar is littered with fly carcasses. Neither of these two are web-builders.

The first jumping spider we kept captive at home made herself a silken enclosure about two weeks after we got her. She sealed herself in and wouldn't come out. We left her alone on a shelf in our study. Several weeks later my husband found some baby spiderlings on his desk. It finally occurred to us to check the silken enclosure. That was the source, dozens were coming out. We tore it open and found the mother's shriveled body. If this happens to you in a class, reading E. B. White's *Charlotte's Web* may help the children savor it. Charlotte the spider dies after making an egg sac, and the hatchlings are later greatly appreciated by Charlotte's pals.

How to Get and Keep Spiders

I don't know of a place to order specific types of spiders other than orb weavers and tarantulas, and they are rather expensive (see Appendix). But spiders are so common, it's easy to catch your own. To do the experiments I've described here, you need one or two web-building spiders and one or two non-web-builders (wanderers).

How to Catch a Web-Builder

I use funnel weavers for the experiments that require web-builders because they're so abundant around my house. Funnel weavers hide at the narrow end of a funnel-shaped web (see Figure 11.4). The floor of the web spreads out into a sheet. There are probably one hundred funnel webs in the ivy across the front of my small house. Many are in the vertical crevices between the downspouts and the wall, uniformly spaced at intervals of about 7 inches (17.8 cm). The symmetry reminds me of a high-rise apartment. On an ivy-covered tree behind our house, there are only four webs, which are spaced at wider but just as regular intervals.

To catch funnel weavers and most spiders, slap a plastic jar down over the spider as fast as you can. After you have the jar over the spider, slide a piece of cardboard between the jar and the wall or ground. Then pick up the jar and replace the cardboard with a lid. Funnel weavers will build a modified web in a jar, which often winds up looking more or less like a silk doughnut lying on the bottom of the jar. The doughnut is a circular tunnel where the spider resides, with irregular strands of silk filling the space above the tunnel. The spider emerges from the tunnel when a victim is snagged on the strands above it.

If you have a jar 1 quart (1 l) or larger, you don't have to have holes in the lid as long as you lift the lid for a moment every day. (This may disrupt the web, so you may

Figure 11.4—A web of a funnel weaver spider, one of hundreds in the ivy on the front of my house.

Figure 11.5 — Jumping spider. Note stocky legs, large eyes in front center.

They're constantly on the move, looking for prey. I find them in odd places — my car, the kitchen table, the living room floor. Most are easy to recognize because of their short stocky legs (see Figure 11.5). They walk at an irregular pace and may jump several centimeters when going after prey. Most jumping spiders are quite small, up to 3/8 inch (1 cm), excluding the legs. A *National Geographic* article (September 1991) on jumping spiders called them "teddy bearish" and they are. Many are fuzzy or have pretty tufts of hair or bright colors to attract mates.

All jumping spiders have a pair of very big eyes (by spider standards) on the front of the head (cephalothorax) and six smaller eyes. They have excellent vision and will turn to face anything moving around them. The big pair of eyes are clearly visible on the larger jumping spiders and, along with the turning behavior, can help you recognize them as a jumper.

The best way I know to catch a jumping spider predictably is to look around the top of fence posts. They like high places — walls, tree branches, etc. There's a jumper at the top of almost every single post of a chain-link fence around a baseball field behind my house in late summer and fall. They hide in silken cocoonlike envelopes, open at both ends. If I poke a twig in one end, the spider runs out the other end into the jar (a second person to hold the jar helps).

prefer air holes.) Feed the spider small insects like flies or moths or young crickets twice a week or so.

If you can't find a funnel weaver, any web-building spider will do. American house spiders (this is their name) are very common. They make tangled, irregularly shaped webs that are seen in corners, especially ceiling corners, in houses. This type of web is called a cobweb. The house spider has a round abdomen that's huge compared to the rest of its body, very frail-looking legs, is light brown and has black streaks and patches (see Figure 11.3). The twenty or so that are behind curtains and windows, behind toilets and on bedroom ceilings in my house right now range in size from 3/4 inch (1.9 cm) or less, including legs. House spiders are easy to catch with a jar, and they build cobwebs readily in the jar.

Black widows are also cobweb weavers and have a body shape that is identical to that of the American house spider. (See the Field Hunt section for more on black widows.) House spiders don't have a dangerous bite and probably don't bite at all.

Most web-building spiders will build some sort of web in a jar, but may not if their normal web is a large orb web or some other type that can't be even approximated in a jar.

How to Catch a Wandering Spider

Jumping spiders are my favorite and are easy to catch too. I stumble upon one every couple of weeks or so.

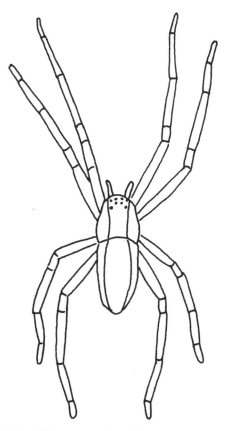

Figure 11.6 — Nursery web spider. Very similar to wolf spider, but less hairy.

If you can't find a jumping spider, any wandering spider (non-web-builder) will do. Look carefully in the grass for a nursery web spider (see Figure 11.6). I find them most predictably in overgrown grass that's been blown or pushed down to make lots of caves underneath. Wolf spiders are found in like places and look very similar to nursery web spiders. Both are large, 3/4 inch (1.9 cm) in length, excluding the legs. In the fall, females are likely to have egg sacs. A female wolf spider will have her egg sac attached to her spinnerets. A female nursery web spider will carry her egg sac with her jaws until near hatching time, then will hide it in a folded leaf.

Any spider you find in the grass or on the forest floor that's not in a web is likely to be a wandering spider. If you look, you will find one! Catch it with a jar and small square of cardboard. Wandering spiders may make draglines crisscrossing a jar, which can be mistaken for a web. If in doubt, put it in a terrarium where it has room to get away from its draglines and make a proper web if it's so inclined.

Housing and Feeding Your Spiders

I usually keep spiders in plastic peanut butter jars. There is no reason to add soil or leaves to the jar; it will only make web-building more difficult and obscure the prey. I keep small jumping spiders in plastic petri dishes because I can see their movements so much better in a petri dish than in a jar, especially their reaction to prey and to each other. Fruitfly vials work nicely too for small non-web-builders. (Petri dishes and fruitfly vials are described in Chapters 7 and 14, respectively.) Large web-builders may need a terrarium.

If spiders are fed adequately, they don't need water. They can last for quite a while without food as well, but I feed them a couple of times a week. Sweep a net through the grass. Almost any little insect out of the grass will do, although it has to be moving. Flies are favorites. Moths are also good prey. You can catch a moth with a porch light at night and a net. Insect larvae (caterpillars, beetle grubs, maggots), other spiders and small bees may or may not be accepted. Pill bugs (roly-polies), slugs, millipedes and worms will probably not be accepted. The prey should not be so large that it completely wrecks the spider's web and should be smaller than the spider itself.

Field Hunt

If the children want to catch their own spiders they can look through leaf litter, in the grass, in shrubs, around windows, on outdoor walls and atop fence posts. Record whether each captive was in a web or not. Substitute your captives for the ones I've suggested for each category: web-builders and wandering spiders.

Poisonous Spiders

Don't let a fear of bites keep you and your students away from spiders. Most spiders either won't bite because they are too timid or can't bite because they're too small. It's still probably a good idea to tell children not to handle any spider. The black widow and the brown recluse are the only two whose bites are dangerous. The bite of any other spider in the United States is either painless or equivalent to an insect bite or sting.

Black widows are virtually identical in shape to the American house spider (see drawing) but shiny black all over except for a red hour-glass marking on the underside of the abdomen. I live in the southeast, where black widows are most common. Most of the black widows I've found have been in dark places like basements or crawl spaces under houses or dark filling station rest rooms or dark cabinets inside my house. The only place I've ever seen them outdoors is a couple of times under big heavy logs or heavy stones. I've never seen one out in the open outdoors. In many parts of the country, especially the northern states, you'll never see black widows at all.

The brown recluse is found in the same type of setting as the black widow—dark corners and out-of-the-way dark cabinets indoors and under heavy stones outdoors. It is yellowish brown and has a dark violin shape on the front half of the cephalothorax. I've never seen one.

Both the black widow and the brown recluse can be avoided by telling children to keep hands out of dark places into which they can't see.

Spiders at School
Getting Ready

All you need to begin observing is a plastic jar with a lid and prey for each spider. Halloween is a good time to do a unit on spiders if you haven't had a hard freeze by then, which would kill many of the adult spiders outdoors. The big orb weavers, like the conspicuous black and yellow *Argiope*, are most easily found in fall. This is the time when many other adult spiders are most abundant after growing and molting all summer.

Observations and Activities
Web-Builders

Some children may not know why spiders have webs. Put a funnel weaver or whatever web-building spider you can find in a jar or terrarium and give it a day or two to build a web. Then throw in a fly or lightning bug or other insect and watch. When the prey gets caught in the web, the spider will grab it and probably wrap it up in silk to hold it securely. The spider will bite the prey to paralyze it and may eat it then (suck it dry) or wrap it more thoroughly and save it for later. If the spider ignores it, the prey may be too big or not moving enough, or the spider may be too concerned about its own safety to be hungry.

Watch then for the children's curiosity to take over. Can we trick the spider by jiggling a twig held against some part of the web? Does the spider attack? Sometimes. What does the spider do with an empty carcass?

Do bigger spiders have bigger webs? Yes, there is a direct relationship between the length of the spiders' legs and the size of the webs. If you have several web-builders of the same type, different sizes, you can show this on a graph (see Figures 11.7 and 11.8). Let the horizontal axis be spider leg length and the vertical axis the web diameter. If you plot several points for several spiders and their respective webs, you should get more or less a straight line or possibly a curved line. You can use that line to predict web diameter for any new spider of the same type. It's easiest to do this with orb weavers, since you don't have to tear up the web to measure the spider. You can record your measurements on a graph (see Figure 11.7). Figure 11.8 provides a blank graph for your measurements.

Wandering Spiders

If you find a spider with an egg sac attached to her abdomen, which some mother spiders do to protect the eggs, remove the egg sac and offer a substitute — a bit of paper or other lightweight object about the size of the egg sac. What does the mother spider do? A mother wolf spider may attach the substitute object in place of the egg sac.

How does a wandering spider react to prey? Most will either ignore the prey or approach rapidly and attack it. They see something small moving and they go for it. Many wandering spiders are able to detect motion only. Jumping spiders are different though. The jumper's two big front eyes have good resolution — that is, they are able to form a clear image of the prey. A jumper's behavior is like that of a toad or a mantis when it first notices the movement of the prey. It will turn the front part of its body to face the prey directly, to fix those two big front eyes on it. This is nice because it signals the viewer (you or me or a student) that the predator has definitely noticed the prey. One advantage of the petri dish for a jumper is that you can look down on the spider and so can see its body swivel more clearly. Can the children tell when the jumper has noticed a new prey item? Get them to articulate how they can tell.

After the jumper has noticed the prey, it may watch for a few moments before jumping on it, or it may decide not to attack. It will almost always turn to face directly something new that's moving, at least momentarily. We have a couple of jumping spiders in petri dishes on the kitchen table where I work. They are startled and hop backward or at least watch me everytime I pick up a book or a paper. In contrast, the spiders in webs in jars never react to me or my activities whatsoever unless I touch the web or pick up the jar. They can't see me, but the jumpers can.

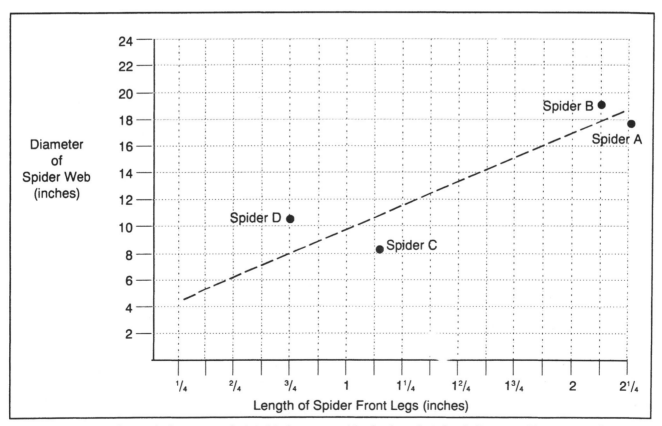

Figure 11.7 — Sample graph showing a relationship between spider leg length and web diameter. The points will probably not conform exactly to a line, but will more or less if your spiders are all the same species.

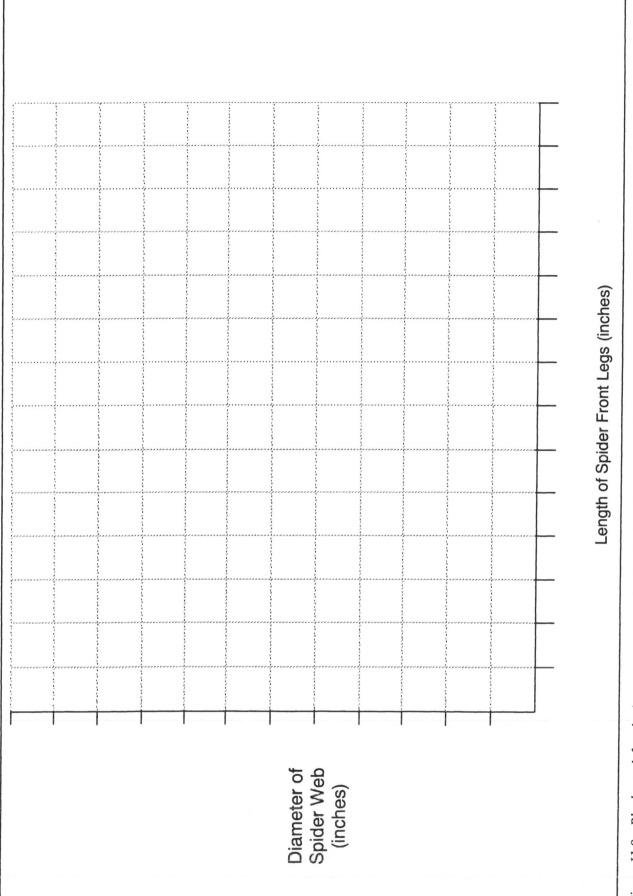

Diameter of
Spider Web
(inches)

Length of Spider Front Legs (inches)

Figure 11.8 – Blank graph for plotting measurements of spider leg length versus web diameter.

It's fun too to watch a pair of jumping spiders react visually to one another. I have a same species pair together in a jar now. (I believe they are the same species because they have identical markings.) The smaller one (not mature) reacts to the larger one by turning to face it head on whenever the larger one moves and by walking backward to get away from it. The smaller one may turn and run if the big one comes too close. The larger one has taken over the smaller one's silken hideout and now keeps the smaller one out. The larger one also gets most of the prey I put in the jar and may eat the smaller one eventually.

If you have two adult jumping spiders of the same species you may see some courtship displays or male-to-male aggression. Adult males usually have some flashy colors or tufts of hair on the front legs and maybe else-where. Female jumping spiders, like female birds, are more usually drab brown or gray. During courtship, males lift their front legs to display their colors and tufts to the females (see Figure 11.2). Two males may display to one another competitively. They may also butt heads or other-wise show aggression. A jumping spider will react to its mirror image as though it's another jumper. A male may turn to face its image and behave aggressively toward it.

Will a wolf spider or nursery web spider or other wandering spider react to its mirror image? Probably not. Although they do detect prey visually, many only detect motion and can't form images at all. A wolf spider can't see its mirror image because it sees only motion. When the wolf spider is walking, everything is a moving blur. When it remains still, its mirror image is still too. Wolf spiders are ambush or sit-and-wait predators, so this type of vision is adequate for them in nature. The spider usually waits motionless, and only the prey is moving, so the prey is visible as movement.

Put a pair of jumping spiders together, a pair of wandering spiders other than jumpers together and a pair of web-builders together. Have the students compare how the pairs react to each other. Jumpers see the best, other wanderers see somewhat and web-builders usually see poorly. Do the children's observations prove this?

Experiments

Remember that the hypotheses I give are just ex-amples. Most are written in the "if ... then" format, but they don't have to be. Your hypotheses will be the predictions made by the class or a particular child. Your result for each experiment will be a statement of how your animals reacted to your experimental setup. Your conclusion is a statement of whether your prediction is confirmed or not. For each experiment, adding replicates increases your confidence in the truth of your conclusion, but they may be omitted if tedious for young children.

Here's a question one child posed after several days of watching a funnel weaver spider eat prey in its web in a jar.

Question: If we put another spider in the jar, would it get caught in the silk like a fly? Or could it walk across the silk like the one that lives in the jar?

Hypothesis: If we put in a second spider, we think the new spider can walk on the first spider's silk without getting caught.

Methods: This is an easy question to test. Allow one spider to build a web in a jar and add a second spider, either of the same species or of a different species. Watch and record what happens. Your control here is watch-ing the intruding spider (or another identical one) on its own silk first.

Result: Your result will be a description of what happened between the intruding spider and the resident spider.

Conclusion: I've had different outcomes here. Often an intruder is able to walk on the existing web, but it is usually killed by the resident, eventually.

What if the intruder is much bigger than the resident? Does the intruder ever kill the resident or coexist with it? If it did kill the resident, what would it do about the resident's web? Use it? Repair it? Spiders often eat their own damaged webs before rebuilding. Would a victorious intruder eat the resident's web to make room for its own web?

Does the result vary according to whether you use a same species pair of spiders or two different species?

Experiment 2

Question: Does a funnel weaver or other web-building spider have to have its web to catch prey?

Hypothesis: If we destroy the funnel weaver's web or put the funnel weaver in another jar, it will still eat prey offered to it.

Methods: Put a funnel weaver or other web-builder in a fresh jar. As a control, keep another funnel weaver in a jar with a web. Offer both prey, like a small cricket. Do both eat?

Result: Your result is a statement of how both spiders responded to the prey.

Conclusion: A funnel weaver in a jar with a web will eat prey readily. A web-builder of any sort will not (in my experience) eat prey without a web. The prediction is not confirmed.

Web-builders are genetically "programmed" to recognize prey by the vibrations of the web. Most web-builders have poor eyesight. But even if they could see the prey, they don't recognize it as food without feeling the vibrations in the web. The vibrations trigger the prey–capture response. The spider doesn't have sense enough to be more flexible in its behavior.

Experiment 3

Question: Do all spiders ignore prey if they are not in a web?

Hypothesis: After seeing the funnel weaver in Experiment 2, we think all spiders have to have a web to catch and eat prey.

Methods: Put a funnel weaver or other web-builder in a fresh jar. Put a jumping spider or other wandering spider in another fresh jar. Larger ones may require a small terrarium. The spiders must be in the jar long enough to get calm (an hour or so) but not long enough to build draglines all over the jar (even non-web-builders may leave draglines when moving around). Put a fly, small cricket or other small prey in each jar. Does either eat?

Result: Your result is a statement of the response of both spiders.

Conclusion: The prediction here is, of course, not confirmed. The web-builder will ignore the prey, but the wandering spider should jump on the prey or otherwise attack it, and either eat it or wrap it up for future use. Most wandering spiders depend on eyesight and not vibration to detect prey. (If the jar has been passed around recently, the spider may be too disturbed to eat.)

Experiment 4

Question: Do spiders have preferences about where they build their webs?

Hypothesis: Whatever the children come up with.

Methods: Set this up as a choice experiment in a terrarium big enough so that either end of it could accommodate a web. Offer different conditions at either end, for example, light and dark, damp sand and dry, a round ball on one end of the terrarium floor versus open space at the other end, an angular object to maximize possible attachment points (like a small lidless shoe box) in one end of the terrarium versus open space at the other end, a dish of water in one end versus an empty dish and so on. Since for any trial the spider could select one end out of indifference instead of a strong preference, you'd have to repeat it several times to be confident of a preference. When a web is dam-

aged, many spiders will eat the whole web (to avoid waste) and start over. So after each choice, you can damage the web and leave it in place to see if your spider does eat it and start over.

If you have a non-web-builder, you can offer it choices too and see where it spends most of its time. If it's a sit-and-wait hunter, where does it hide?

Result: Your result will be a statement of your observations of your spiders.

Conclusion: Depends on the type and size of the spider and the choices offered.

Experiment 5

Question: Will tearing the web up daily or spraying the spider with water cause the spider to change the location of its web? Can the spider be induced by other means to change the location of the web?

Hypothesis: We think the spider will build in a new location if we damage its web.

Methods: Damage the web somewhat each day with a stick or spray the spider with water or disturb it in some other way. Withholding food from it is one option. Will hunger make it move? The spider has to be in a terrarium or other container big enough to have another choice of locations. Your control is another spider of the same type that is not being bothered, sprayed or starved.

Result: Your result is a statement of your spider's reaction.

Conclusion: Some spiders can be remarkably persistent about building a new web daily in the same place. After all, webs are torn up a lot in nature. Some spiders routinely eat the whole web every night and start over. Others may move if disturbed, particularly if they themselves are menaced. Water may or may not bother the spider, depending on the species and the force of the water. Usually not. In my experience, starvation does not usually cause a spider to move.

Experiment 6

Question: If two funnel weavers are in the same jar and there's not room for two webs, will they build a web together?

Hypothesis: We think two crowded spiders will build a web together.

Methods: Put two funnel weavers or other web-building spiders in a jar together. As a control, have a single one in another jar to make sure this type of spider will build in a jar.

Result: Your result is a description of the actions of your spiders.

Conclusion: In general the prediction here is not confirmed. Usually neither will build a web. One may, or possibly both may squeeze in a small web, but certainly they won't build one together.

Experiment 7

Question: Will spiders build webs in the dark?

Hypothesis: If we put the jar in the dark, the spider can't see to build.

Methods: Put two web-building spiders of the same type in two jars. Put one jar in the dark and leave one in a well-lit room. Does the one in the dark build a web as well as the one in the light?

Result: Your result is a statement of your spiders' activities.

Conclusion: The prediction here is not confirmed. Since web-builders have poor eyesight, they don't rely on vision much or at all for web-building. Most can build a normal web in the dark. Can a web-builder catch prey in the dark?

Experiment 8

Question: How does darkness affect prey capture?

Hypothesis: Since web-builders can't see well, we expect that they can catch prey in the dark. Since wanderers, especially jumpers, see well and use their vision to catch prey, we expect that they can't catch prey in the dark.

Methods: Have a web-builder with web intact in one jar. In another jar have a wandering spider, preferably a jumping spider. Take both jars into a closet or other room that can be made very dark. Add prey, such as a small cricket or moth, to each jar at the same time and turn off the light quickly. Check the spiders after ten minutes or so. Have both caught their prey?

Result: Your result is a statement of what happened with your two spiders.

Conclusion: The prediction is confirmed. Since web-builders rely on tactile detection of web vibrations to find their prey, darkness has little effect on their prey capture. Since wanderers rely mostly on visual detection of prey, complete darkness is a serious handicap. If you get different results, what explanations can the children think of?

Experiment 9

Question: Will spiders build webs in the cold?

Hypothesis: If we put one jar in the refrigerator, the spider will be too cold to build.

Methods: Put two web-building spiders of the same type in two jars. Put one jar in the refrigerator and leave one at room temperature. Does the one in the refrigerator build as well and as soon as the one at room temperature?

Result: Your result is a description of your spiders' activities.

Conclusion: Depends on the temperature of the refrigerator and the type of spider. Some spiders will build normally in the refrigerator (which is also dark). Can they catch prey in the refrigerator?

Experiment 10

Question: Do particular kinds of spiders prefer certain types of prey? Must the prey be moving?

Hypothesis: Whatever the children predict.

Methods: You can do this with either a web-building spider in a web or a non-web-builder. Offer one spider two different types of prey at the same time and record which prey is taken. To be sure there really is a preference, you'd have to offer the spider the same choice of prey more than once. Do different kinds of spiders share preferences?

Result: Your result is a statement of your spiders' choices, or abstentions.

Conclusion: Prey must be moving. Spiders generally prefer flies or other flying or actively moving insects. They will sometimes accept wormlike animals like beetle larvae (grubs) or fly larvae but not as readily. What about caterpillars, earthworms or small slugs? Prey usually must be smaller than the spider.

A spider's hunger can affect its preferences. A hungry jumping spider has an abdomen that's smaller in circumference than its cephalothorax and looks caved-in. Watch its abdomen plump out after it's fed. A hungry jumping spider will accept prey that it ignores when well fed.

CHAPTER 12

Praying Mantises — The "Smartest" Insects

Introduction

Mantises are probably the most interesting insect in this book. They seem much too intelligent to be only insects. My family has been totally charmed by the many we've kept as pets. In this chapter I'll describe the features that I think set them apart from other bugs. I'll also describe their predatory behavior and how children can involve themselves in feeding the mantis. The chapter also outlines several experiments to investigate prey recognition, habitat choice, climbing behavior and more.

Figure 3 in the Postscript provides a range of questions and answers comparing behavior of the predators discussed in Chapters 8 to 13. A list of the questions represented in Figure 3 is provided in Figure 4, which can be photocopied and handed out for the children to answer.

Materials

1. A mantis. You can order egg cases from a biological supply company (see Appendix) or catch one outside (instructions later in the chapter).
2. A terrarium at least about 6 by 6 by 10 inches (15.2 x 15.2 x 25.4 cm).
3. A lid for the terrarium that is not airtight.
4. Live prey for the mantis. This is not as hard as you might think. I'll tell you how to find suitable critters in the Field Hunt section. (See also Chapter 2 for suggestions on how to attract and trap bugs for the mantis.)

Background Information

At first glance mantises look a bit like spiders because of their long legs. Their appearance put me off at first until I watched one long enough to realize that the resemblance to spiders stops with the legs. In many ways their behavior is more like that of a cat or even a person.

Our first captive mantis, whom we eventually named Mantie, intrigued us the minute we brought her inside by turning her head to look at each of us in turn. I'd never seen another insect turn its head — it's odd how far this went in making her look intelligent and sentient, even sort of human.

Figure 12.1 — An adult Chinese mantis on my back deck railing, looking at the camera. Her rounded abdomen is typical of females full of eggs. Note the triangular face and round eyes that give her a sentient look, and the spines on the two front legs that help grip prey.

The head-turning made her seem interested in us, which I think was not entirely an illusion. And her face looked recognizably like a face, which is more than can be said for most insects. Like all mantises, she had a heart-shaped face with two round eyes and a little pointed mouth (see Figure 12.1). She held her front legs folded in front of her as if she were praying. We learned in time that she used her front legs more as arms than legs, for holding prey and climbing, not for walking. This too made her seem less insectlike and more human.

Preying

Mantises are predators (they eat only live prey), which is where the catlike behavior comes in. Mantises don't actively search for prey as some predators do. A cheetah, for example, can chase down its supper, but a mantis can't walk very fast. A mantis hunts by sitting very still and waiting. If a mantis sees a cricket or a fly out of reach, it will creep slowly toward it. Its body stays very level as a cat's does, only the legs move, to avoid startling the prey. When the mantis gets within striking distance, it will sometimes sway gently back and forth before it strikes. I don't know why — to improve its depth perception? I asked a friend why baseball players sometimes sway back and forth before some impending action, like batting. He said, "You can move faster if you're already moving when you start." Maybe that's why mantises sway.

The strike from start to finish lasts just a fraction of a second. If you blink you'll miss it. A mantis doesn't take a step when it strikes; it merely leans forward and extends its long front legs lightning-fast, grabs and returns to the starting position. The front legs are jointed and clamp the prey in a scissor hold. Spines along the front legs hold the prey in place. The mantis takes small bites, eating the prey alive, and eats almost the entire thing from "head to toe." I have to admit watching the mantis eat is a little grisly sometimes. Mantie once ate a pet salamander I had, which horrified me. But it was my fault, not hers, for leaving the salamander where she might find it.

Mantises will readily take prey from your hand. I've never had one grab my finger by mistake. That's good because the spines might hurt. I usually offer crickets when I feed by hand so I can hold the tip of the cricket's long legs and keep its body away from my fingers. My own children will feed the mantis by hand, but I think it takes a good bit of familiarity with the mantis for a child to be so inclined. I've never been able to feed one by hand with a class gathered closely around. The mantis is too distracted by the unaccustomed activity of a crowd to be interested in eating. It will eat in the classroom after it gets used to its surroundings.

Feeding a mantis by hand is what I like best about keeping mantises. It's just icky enough to give me a thrill.

Grooming

Something else about mantises that I really like is how they clean themselves. A mantis will clean its legs with its mouth after a meal. Then it uses the front legs to clean its head and face, as a cat does. It cleans its back legs too. A mantis really reminds me of a cat with the tip of that back leg in its mouth. I'm not sure how they do it with no tongue, but they do.

Reproduction

Mantises mate in late summer or early fall. The male stands on the female's back, the tip of his abdomen curved up to join hers. (Kindergartners recognized this as "riding piggyback.") I've seen mantises stay in this position for a couple of days. The female may eat the male or just chew off his head after the mating is over.

A female full of eggs has a rounded underside to her abdomen. (A male's abdomen is slender.) Because she's heavy, she can't fly and is hence very easy to catch. Probably eight out of ten adult mantises I or others catch turn out to be pregnant females, which is fortunate for those of us who want egg masses.

The female lays her eggs usually one to two weeks after mating. She'll lay them in captivity readily, usually two or more egg masses. The mantis begins egg-laying by expelling a wad of foam from the tip of her abdomen onto a twig or the side of the terrarium. The eggs are suspended in the foam, which hardens into an egg case. They will hatch in the spring if fertile. (See Chapter 13 for ideas about what to do with the hatchlings.)

All mantises die after the eggs are laid, in autumn, no matter how well you care for them. They may die abruptly or weaken and stop eating gradually over a period of a month or so. If you lay a dead mantis on its back in a dry and airy spot, it will dry out without any odor and can be kept indefinitely for viewing.

Defensive Behavior

I'm curious about what specifically triggers a mantis to react the way it does when frightened. If you move your hand toward an adult suddenly, it will open its wings to make itself look bigger and more menacing. It draws its upper body and forelegs back, poised to strike — somewhat like a snake. The mantis draws back much farther when frightened than it does before making a food strike. And it may strike at your hand, although not trying to grab it but apparently just to bump it. Young ones do the same thing when frightened, but without opening the wings because they have none.

In some adult mantises I've seen a completely different reaction to being frightened, a reaction I think evolved to conceal them rather than to threaten the intruder. I had one mantis in particular that did this every time I took the lid off of her terrarium. She froze with her body held vertically and her forelegs extended vertically above her. This posture made her look much more like a stem, and I suppose in general makes a mantis less visible to potential predators. Many of the baby mantises I have now in an insect sleeve cage (see Figure 2.3e) adopt this posture when I spray water droplets through the mesh top of the cage.

This type of behavior — cryptic posturing — occurs other places in the animal kingdom. Bitterns are a type of marsh bird with vertical streaks on the breast. When startled, the bittern will freeze with its head thrown back, so that the vertical streaks on its throat and breast blend in with the marsh grass. It's effective enough that I've never been able to spot one, after years of searching. Any behavior or physical feature that helps an animal blend in with its background can be called cryptic. The mottled brown skin of a toad is cryptic coloring, as are the spots on a fawn, the stripes on a tiger. It's easy to think of many examples of cryptic coloring, less easy to think of examples of cryptic posturing. Why do some mantises strike when startled, while others freeze in a vertical position?

How to Get and Keep Mantises

Several species of mantises live throughout most parts of the United States. If you want one, you can try catching one outdoors.

Most of the adults I've had I have simply stumbled on unexpectedly around the outside of my suburban house — on the porch, an outdoor window sill or a screen. Keep your eyes open all the time for one and tell your students to, especially in August, September and October. I usually find two or three per summer. I've never purposely gone out in search of an adult and found one. I have, however, been successful in catching many very small and recently hatched mantises with a net. The best net to use is a long-handled sweep net with an opening of about 15 inches (38.1 cm). The mesh part of the net is almost 40 inches (1 m) long and cone-shaped. You can order a sweep net from a biological supply company (see Appendix). Or you can use any net with a handle — a large fish net or butterfly net. The best place to look is in areas of overgrown weeds that are waist high or taller. Sweep the net through the tops of the weeds quickly. The advantage of a sweep net is that the animals are swept to the tip of the long net and can't get out easily, giving you time to get your jar ready. The baby mantises jump — be fast! The babies are also on twigs of shrubby trees in overgrown areas. They are not in forests but in places like overgrown fields, the weeds along a creek or ditch or the edges of fields.

If you can't find a mantis outside, you can raise your own from an egg case. See Chapter 13 on baby mantises for a description of how to look for egg cases outside or how to order one.

Keeping a single mantis is relatively simple. The terrarium I use is about 16 by 8 by 8 inches (40.6 x 20.3 x 20.3 cm). It should have a multibranched twig in it that doesn't rock for the mantis to climb on. A mantis who has nothing to climb is not happy. You'll need a lid to keep the mantis inside, but not an airtight one. A cloth lid is ideal. You can affix it to a wood frame or a rectangle that fits around the top of the terrarium (see Figure 12.2), or you can use a rubber band or just tape it on. The mantis won't try to squeeze under the edges so it needn't be tight. Keep the floor bare so the mantis can spot its prey.

For a baby mantis the first enclosures should be small. A tiny mantis in a large terrarium will never be able to find its prey. For a mantis 1 inch (2.5 cm) long, an 8-ounce (.25 l) drinking glass is big enough. I don't use twigs for very small enclosures because a small mantis can climb the side of the enclosure. As the mantis molts and grows, get bigger enclosures.

A mantis can eat prey almost as large as itself. The easiest way to feed a large mantis is to set out a funnel trap (see Figure 2.3b) baited with a quarter-sized piece of raw chicken, liver or fish. You'll catch big flies. Chill them for two and a half minutes in the freezer, then dump them in the mantis's cage. They also like moths, crickets, beetles, grasshoppers, just about any insect. They don't like slugs, caterpillars or roly-polies. I find field crickets by looking under boards or under sheets of plastic on the ground and especially inside piles of old damp grass clippings. Camel or cave crickets hang out on the inside walls of sheds or basements. You can catch grasshoppers the same way I catch baby mantises, by sweeping a long-handled net through the tops of tall grasses. You can get moths by turning on your porch light at night. Use a plastic cup or jar to clap over one or whack it lightly with a rolled-up newspaper. A mantis will eat a wounded creature, as long as it's moving. I have had them eat freshly dead crickets that I've wiggled by the legs. They may even eat raw hamburger if you wave it in front of them with tweezers. You can make a drop-trap with a tin can to catch various critters (see Figure 2.3a). Baby mantises like fruitflies. (See Chapter 14 for information on how to trap or raise fruitflies.) They also like *Tenebrio* beetles, adult mealworms, which are easy to raise (see Chapter 16).

A mantis will eat prey much smaller than itself, but if the prey is very small, make sure the mantis gets enough to eat. It will eat several times a day if given the opportunity, but twice a week is enough to sustain one.

Field Hunt

I don't recommend taking children on a field hunt for adult mantises, because you're unlikely to find one. They blend in quite successfully with their surroundings and sit very still. Even if you look right at one, you probably won't see it. I've spotted an adult mantis in its natural habitat (tall grasses and shrubby areas) only once.

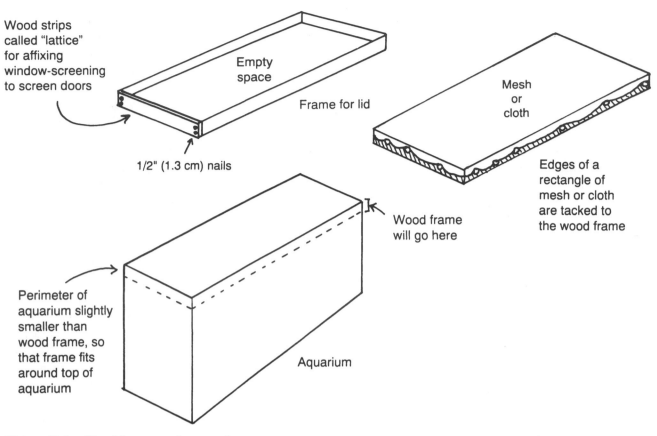

Wood strips called "lattice" for affixing window-screening to screen doors

Empty space

Frame for lid

1/2" (1.3 cm) nails

Mesh or cloth

Edges of a rectangle of mesh or cloth are tacked to the wood frame

Wood frame will go here

Perimeter of aquarium slightly smaller than wood frame, so that frame fits around top of aquarium

Aquarium

Figure 12.2 – Wood frame top for aquarium.

Show your students pictures of mantises and ask them all to look in August, September and October. It's easy to catch an adult female with a jar. If you put the open jar slowly in front of her or over her, she'll probably step into it.

Baby mantises are fairly easy to catch with a net. I've never caught one longer than about 1 1/4 inch (3.2 cm) with a net. [Hatchlings are about 3/8 inch (1 cm); adults of some species are up to 4 inches (10.2 cm).] See the Field Hunt section of Chapter 13 for information on finding babies and egg cases.

A Mantis at School

Getting Ready

All you need to begin is a mantis, a terrarium, a lid, a twig for climbing and food.

Observations and Activities

What seems to impress children the most about mantises is holding them (see Figure 12.3). The first class I took a mantis to was a first-grade class. As the children sat gathered around watching me unsuccessfully try to feed the mantis, almost every one of them clamored and begged to hold it. They could see she was sitting very calmly on my

wrist, and there was no menace involved. But there were too many of them to hand it around so we couldn't do it. After they all sat down at their desks, the mantis decided to eat and I walked around to each seat so each child could see. One little boy, Kenny, put his head down on his desk and declined to look. But as I went to put the mantis away, there was Kenny. "Can I hold it please?" Everyone else was on to some other lesson. "Sure, Kenny." He flapped his hand out calmly, trustingly, and recoiled only slightly when he felt its tickling feet. This was a full-grown Chinese mantis, the largest, at about 4 inches (10.2 cm). He stared intently as the mantis began her trek up his arm, as they always do in their yearning to climb. When it passed his elbow, he asked me to take it. Then he beamed at me from ear to ear. He was very pleased with himself.

A mother asked me to tutor her ten-year-old girl who was doing a school report on a mantis she had found. The girl's mother wanted her to interview me on the life history of mantises. The daughter dutifully asked a few questions and wrote down the answers, but with no enthusiasm. What she really wanted me to do was show her how to hold it to impress her younger siblings, her mom, me and herself. I showed her how to put her hand down slowly in front of the mantis and allow it to step on. It usually will because your arm is something to climb. If you move too

Figure 12.3 — A sequence of photographs. Sarah enjoys the first part of an adult Chinese mantis's walk on her right arm. Mantises always climb whatever's available, so it heads for the top. Sarah tries to transfer the mantis to her left hand, but it steps over instead and continues upward toward her neck.

suddenly you'll frighten the mantis, and it may strike at you. The daughter accomplished her goal, easily and proudly. She even let it walk up the back of her neck, something most people can't tolerate (me included). I heard from her mom that the mantis was a big hit at school, and she was asked to take it around on her arm to some other classes. She felt good about that.

So, if you can manage it, it's probably a good idea to let those who want to hold it. I've let many captives out of the cage and they generally don't fly unless frightened. But it may wander away if you leave it out all day.

If you let the children feed it and watch it eat for several days, they may come up with some questions you can address experimentally.

Experiments

Remember that the hypotheses I give are just examples. Most are written in the "if … then" format, but they don't have to be. Your hypotheses will be the predictions made by the class or a particular child. Your result for each experiment will be a statement of how your animals reacted to your experimental setup. Your conclusion is a statement of whether your prediction was confirmed or not. For each experiment, adding replicates increases your confidence in the validity of your conclusion, but they may be omitted if tedious for young children.

What characteristics of potential food cause the mantis to recognize it as potential food? People recognize food by sight and smell. Does a mantis recognize the shape and color of a cricket? Does it recognize the shape and color of all the animals smaller than itself that it could eat? That's a lot of different animals to recognize for an insect, even if it is a smart-looking insect. Is it something about the smell that they recognize? Do all prey make some sort of noise? The answer is something that children probably will not guess, although it is very simple, because it is so different from what we look for in food. There's one thing that all mantis meals have in common: They're all *moving*. Movement is what attracts mantises' attention, what signals their brains that the object before them is a potential meal. How efficient! It's much simpler to recognize movement than to recognize hundreds of kinds of creatures.

You can help children discover this on their own simply by either suggesting or seeing to it that the children offer both dead and live prey. If you tell them to bring in an insect and don't specify that it be alive, they'll bring dead ones. They may notice spontaneously that dead prey are ignored. If not, ask them if the prey that were struck at were dead or alive.

It's good to lead them at this point to a suspicion that being dead or alive has something to do with it. Conduct an experiment to get a definitive answer. Experiments 1 and 2 address the issue of prey recognition.

Experiment 1

Question: Will a mantis eat a dead insect?
Hypothesis: We think our mantis will eat any bug, dead or alive.
Methods: Put a live bug and a dead specimen of the same type in the terrarium. Crickets are a good choice, because live ones move a lot. A live moth may sit still for hours. Watch until one is eaten or at least struck at.
Result: Your result is a statement of your mantis's actions.
Conclusion: The prediction is not confirmed. A mantis will eat or at least strike at live prey, but it will ignore dead prey. If your mantis ignores the live prey too, it may be upset by too much activity around it, it may not be hungry or it may object to that particular prey type for some reason. Keep trying.

Experiment 2

Question: Do mantises ignore dead prey because they are dead and rotting, or because they are not moving?
Hypothesis: We think our mantis ignores dead things because they smell bad.
Methods: Hold a freshly dead cricket by the back legs with a pair of tweezers and jiggle it in front of the mantis. You may want to withhold food from the mantis for a day or two before you do this. You can kill the cricket painlessly by freezing it. This will leave it looking intact. Freezing an insect is not as cruel as it sounds because they are cold-blooded. They don't shiver and feel miserable; they simply slow down gradually until they stop.
Result: Your result is a statement of your mantis's response to the cricket.
Conclusion: The prediction is not confirmed. The mantis will eventually strike at the cricket and eat it. Mantises ignore dead prey because they are not moving. It may take persistence and trying different amounts of jiggling. A mantis that's overstimulated by little hands waving around it will usually not eat.

Try the same thing with a piece of hamburger, then a piece of apple. Does taste have something to do with acceptance of food after capturing it?

Why do mantises choose the places they do to wait for prey? Why don't we see them on the forest floor?

Experiment 3

Question: Why do mantises climb? Will a mantis in a high place catch flying prey faster than a mantis in a low place?

Hypothesis: We think a mantis in a high place will catch flying prey faster than a mantis in a low place.

Methods: Offer a mantis a moth in a cage with twigs whose branches reach almost to the top. At another time offer the mantis a moth in a cage with nothing on which to climb. Do it simultaneously if you have two mantises and two cages. Record how long it takes the mantis to catch the moth in each cage. Which mantis is the fastest? Repeat each trial several times if you want to be sure the results are not due to chance alone.

Result: Your result is a statement of the time required to capture the moth in each situation.

Conclusion: The prediction is confirmed. A mantis will usually catch a moth faster in a cage with twigs to climb on.

Experiment 4

Question: Does climbing help mantises catch nonflying prey, like crickets? Does a mantis in a high place catch nonflying prey faster than a mantis in a low place?

Hypothesis: We think climbing helps mantises catch all prey.

Methods: Set up one terrarium with climbable twigs as in Experiment 3. Set up the other with no twigs. To be realistic you should put leaf litter on the floor of each cage, because a cricket in nature will hide. Offer a mantis a cricket in each cage and record how long it takes to capture the cricket in each cage. Then try the experiment again with a bare floor in each cage.

Result: Your result is a statement of the time required to catch the cricket in each situation.

Conclusion: The mantis will probably never catch a cricket in a cage with leaves on the floor. In the cage with a bare floor, it'll catch the cricket, but twigs won't make any difference. Climbing does not help catch nonflying prey.

Experiments 3 and 4 bring up the issue of different predator strategies. Mantises are sit-and-wait or ambush predators. This strategy works well for flying prey that might come to rest next to a mantis. It does not work well for concealed prey, like crickets. Many predators, like towhees and other birds, will actively search through the leaf litter for prey, flipping over leaves with their feet. A mantis will never turn over objects to expose prey as a towhee will, and most insects on the ground are hiders. Can

the children think of other examples of either strategy? What strategy does an ant lion (Chapter 10) use? How about spiders? Frogs? Anteaters?

Maybe the students can come up with other experiments to find how the mantis's strategy does or doesn't work with various types of prey. Can they think of a nonflying prey that doesn't hide?

Experiment 5

Question: Does the twiggy shape and green or brown coloring of a mantis help it to hide from its enemies?

Hypothesis: We think the mantis's shape and color help it to hide from its enemies.

Methods: Release your mantis in a bush while the children aren't looking. At the same time, place a small red ball no bigger than an egg in the bush. Substitute anything that's a different shape and color than the mantis but not much bigger. Ask the children, one at a time, to find the mantis and the ball. How many children spot the ball first? How many spot the mantis first? Does the mantis's shape and color help to conceal it?

Result: Your result is a statement of the number of children spotting the ball first and the number of children spotting the mantis first.

Conclusion: The prediction is confirmed. A mantis in a bush is very hard to spot. I've spotted a mantis in its natural habitat only once or twice in my life. Almost all of the adults I catch are those who have strayed onto a sidewalk or porch or the wall of a building, where they are much easier to see.

Experiment 6

Can a mantis learn from experience? Specifically, will a mantis be able to catch crickets faster after a two-week diet of crickets? The ability to improve its efficiency as a predator would be to the mantis's advantage. But is its brain capable of learning? Ecologists recognize several components of foraging or prey capture: (1) search, (2) pursuit, (3) capture and (4) handling (which includes eating). Many animals have been shown to be able to improve their efficiency, at each step, with experience. Obviously, a predator such as a lion, that learns predator skills in part from its mother, would improve with experience. But what about an animal whose behavior is not learned from a parent but is completely instinctive? You can do a separate experiment with each component of prey capture. I've outlined an experiment to test the mantis's ability to spot prey faster with experience.

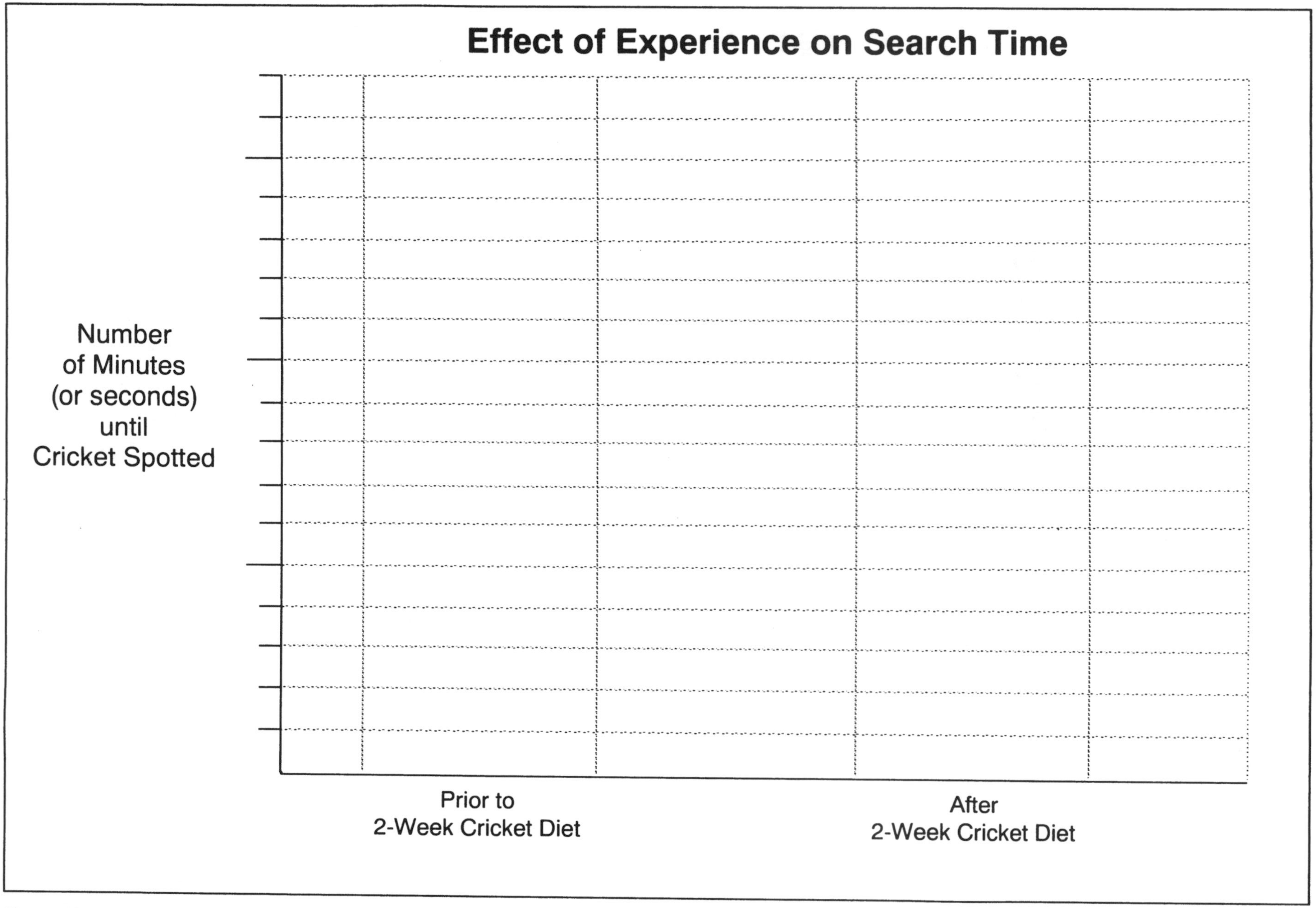

Effect of Experience on Search Time

Number
of Minutes
(or seconds)
until
Cricket Spotted

Prior to
2-Week Cricket Diet

After
2-Week Cricket Diet

Figure 12.4 — Blank graph on which to record your results for Experiment 6. (See Figure 3.4 for an example of a completed histogram.)

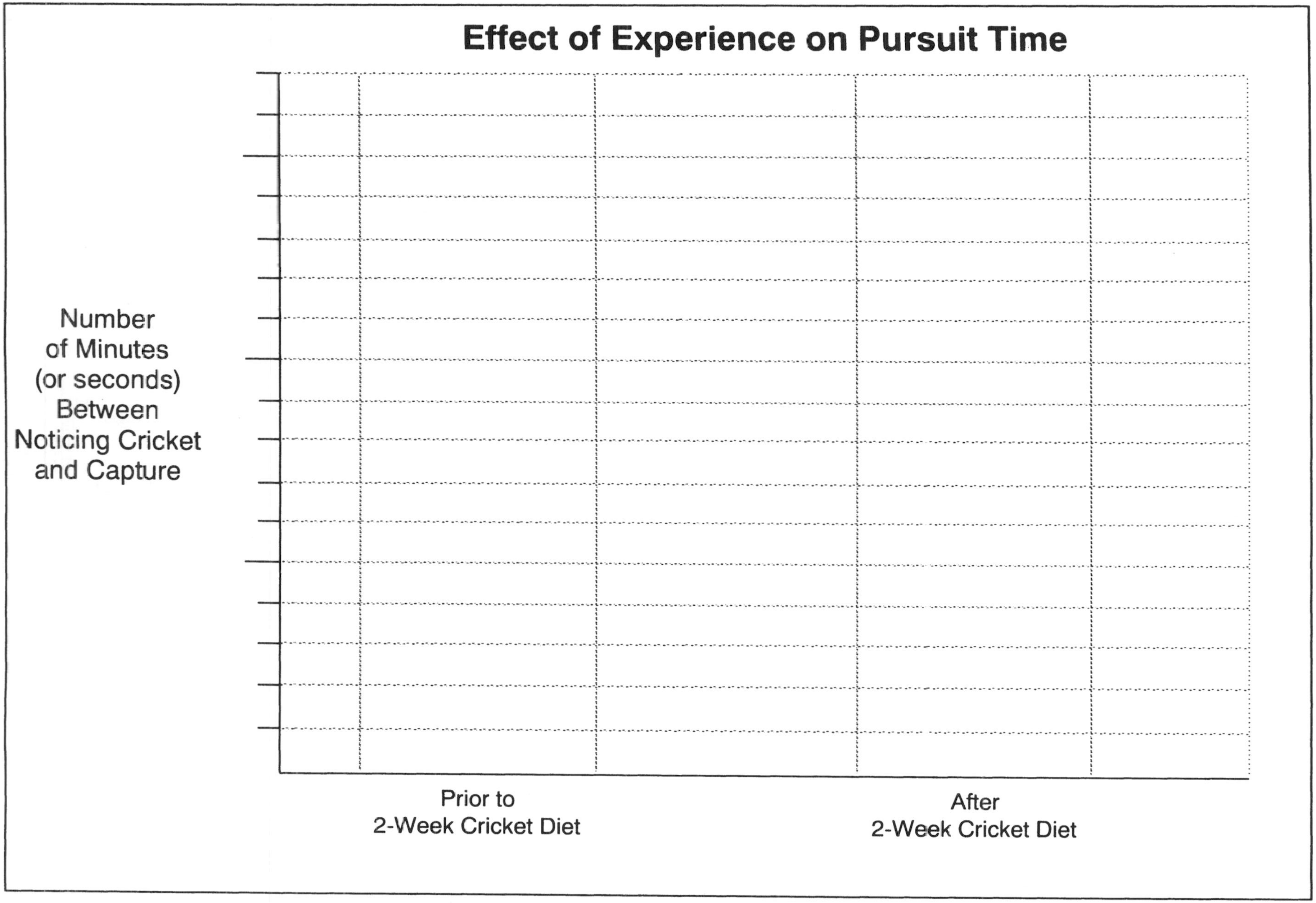

Effect of Experience on Pursuit Time

Number
of Minutes
(or seconds)
Between
Noticing Cricket
and Capture

Prior to
2-Week Cricket Diet

After
2-Week Cricket Diet

Figure 12.4 — Blank graph on which to record your results for Experiment 6. (See Figure 3.4 for an example of a completed histogram.)

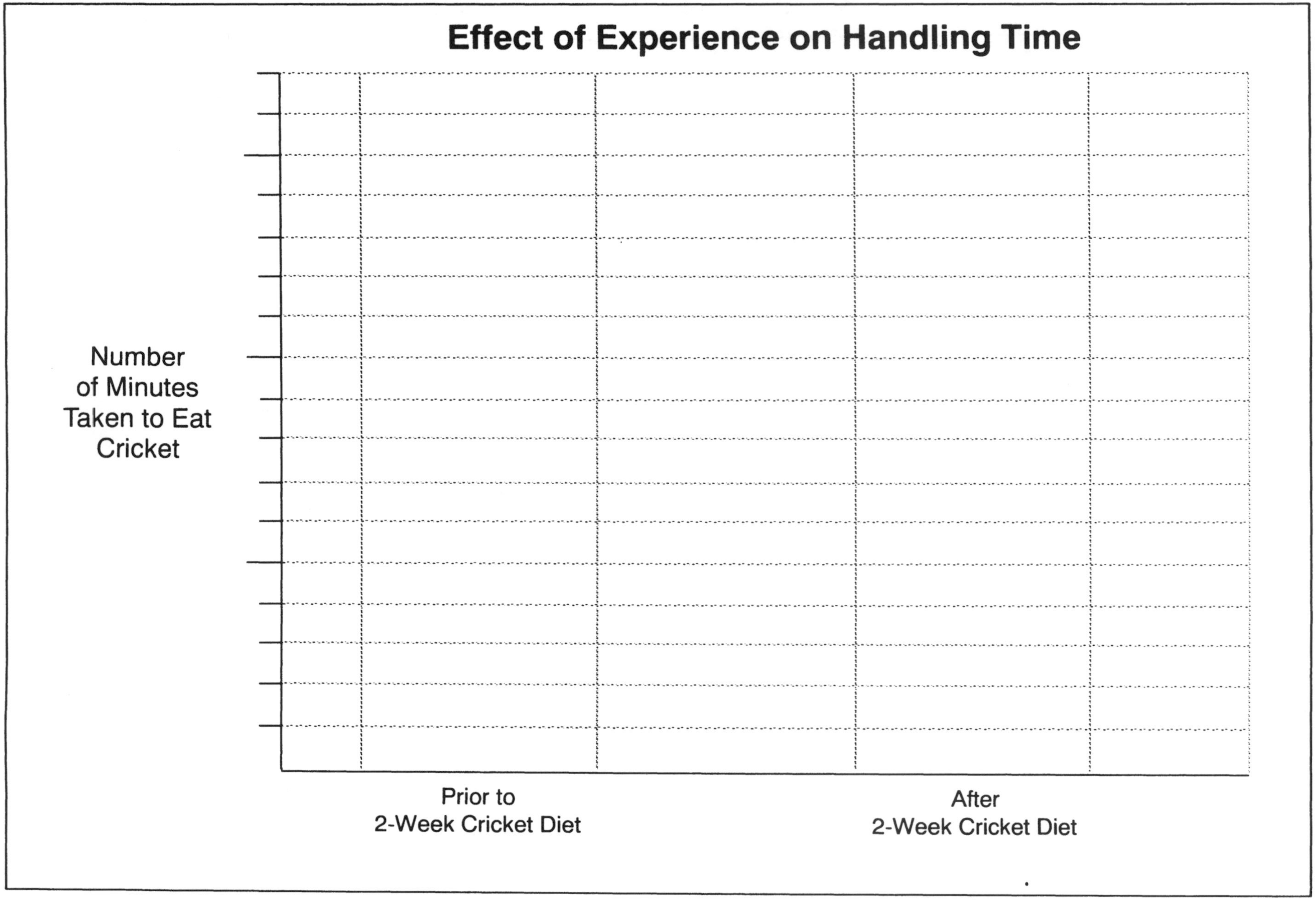

Effect of Experience on Handling Time

Number
of Minutes
Taken to Eat
Cricket

Prior to
2-Week Cricket Diet

After
2-Week Cricket Diet

Figure 12.4 – Blank graph on which to record your results for Experiment 6. (See Figure 3.4 for an example of a completed histogram.)

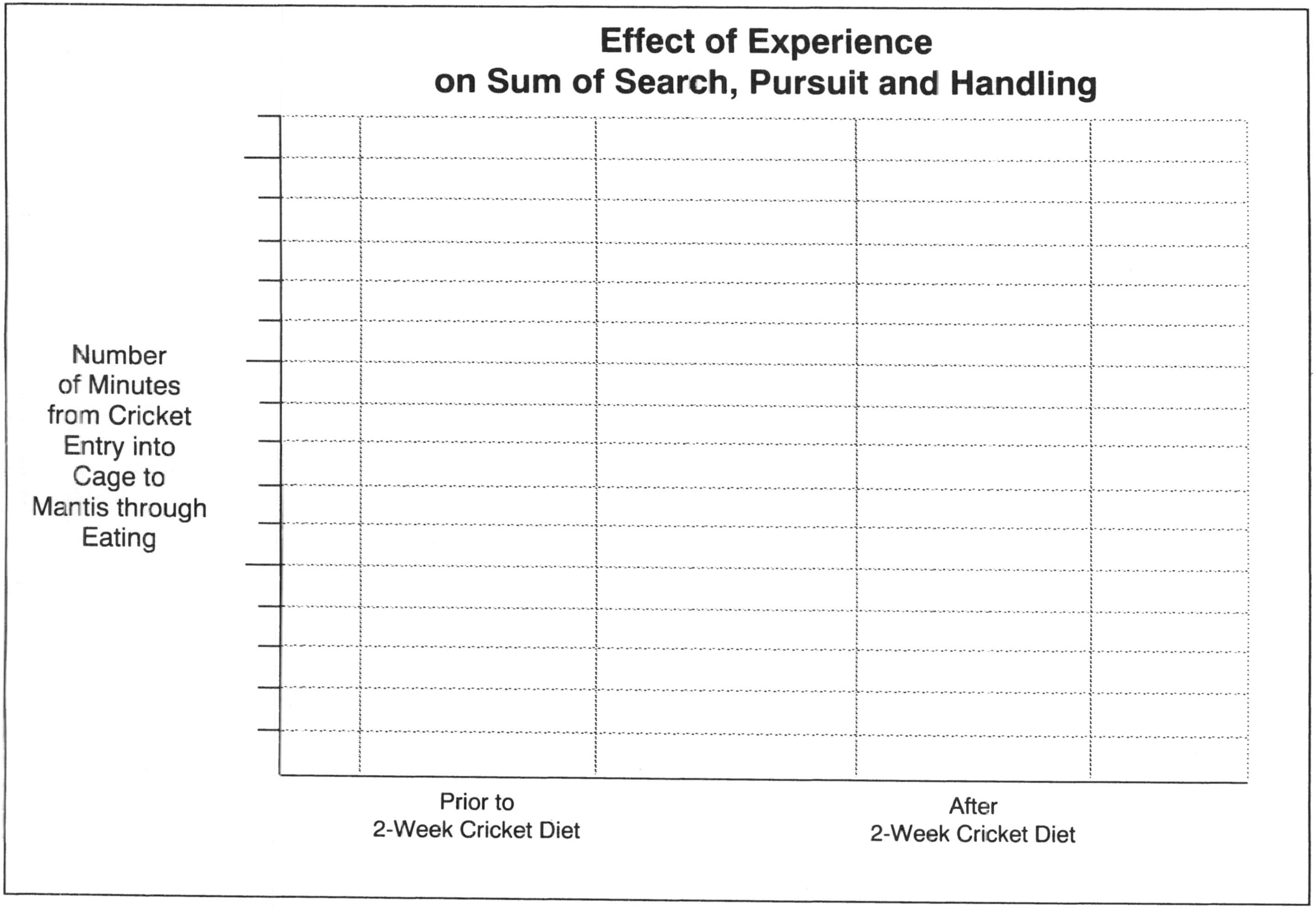

Effect of Experience
on Sum of Search, Pursuit and Handling

Number
of Minutes
from Cricket
Entry into
Cage to
Mantis through
Eating

Prior to
2-Week Cricket Diet

After
2-Week Cricket Diet

Figure 12.4 — Blank graph on which to record your results for Experiment 6. (See Figure 3.4 for an example of a completed histogram.)

Prey Offered	Prey Ignored	Prey Struck at and Dropped	Prey Eaten
Slugs			
Caterpillars			
Pill bugs			
Mealworms			

Figure 12.5 — Blank table on which to record your results for Experiment 7.

Question: If I feed my mantis a cricket every day for a week or two, will the mantis spot the cricket faster at the end of the week than it did at the beginning?

Hypothesis: We think the mantis will spot a cricket faster after a two-week diet of crickets.

Methods: At the beginning of a two-week period, and again at the end of a two-week period, record how long it takes your mantis to notice a cricket. Measure the time from when the cricket is first put in the cage to when the mantis notices the cricket. (Because the mantis can turn its head, it's obvious when the mantis is watching something.)

Use crickets that are more or less the same size for the tests and be consistent in how far from the mantis the cricket is introduced into the terrarium. Feed the mantis nothing but crickets in between the two tests.

Alternatively, you could measure the other components of prey-capture: the time from when the mantis notices the cricket to when it captures the cricket (pursuit), the time from capture until the time eating is finished (handling) or the sum of search, pursuit and handling. The capture itself is almost instantaneous for a mantis. Do the other components of foraging improve with experience?

Result: Your result is a statement of your mantis's response. You can record your results on the histograms in Figure 12.4. Figure 3.4 provides an example of a completed histogram.

Conclusion: The prediction has not yet been confirmed.

It's easy to experiment with what type of prey mantises will accept. I've been surprised at some of the things they've refused to strike at, such as slugs and caterpillars. They'll grab roly-polies and bite them but then drop them. It would be interesting to see if they'll eat sow bugs, which look like roly-polies but can't roll up. I've seen a mantis outdoors eating a large wasp, which surprised me. Is the mantis's exoskelton impervious to stings? The largest animals I've seen mantises eat are a 4-inch (10.2 cm) salamander and a 1 1/2-inch (3.8 cm) tough grasshopper.

Here's a sample question.

Question: Will a mantis eat a mealworm (a beetle larva, see Chapter 16)?

Hypothesis: We think our mantis will eat a mealworm.

Methods: Put a mealworm in the terrarium with the mantis.

Result: Your result is a statement of your mantis's response. You can record your results on the table in Figure 12.5.

Conclusion: The prediction is confirmed. A mantis will eat a mealworm.

CHAPTER 13

Baby Mantises

Introduction

Praying mantises are large predatory insects with a distinctive appearance. Most insects use all six legs for walking, but mantises use the first two for grabbing and holding prey. When at rest, these legs are held folded in front, resembling hands held in prayer. The Chinese mantis, one of the largest and most common species and the one I've used most for the activities and experiments in this chapter, is 4 to 5 inches (10.2–12.7 cm) long at adulthood in late summer (see Figure 13.1).

Chapter 12 deals with adult mantises. I've put baby mantises in a separate chapter because I always cover them separately with classes. This is because adults are available only in the late summer and fall, and babies are generally available only in the spring. I usually have only a couple of adult mantises at a time because they need large containers. But it's not hard to keep thirty babies at one time. Each child can keep one in a small container at his or her desk. The activities and experiments involving baby mantises focus on their growth and molting, and their effect on one another. Most of the experiments involving adults are related to their predatory behavior. The babies are predators too, of course, so many or all of the experiments described for adults can also be done with babies. But most of what I describe for babies can't be done with adults.

Figure 3 in the Postscript provides a range of questions and answers comparing behavior of the predators discussed in Chapters 8 to 13. Figure 4 provides a list of the questions represented in Figure 3, which can be photocopied and handed out for the children to answer.

Materials

1. Baby mantises. To have enough for a whole class, you'll probably need an egg case, which you can order from a biological supply company (see Appendix). You can possibly find one outside. You may be able to catch a lot of baby mantises with a sweep net outside, but probably not thirty. (See the Field Hunt section in this chapter for more about finding eggs and catching babies.)

2. One *Drosophila* culture vial for each baby mantis. The vials are clear plastic cylinders 4 by 1 1/4 inches (10.2 x 3.2 cm), which can be ordered from a biological supply company. (*Drosophila* are fruitflies and are used commonly in biology labs, so even a science hobby shop may have vials and plugs.) Small clear jars such as baby-food jars will do, although vials are easier. The tiny colored candy for sprinkling on cakes come in clear plastic vials that are very similar to

Figure 13.1 — Adult Chinese mantis with arms outspread as though to be picked up.

Drosophila vials. You could ask each parent to donate one.

3. Foam rubber *Drosophila* vial plugs, which can be ordered from a biological supply company.

4. One cotton swab for every vial to provide water.

5. Fruitflies or aphids or other small insects to feed the mantises. Fruitflies can be ordered, cultured or trapped (see Chapter 14 for information on flies, Chapter 15 for aphids). Wingless fruitflies from a biological supply company are the easiest prey for very small mantises. Mantises over two to three weeks old can easily eat wild fruitflies you can trap.

Background Information

Mantises are fascinating creatures. They seem very intelligent and display an array of behaviors that seem very un-insectlike. They groom themselves like cats. They turn their heads and watch us like people. They use their "arms" to hold their food like monkeys. They stalk and capture prey like the most ferocious predators. The larger ones are easier to observe, but the babies do all these things too. Adults move slowly and deliberately and are easy to hold; babies run fast and jump, so they are harder to handle without losing them. They are easier to handle as they grow.

The easiest way to get baby mantises is to get them before they hatch in an egg case. Adult mantises lay their egg cases in the fall, before they die. The eggs normally hatch in late spring, although egg development can be accelerated by keeping them indoors. Each egg case will yield fifty to one hundred babies or nymphs. Mantises are one of those insects that undergo incomplete metamorphosis,

which means that they have no larval or pupal stage in development. Rather, the hatchlings are tiny replicas of the adults, properly called nymphs (see Figure 13.2). The only adult features they lack are wings and sexual maturity. (There is no way to distinguish their gender before adulthood.)

Watching an egg case hatch is a thrilling experience. The babies come squeezing out head first through cracks in the egg case. Less than 3/8 inch (1 cm) in length, they look like white worms or skinny fish with two black eyes. The head-first entry and the wet and squeezed appearance of the new arrival remind me somewhat of a human birth. But they keep coming and coming! Dozens ooze out and dangle upside down en masse as their newly exposed exoskeletons harden and their skinny little white legs unfold. Within minutes, they're off and running, one by one, until the terrarium is filled with miniature mantises.

The baby mantises won't eat for a day or two after hatching; then they will eat fruitflies, aphids or other small insects. They strike at and grab their prey with their spiny forearms lightning-fast, just as the adults do. The prey is held tightly with one or both forearms and munched slowly until nothing remains.

Molting is probably the most remarkable and conspicuous feature of captive hatchlings. An insect's skin, more properly called the exoskeleton, is stiff and provides support for its body. The exoskeleton doesn't grow, so the animal must shed the exoskeleton as its body grows. A new, soft one forms underneath before the old one is shed, or molted. After the new exoskeleton is exposed, it expands a little and then hardens. Mantises molt about six to nine times before reaching adulthood. In my experience, their first molt (after the molt that occurs during hatching) comes at the age of about twelve days if they are fed fruitflies more or less continuously. The growth rates of cold-blooded animals vary a great deal depending on quantities of food and temperature. The time to the first molt can vary considerably too, since it depends on the growth rate. (Cold-blooded is actually a misnomer because they may not be cold at all. The proper term is poikilothermic, which means that they cannot regulate their body temperature internally as we homeotherms do, but must regulate it behaviorally by sitting in the sun or shade, etc.)

How to Get and Keep
a Baby Mantis

I order egg cases from a biological supply company, or use an egg case from a female captive of the year before. The egg cases are usually attached to a twig or the side of the terrarium and should be kept suspended so that the hatchlings can hang upside down from it as their new exoskeletons harden. You may be able to find one outside (see the Field Hunt section in this chapter).

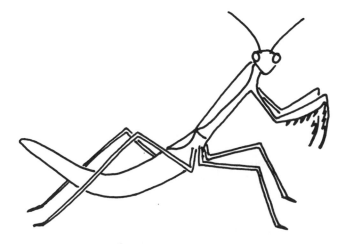

Figure 13.2 — Baby mantis or nymph. The nymph, which lacks mature functional wings, is 1/4 to 3/8 inch (.6 cm–1 cm) at hatching, up to 3 inches (7.6 cm) or more before the final molt to adulthood.

The hatchlings will begin to disperse as soon as their exoskeletons harden, so the egg case must be kept enclosed in a terrarium or other enclosure with a cover that allows at least a little air to circulate.

Most mantis egg cases hatch over a period of one to two hours. Others, like the egg case of the Carolina mantis, produce one or two hatchlings every couple of days for a couple of weeks or longer. There are several species of mantises in the United States, and the number of hatchlings can vary from the usual fifty to one hundred. If you want your students to keep individual mantises alone in vials at their desks, you can remove the hatchlings from the terrarium as soon as they are moving around. A small mantis will step into a vial if you goose it from behind with a cotton swab or a vial plug

They can be kept together safely for a while but will eventually begin to eat each other. How soon depends on how well they are fed and how crowded they are. I kept ten or so in a container the size of a hat box (an insect sleeve cage, see Chapter 2) for two months before I saw any cannibalism. Other times I've seen cannibalism within three to four days of hatching.

Feeding

The easiest way to feed baby mantises is by raising your own fruitflies. It takes about six vials of breeding fruitflies to feed thirty vials of baby mantises for two weeks. Maybe more. (See Chapter 14 for instructions.)

To feed baby mantises in a terrarium, just dump fruitflies into the terrarium every day. One fly per mantis per day is enough. If the fruitflies are winged, you'll need to chill the fly vial in the freezer first for sixty to ninety seconds to paralyze the flies temporarily, so they won't fly away during transfer. If they are vestigial winged fruitflies, no chilling is necessary. (This flightless and almost wingless variety has to be ordered.)

Most of the baby mantises will hang upside-down from the lid of the terrarium, which can be a problem at feeding time. If your terrarium is crowded (fifty to one hundred babies), some of them will escape every time you lift the lid. Thinning the population can help. Escapes can be avoided altogether by keeping the mantises in an insect sleeve cage instead of a terrarium. These can be ordered from a biological supply company (see Appendix) or made with a household bucket and piece of cloth (see Chapter 2 for an illustration and instructions).

If your mantises are in separate vials, you can feed them by tapping two or three flies into each vial. You'll have to chill the flies first if they're winged, as described above. If they're vestigials or flightless flies, no chilling is necessary, but you need to smack the bottom of the fly vial before opening it to knock all the flies to the bottom. Then you can quickly tap out a couple of flies at a time.

You can trap fruitflies easily when it's warm, but probably not enough to feed thirty baby mantises unless you have several traps. All you need to trap flies is a jar and some rotten fruit (see Chapter 14). Bigger fruitflies that you may catch in traps need to be chilled for 150 to 180 seconds.

Baby mantises like aphids, so if you can find a weed outside with aphids you may have an endless supply of food (see Chapter 15). Aphids don't move much though, so it sometimes takes the mantises a while to notice them.

After the mantises have molted once or twice, they're big enough to handle baby crickets. In the spring, I find baby crickets easily under boards and under garbage cans, etc. A piece of cardboard will scrape them into a jar. Most get away, but if I come back in an hour they're back in position.

Watering

To provide moisture to mantises in a terrarium, spray the inner walls of the terrarium once a day with small water droplets from a plant sprayer. Hatchlings will get stuck and drown in big drops. To water those in vials, keep the wet end of a cotton swab in the vial, the central shaft of it held in place between the stopper and the vial, with the dry end sticking out of the vial (see Figure 13.3). It's easy to remove the cotton swab every day to rewet it, without removing the stopper. The students can do this easily (see Figure 13.4). When you have flies in there you won't want to remove the stopper. Be sure the mantis is not standing on the swab before you remove it.

Figure 13.3 — Drawing of a Drosophila *culture vial with a cotton swab in place.*

Figure 13.4 — Tyewanda and Austin dip their cotton swabs in water before replacing them into their vials.

If you're using baby-food jars instead of vials, use cloth lids secured with rubber bands. You can water the mantises by moistening the cloths.

Field Hunt

At the right spot and the right time, baby mantises are easy to catch with a net. I live in a suburban area, but behind my house is a ditch and an area of overgrown grasses and wild shrubs. If I run a sweep net quickly through the top of the waist-high grass in late spring, I get a lot of baby mantises in the net even though I can't spot them in the grass. [A sweep net is a long-handled net for catching insects (see Figure 13.5).] The mesh part of the net is almost a meter long and has an opening of about 15 inches (38.1 cm). The length enables you to pinch it shut and keep insects trapped while you get your jar ready to receive them.

Egg masses are found in the same sorts of places. They're stuck to the top or middle of tall grasses and stems, usually at knee or waist height. Egg masses start out as foam, deposited around a stem. The eggs are imbedded in the foam, which hardens to protect them. The result is a light brown, walnut-sized, irregularly shaped mass with a rough irregular surface (see Figure 13.6). If you find a perfectly smooth and round thing about the same size, it's an insect gall and not a mantis egg case.

Carolina mantis egg cases are smaller and conform somewhat to the shape of the stem. They are very hard to spot in nature.

Baby Mantises at School
Getting Ready

Start your six vials of fruitflies two weeks before you plan to put the mantises in individual vials, because it takes about that long to go from egg to adult fly (see Chapter 14 for instructions). If you have a bunch of mantis hatchlings

and no flies, you can order the flies from a biological supply company and probably get them in just a few days. Most of the mantises will survive a few days without food.

If you plan to let each student have his or her own mantis, you need a vial with a stopper or some alternative enclosure and a cotton swab for each one. The mantises should be in the vials when you give them to the children, unless you're willing to have a lot of mantises escape. Caution the children about twirling their cotton swabs. I had a student once who twirled his swab absentmindedly while his mantis was standing on it. The mantis got wrapped around the swab and flattened and poor Christopher was horrified.

You can feed the mantises yourself, but children age eight and up can learn to do it easily enough. I find it works better to have the students transfer a couple of flies to an empty vial first, then from there into the mantis's vial (see Figure 13.7). That way they don't have to worry about containing the mantis and a vial full of flies at the same time. Anytime you or they get ready to open a vial, whack the bottom of it hard first to knock the mantis or flies away from the top. Otherwise mantises and flies will run out (see Figure 13.8).

Figure 13.5 — Sarah and Alan with sweep net.

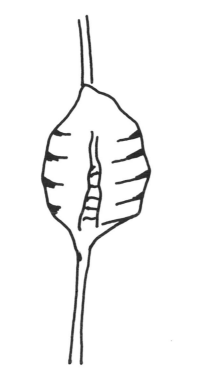

Figure 13.6 — A mantis egg case, about 1 inch (2.5 cm) tall.

Observations and Activities

If every child has his or her own mantis, just watching them eat and molt is interesting enough that you can stop there if you want to. A first-grade class and a third-grade class I gave mantises to last year kept them for two weeks, which worked out well. The vials stayed in the grooves in the desks intended for pencils. After two weeks the children showed no signs of losing interest, but the feeding routine can get tiresome if the teacher is doing it all. You may also run out of flies after two weeks, unless you started six more vials two weeks after you started the first six. I handed the mantises out when they were about a week to ten days old. During the two weeks that the children had them, all but one of the mantises molted, although fewer than half of the children actually saw the mantis in the process of molting.

The most exciting aspect of keeping baby mantises captive is watching them molt. Explain to the children that we and all vertebrates (fish, mammals, birds, amphibians and reptiles) have skeletons on the inside. Some of the children may be able to tell you why we have skeletons — to support our bodies. Explain that an insect has a skeleton outside its body. Its skeleton is a stiff skin that supports its body. "Exo" means "outside." They may guess a couple of other animal groups that have exoskeletons. Several children in the first-grade class I worked with suggested snakes as an example, and that's good thinking, but snakes shed their skins not exoskeletons. Snakes have an internal skeleton like we do. A snake's skin provides no support.

The first time a child (or anyone) sees an insect in the process of molting, he or she is likely to be very impressed. My most vivid memory of sharing baby mantises with children is of the morning I discovered a first-grader named Emily watching her mantis molt. Hers was the first in the class to molt. She was grinning from ear to ear and ran to greet me as I entered the room. I asked her to tell me exactly what she saw. She said the head came out first and it was all white. At first she thought it was dying, but then she realized what was happening.

Watching the mantises eat is fun too. If you keep the mantises in the class for two weeks, almost all of the children will see the mantis in the process of eating a fruitfly (which takes a minute or two), but very few will see it strike or grab the fly (which takes a fraction of a second). The mantises often eat first thing in the morning because the children's arrival disturbs the flies. The flies' movement causes the mantises to notice them. Many children will see the mantis eat every day yet will continue to find it interesting every time. When children are interested in something, their powers of observation are amazing. There was a little boy in this first-grade class named Sam who attracted my attention because he seemed such an underdog. He was a low achiever, "learning disabled" and unconventional in both speech and behavior. He was mocked and bullied sometimes by the other children. One day as I put new flies in the vials Sam told me that he'd noticed his mantis had bumps on its arms. He was referring to the spines on the forelegs. I asked him what he thought those bumps might be for. He said, "To help it hold on to its fly so it can't get away." I had not planned to even mention the spines to the children because I thought they were too tiny to see. Sam was one of those who surprised me.

Figure 13.7 — Tyewanda and Austin prepare to tap a couple of fruitflies from their Drosophila *culture vial full of flies into an empty vial.*

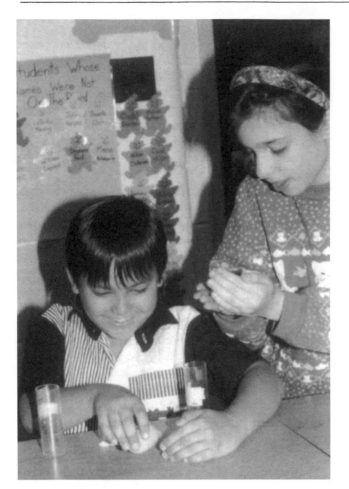

Figure 13.8—Mena and Clint round up a couple of escaped mantises.

He was the only one in the class who noticed the bumps, let alone figured out their function. It was fun to hear him tell the class his discovery.

It might be a good idea to have a photograph of an adult mantis with something to give it scale, as well as an egg case for the children to look at. The children forget that their own captives are babies without something to remind them. Aphids molt too and if you're using aphids as mantis food, the aphids will leave tiny white exoskeletons in the vial. The children will think these little white specks and any dead aphids are their mantises' eggs, unless they have some concrete reminder that their mantises are babies themselves.

You can use the table in Figure 13.9 to record daily tallies of the number of mantises seen eating or molting.

Experiments

Remember that the hypotheses I give are just examples. Most are written in the "if … then" format, but they don't have to be. Your hypotheses will be the predictions made by the class or a particular child. Your result for each experiment will be a statement of how your animals reacted to your experimental setup. Your conclusion is a statement of whether your prediction was confirmed or not. For each experiment, adding replicates increases your confidence in the validity of your conclusion, but they may be omitted if tedious for young children.

Experiment 1

Question: Will a mantis who is fed more molt sooner?

Hypothesis: A mantis that is fed more will molt sooner than one that is fed less.

Methods: Have two or more mantises from the same egg case. It's important that they be the same age. Feed one mantis six flies or more per day every day. Feed the other mantis one fly every other day, which is certainly enough to keep it alive. Record which molts first. Use more than one pair to have confidence in your results.

Result: Your result is a statement of the date each mantis molted.

Conclusion: The prediction is confirmed. Mantises that eat more should molt sooner, because they grow faster. A mantis or any insect molts when it outgrows its exoskeleton.

A variation of this is to feed one mantis more consistently until adulthood. The mantis that is fed more should mature at a larger size and molt more times (about nine times) than one that is fed less (about six molts).

Experiment 2

Question: Will a mantis that is kept warmer molt sooner?

Hypothesis: A mantis that is kept warmer will molt sooner. (The children may have no idea what to hypothesize here. An unrealistic hypothesis is fine.)

Methods: You need two very young mantises the same age and size. Keep one in a cold place. Anything down to 40 degrees F (4.5° C) is alright. Keep the other one in a warmer place, anything up to 90 degrees F (32° C). A temperature difference of only 10 or 20° F (-12–-6.5°C) may be enough to make a difference. Feed them both adequately and equally (at least two flies per day). Which one molts first?

Result: Your result is a statement of which mantis molted first. You can record your results on the table in Figure 13.10.

Conclusion: The prediction is confirmed. The one kept warmer should molt sooner, because warmth speeds the development of mantises and all other "cold-blooded" animals.

If both mantises are kept hungry, the warmer one may not grow faster. A lack of food may limit its growth rate.

Day (starting the day you get them)	Number of Mantises Seen Eating	Number of Mantises Seen Striking	Number of Mantises Molting	Number of Mantises Seen in the Act of Molting
1				
2				
3				
4				
5				
6				
7				
8				
9				
10				
11				
12				
13				
14				
15				
16				
17				
18				
19				
20				
21				
22				
23				

Figure 13.9 — Blank table on which to record daily tallies of the children's observations.

The Effect of Cold on the Growth Rate of Mantises

Date Molted
(average if a group)

Mantis 1 or Group 1
(kept cold)

_____

Mantis 2 or Group 2
(kept warm)

_____

Which one or which group
molted sooner?

_____

The Effect of Interference on the Feeding Rate of Mantises

	Vial Containing One Mantis	Vial Containing Two Mantises
Number of flies consumed over _____ hours	a. _____	b. _____
Number of flies you would expect to be consumed in the vial with two mantises if they each ate as much as the solitary mantis		c. _____ (c is equal to 2 x a)

Were the two mantises housed together affected by one another?
If b < c (*significantly* less than), then the answer is yes.
If b = c or b > c, then the answer is no.

Figure 13.10 — Blank table on which to record your results for Experiments 2 and 3.

Experiment 3

Mantises are normally solitary creatures. They disperse soon after hatching and probably never see each other again. If forced to stay together in one enclosure, the hatchlings will eventually eat each other. The only time they come together as adults is to mate, and the females may eat their mates if they are hungry. So we might expect that two mantises cooped up together would be wary of each other. Are they? How can we tell if they are aware of one another or distracted by one another?

One way is to see if they eat normally when another mantis is around.

Question: Do mantises interfere with one another's prey capture?

Hypothesis: A mantis will eat fewer flies if another mantis is present, but not because the other mantis eats the flies.

Methods: Before starting the experiment, you need to determine how long it takes a single small mantis (of the size you have) in a vial to eat ten fruitflies. Let's say you determine that it takes about twenty-four hours. For the experiment, you'll need at least two vials. Into one vial put two small mantises and twenty fruitflies. Close the vial with a sponge (foam rubber) stopper. Into the other vial put one small mantis and ten flies and close the vial with a foam rubber stopper. Push the stopper down into the second vial so that the single mantis has only half the space available in the first vial. You want to be sure that the amount of space available per mantis is constant. Then you'll know that the amount of space available is not responsible for the results. Leave the mantises in the vials for twenty-four hours, or whatever time you determined. Then count how many fruitflies are left in each vial.

To be confident that your results are not due to chance alone, you may want to set up several replicates of each situation.

Result: Your result is a statement of the number of flies left in each vial after twenty-four hours. You can record you results on the table in Figure 13.10.

Conclusion: The prediction is confirmed. When I've done this experiment I've found that the mantis alone consumed more flies than either of the two placed together. For example, after the predetermined number of hours the single mantis had consumed eight flies, while the two mantises together had consumed only a total of three flies between them. If they were eating at the same rate as the single mantis, they should have eaten sixteen flies together. The proximity of another mantis does seem to interfere with normal behavior. This is to be expected in a solitary and cannibalistic creature like a praying mantis.

INSECT REPRODUCTION

CHAPTER 14

The Two-Week Life Cycle of Fruitflies

Introduction

Perhaps the most interesting feature of fruitflies is that you can see the entire life cycle, from adult parent to adult offspring, in two weeks. I don't know of any other insect that reproduces that quickly in captivity. What's more, they'll go through the whole cycle twice (to adult grandchildren) in a vial that fits in the palm of your hand, with no maintenance or notice required whatsoever. There's something compelling about this little self-contained world. Fruitflies are handy prey for many of the predators in this book.

The experiments herein address various factors affecting development, food requirements and more.

Figure 6 in the Postscript provides a range of questions and answers comparing the life cycles of the organisms discussed in Chapters 14 to 16. A list of the questions represented in Figure 6 is provided in Figure 7, which can be photocopied and handed out for the children to answer.

Materials

1. One-quart or 1-liter jar for making a fly trap. (Three jars for Experiment 1.)
2. Rotting fruit for the fly trap.
3. Fruitfly vials and stoppers from a biological supply company (see Appendix) or other small containers like baby-food jars. One per student or per group, plus at least five for your stock populations.
4. Cloth lids for baby-food jars and rubber bands to secure the lids.
5. Dried banana flakes from a biological supply company (see Appendix) or ripe bananas.
6. One packet of active dry yeast, the type used for making bread.
7. Freezer for Experiment 1.
8. Alternative foods for Experiment 3.
9. Refrigerator for Experiments 4 and 5.
10. Dark room for Experiment 7.
11. Terrarium and lid and lamp for Experiment 8.
12. Dark cabinet for Experiment 9.

Background Information

Most of us think of a housefly when we hear the word "fly." But did you know that mosquitoes are flies too? Flies are actually a huge and diverse group. Those I work with most are fruitflies, because they're easy to trap and easy to maintain in captivity. They reproduce happily in small containers, and their food doesn't smell bad. Many of the various flies that resemble houseflies lay their eggs on rotting meat so you'd have to provide that to raise them. They sometimes carry dangerous bacteria on their feet from landing on carrion and feces. My office mate in graduate school was studying the community of flies that breed on carrion. He had to have an area that was recessed into the wall with an exhaust fan to keep them indoors, and still the stench pervaded our lab. (He also had to have a 10-foot (3 m) pole with a scoop on the end to "sample" the flies breeding on road kills.) So, I stick to fruitflies. They are attracted only to fruit. Although rotten fruit has bacteria in it, it's not dangerous bacteria.

The only disadvantage to fruitflies is that they are smaller and harder to see. For me, however, the advantages outweigh this one drawback.

Flies are insects of course so they have three body parts (head, thorax and abdomen) and six legs, as all insects do. Being insects, flies have the same type of life cycle as most insects. They go through what's called complete metamorphosis. From the egg hatches a wormlike larva. A fly larva is often called a maggot. The larva eats and grows, shedding its skin, or exoskeleton, several times. After it reaches a certain size, it leaves its larval food source and pupates. Some insects, such as moths, spin a cocoon around themselves to pupate, but the fly's larval skin hardens into a tough casing instead. Inside that casing the body of the larva transforms into that of an adult fly. This stage of transformation is called the pupa. The pupa does not move around or eat. It looks like a tiny fat cigar. When the adult fly inside is ready, it emerges from the pupal casing.

The wings are crumpled when the fly first emerges, but as blood is pumped into their blood vessels, the wings straighten out and harden. Then it can fly. The period following emergence is a very vulnerable period for winged insects, because they can't yet fly to escape predators. The life of an adult fly is usually brief, only a couple of weeks. Within a day or two of emerging, it seeks another adult fly of the opposite sex. The male courts the female to coax her into accepting him. Courtship behaviors vary according to species, but usually involve wing movements, foot movements (tapping the ground or the female) and/or walking in circles or half-circles around the female. The species I have the most of (*Drosophila melanogaster)* are tiny [1/16 inch (1.6 mm)], but I can easily see the male following the female around vibrating his wings. If the female is not ready to mate, she may fly away from the male's pursuits or ignore him.

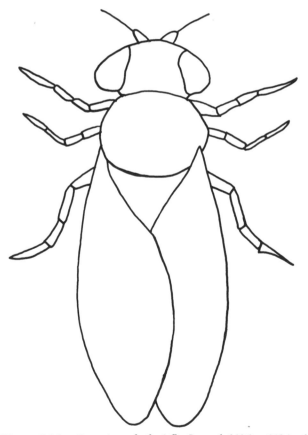

Figure 14.1 — Drawing of a fruitfly. Length 1/16 to 1/8 inch (1.6–3.2 mm), depending on species. They are yellowish or brownish in color.

If she is ready, she will allow the male to stand on her back as they mate. When she is full of eggs, her abdomen will look swollen and white and easy to see, even though they are so tiny. She'll lay her eggs when she has rotting fruit to lay them on. (I'll describe in the next section how to provide a suitable place for egg-laying.)

The fruitflies you get when you order from a biological supply company are *Drosophila melanogaster*. In addition to their tiny size, you can identify them by their bright red eyes. When biologists or those who study insects refer to fruitflies, they generally mean *Drosophila melanogaster*. If you leave a bowl of fruit sitting out on your kitchen counter and notice tiny flies on it that scatter when you pick up a piece of fruit, they are most likely *Drosophila melanogaster*. They are referred to also as the red-eyed fruitfly or the common fruitfly. There are many other species in the family of fruitflies, which is the *Drosophilidae*. Once you've seen a red-eyed fruitfly, you'll recognize the others by their similar, almost identical, body shape (see Figure 14.1), even though other species lack the red eyes and may be twice as large. When looking them up in a field guide, look up *Drosophila*, because field guides sometimes use unfamiliar common names, such as pomace flies.

Fruitflies are commonly used in biology labs because their generation time is so short (fruit doesn't last long in nature), and they have a lot of offspring. This makes them convenient for studies of genetic mutations — how subsequent generations are affected by genetic changes and so on. They also have an unusually large chromosome that's more easily studied with microscopes than the chromosomes of other organisms.

How to Get and Keep Flies

You can order fruitflies (*Drosophila melanogaster*) from a biological supply company (see Appendix), or you can catch your own. Catching flies is something I do on a daily basis in spring and summer, not because I love flies but because I feed them to so many other captives. Just about all the predatory insects in this book will eat fruitflies, with the exception of ladybug beetles.

The traps seem too easy to work as well as they do. I put a piece of rotting fruit in the bottom of a 1-quart or 1-liter plastic peanut butter jar. I lay the jar on its side with the lid off and the opening slightly lower than the bottom so rain won't collect in the jar. It works best when placed near a garbage can or compost pile, or near some other already existing rotting vegetation. When the weather is hot, the jar needs to be in the shade or the fruit dries out too quickly. Aging grapefruit rinds work best for me, although banana peels, apple cores or cantaloupe rinds work too. Leave the jar for twelve to twenty-four hours. When you return, creep up on it slowly. Very slowly put the lid on the jar without touching the jar in any way, otherwise the flies will see you or will feel the jar move and exit before you can trap them. You may find from five to one hundred fruitflies of various sizes in the jar. If you don't find any, leave something large like a watermelon rind or several grapefruit rinds out in the open for several days, then remove them and leave the trap in their place.

When setting up the trap, put an inverted funnel of cardboard in the mouth of the jar to funnel the flies in toward the bait and make exit difficult. This isn't necessary if you move slowly when closing the jar to trap the visitors, but sometimes children like making the funnels. When the rotting fruit is dried out, it needs to be replaced.

Now you have a jar full of flies. What do you do with them?

If you just want to examine them, you can anesthetize them temporarily by putting the jar in the freezer for ninety seconds or so. If that's not long enough, check every twenty to thirty seconds after that until they stop moving. You can anesthetize them by putting some dry ice in the jar until they stop moving. Flies can be easily moved around with a fine paintbrush.

You may want to feed your flies and provide what they need to reproduce so you can observe their life cycle. That's really the interesting part. I use fruitfly culture vials from a biological supply company (see Appendix). They're plastic cylinders, about 1 1/4 inches (3.2 cm) in diameter and 4 inches (10.2 cm) tall, that come with a sponge plug. The sponge allows air to circulate while keeping most of the moisture and all of the flies inside. I use the vials for a lot of other bugs as well—praying mantis hatchlings, aphids, ladybugs and small spiders. They're handy for keeping in a shirt pocket on a walk in case you spot an interesting bug. I get a lot of requests from children for the vials. Kids find them fascinating because they look exotic and scientific and are fun to handle.

You can also use baby-food jars or any small jar with a cloth cover secured with a rubber band. Among other things fruitflies eat yeast that grows on bananas. To feed them in the culture vials, put in a mixture of bananas and yeast before you put in the flies. I buy banana flakes from a biological supply company for this purpose. One tablespoon (15 ml) of flakes and 1 tablespoon (15 ml) of water make about 1 inch (2.5 cm) of goop in the bottom of the vial (no stirring necessary). Sprinkle about ten grains of yeast over the banana mixture. Don't put too much yeast or the mixture will rot and start to smell bad. You can make your own culture medium by mashing about 1 tablespoon (15 ml) of banana with about 1/8 teaspoon (.63 ml) of water and putting it into the bottom of a vial. Add yeast as described. One disadvantage of using mashed banana is that it will get moldy eventually. The banana flakes have an antimolding agent mixed in. If you use baby-food jars instead of vials, cloth won't keep moisture in as well as the sponge so you'll need to watch the food and maybe spray it with water if it starts to dehydrate.

Add at least eight to ten adult flies that are the same size and look like the same species. The flies will lay eggs on the banana mixture. If you want to see the eggs, put in some black cloth or paper or black banana peel, otherwise they'll blend in with the pale banana. After you've set up the culture and added the adult flies, it requires no maintenance at all. (A "culture" is a container in which organisms are or will be reproducing.) Fruitfly eggs hatch into larvae that grow to a length of about 1/8 inch (3.2 mm). The white larvae will be visible wiggling around just under the surface of the banana mixture about one week after starting the culture. (In nature they burrow into rotten fruit.) About eight or nine days after starting the culture, they'll begin leaving the banana mixture to pupate on the sides of the vials. The pupae look like reddish brown cigars, 1/16 to 1/8 inch (1.6–3.2 mm) long. They do not move or eat. New adult flies will begin to emerge from the pupal cases about two weeks after you started the culture and will continue to emerge for about another week. The new flies will begin to lay eggs themselves about two days after emerging. These eggs will also take about two weeks to hatch, go through metamorphosis and reach adulthood. About four and a half weeks after you started the vial you'll begin to get a third generation of adult flies, the grandchildren of those you started with.

When the level of banana mixture gets low in the container, simply start a new vial, adding at least ten adults. This way you can keep your fly population going indefinitely. Each female probably lays a hundred eggs so there are a lot of adults coming out. If you order fruitflies from a biological supply company, you can get vestigial flies that have no wings. The no-wing condition is a genetic mutation that is passed on to their offspring. They're called vestigials because their wings are vestigial, which means that they are only a vestige of the normal wing. Vestigial flies are much easier to use to feed ant lions and baby praying mantises than are winged flies because they can't escape as easily. You can use winged flies to feed predators, but you may need to anesthetize them by chilling them in the freezer (for one to two minutes, depending on size) so they can't escape as easily.

Field Hunt

You can catch flies by sweeping through tall grass with a net, but they are unlikely to be fruitflies. If you want to hunt for fruitflies instead of setting a trap, hunt around garbage or rotting vegetation. The best way to be sure you're getting fruitflies is to trap them, as described above.

Flies at School
Getting Ready

Order vials and banana flakes about a week before you need them. If you have thirty students and want every child to have his or her own vial of flies, you need to start about five vials three weeks in advance to have enough to give each child ten flies. You can instead rely on trapping to start the class' vials, but you'll need to have a lot of traps or else stagger the students to start their cultures on successive days. If you plan to let the students add the flies to their own vials, you'll need twice as many flies because a lot of them will escape.

Observations and Activities

Start with adult flies for observation. Bring in a culture vial you've started or trap some flies. Since the children are used to thinking of flies as houseflies, you may want to ask them to describe how the fruitflies are similar to and different from houseflies. If they ask, you can tell them the definition of a fly: an insect with one pair of functioning wings and a pair of back wings that are just small knobs called halteres. The function of the halteres is to help maintain balance during flight, but you can't see the halteres on fruitflies with the naked eye.

You can freeze a few flies by putting them in a jar in the freezer for ten minutes or more. Ask the children to draw the flies and label their body parts as well as they can

Figure 14.2 — Tanielle scoops up water to put on her banana flakes while Zack wonders about the yeast grains in the yogurt cup.

(see Figure 14.1). This is a good time to explain the life cycle — egg, larva, pupa and adult.

In setting up the vials, children can measure out the banana flakes and water and yeast themselves (see Figure 14.2). I like to start out by showing a couple of students how to do it, then having them show the next pair, who shows the next pair and so on. Make frequent quality control checks to make sure they don't drift too far afield from the original directions, especially with too much yeast. When all the vials or jars have had culture medium (bananas, water and yeast) added, either you or the children add the flies. Unless I have a great overabundance of flies, I add the flies myself. If you do let the children do it, spread the flies you have over a great many empty vials before turning them over to the children, so if a vial is dropped you won't lose half your flies.

To add flies from a culture vial to a new vial, it's essential that you first tap the bottom of your culture vial on the tabletop firmly to knock the flies to the bottom of the vial. After this you'll have a few seconds to tap eight to ten flies into the new vial. You need this many to be sure that at least a couple of them are fertile females. Replace both stoppers quickly! It's a good idea to write each child's name on his or her own vial using masking tape or file-folder labels.

I give each child a chart for recording daily observations and counts (see Figure 14.3). They can release the parent flies after five or six days because by then the flies have already laid plenty of eggs. With the parent flies gone, the children can take the stoppers out of the vials to look for larvae more carefully. They'll notice about day six or sooner that the banana mixture is more liquid than it was, and they may be able to see the movement of larvae under the surface of the stuff. (The larvae secrete enzymes to soften their food.) The children can see the larvae under the surface by looking through the side of the vial too. Keep a record for how many children spot larvae for the first time each day.

By day eight most children will have larvae climbing up on the sides of the vials to pupate. Even though you've told the children what to expect, many won't understand what's happening. Every morning for a week or so the children will find more of the little reddish brown pupal cases on the sides of the vials, and they'll enjoy counting them (see Figure 14.4). The children can see two respiratory tubes that look like short antennae projecting from one end of each pupa in larger species of fruitflies.

I find that I need to keep going over and over how these white wiggly things and reddish brown cigars relate to the insect life cycle, even if the children can recite the stages of the life cycle perfectly. How do the words larva, pupa and adult relate to what they're seeing? Remind them that the larvae are eating the banana and yeast mixture. Many children tell me their larvae are eating each other (or fighting or mating or something, all of which don't happen with fly larvae).

Name _____

Tiny white worms called larvae will hatch from your flies' eggs. The larvae will eat your banana mixture. You may be able to see them. Soon they will crawl up onto the clear plastic. Then you can see them moving on the plastic. They will turn into pupae on the plastic. Pupae look like tiny brown cigars. Pupae do not move. An adult fly will come out of each little cigar, or pupa. All this will happen in the next two weeks.

Write down how many larvae and pupae you see every day for the next two weeks as best you can. If you can't count them all, just write "many." Larvae are white worms; pupae are brown cigars.

DAYS
after starting
vial

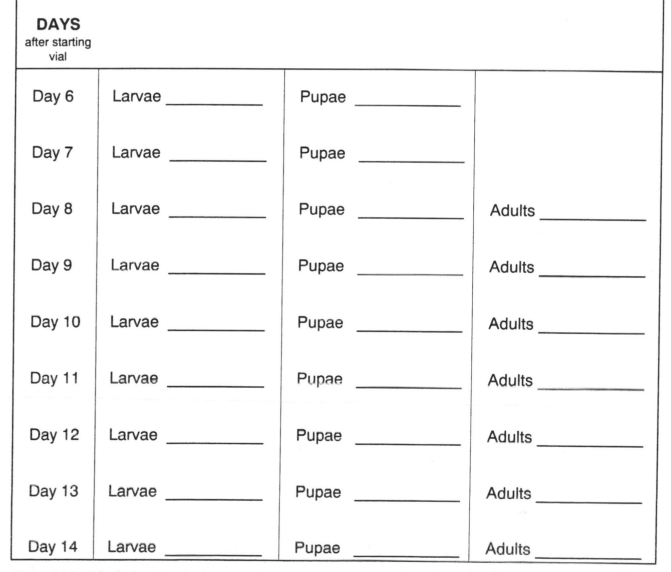

Day 6	Larvae _____	Pupae _____	
Day 7	Larvae _____	Pupae _____	
Day 8	Larvae _____	Pupae _____	Adults _____
Day 9	Larvae _____	Pupae _____	Adults _____
Day 10	Larvae _____	Pupae _____	Adults _____
Day 11	Larvae _____	Pupae _____	Adults _____
Day 12	Larvae _____	Pupae _____	Adults _____
Day 13	Larvae _____	Pupae _____	Adults _____
Day 14	Larvae _____	Pupae _____	Adults _____

Figure 14.3 — Blank chart on which to record your daily counts of larvae, pupae and adults.

Figure 14.4 — Claire records the number of pupae in her vial on her table.

One child in a second-grade class I worked with was the son of a teacher and had had his own vial of fruitflies at home for months. He rolled his eyes to signal his boredom when I told the class we were going to raise fruitflies. But on the day his larvae first became visible, he didn't know what they were — another reminder that seeing is not necessarily understanding when it comes to critters!

The original adults probably laid eggs every day they were in the vial, so if you left the originals in their vials for a week, they'll get new adults emerging every day over a period of about a week.

Experiments

Remember that the hypotheses I give are just examples. Most are written in the "if ... then" format, but they don't have to be. Your hypotheses will be the predictions made by the class or a particular child. Your result for each experiment will be a statement of how your animals reacted to your experimental setup. Your conclusion is a statement of whether your prediction was confirmed or not. For each experiment, adding replicates increases your confidence in the validity of your conclusion, but may be omitted if tedious for young children.

Experiment 1

Question: How does the degree of rottenness of the fruit affect the flies' interest? Will they come to a jar with fresh fruit or only rotting fruit?

Hypothesis: If we offer the flies rotting fruit and fresh fruit, they'll like them about the same.

Methods: Get one grapefruit and three jars. Cut the grapefruit into thirds or quarters. Freeze one piece and leave the other two covered at room temperature. After three days, freeze a second piece that has been at room temperature. After three more days, put the piece that has been at room temperature into a jar and put the two pieces from the freezer into two other jars. Put the three jars outside on their sides, without lids, not more than a foot (.3 m) or so apart. After one day return and put lids on them, slowly, as described earlier. Which one has the most flies? You may get more meaningful results on this one if you do two or three replicates of each setup. You can substitute other fruit, but fruitflies seem to be strongly attracted to grapefruit.

Result: Your result is a description of what turned up in each jar. You can record your results as a histogram (see Figure 3.4 for an example of a completed histogram). A blank graph for your results is provided in the Appendix.

Conclusion: The prediction is not confirmed here. In my experience, the older the fruit is, the more the flies like it, until it begins to dry out or turn liquid. Fruit in jars outdoors often dries out before it rots completely. In nature drying is probably less common.

Experiment 2

Question: Do flies detect their food by sight?

Hypothesis: Flies use sight to detect their food. If we put food out of sight they won't find it.

Methods: You need two vials of flies, with approximately equal numbers. You also need two grapefruit halves three to six days old. You're going to put one vial of flies with a grapefruit in the dark and the other vial of flies and grapefruit in the light. You can accomplish this with two small rooms of approximately equal size, like closets or bathrooms, if you have one that can be made completely dark. If so, release one vial of flies in a well-lit room at a good distance (across the room) from the grapefruit. Release the other vial of flies in a completely dark room at a good distance from the grapefruit. Return at intervals of fifteen minutes or so and check the grapefruit in the light room until it has a number of fruitflies on it. Then count the flies on both grapefruits. Which has more flies? If you don't have two rooms, invert a cardboard box over one grapefruit with only a small crack along the bottom. The box needs a window in the top that can be covered with a book to block out light, but opened when the time comes to count the flies. Cover the other grapefruit with something transparent — a glass dish or a box with a plastic wrap window — and leave a crack along the bottom where flies may enter. Release only one vial of flies between the two boxes. Watch the grapefruit in the transparent box until it has a lot of flies on it and count them. Then slowly open the "window" on the top of the dark box and count the number of flies on that grapefruit. Which has more?

Result: Your result is a statement of your fly counts and other observations. You can record your results as a histogram (see Figure 3.4 for an example of a completed histogram). A blank graph for your results is provided in the Appendix.

Conclusion: The prediction is not confirmed. Flies locate food mainly by a sense of taste or smell, so the dark should have little effect on their ability to find the food.

Another way to go about this is to offer two items, one of which smells and tastes like food, but neither of which looks like food. Wet one rag with grapefruit juice and another with water and release a vial of flies between them. Do flies go to either one? More flies on the grapefruit-soaked rag suggests that smell or taste plays a part in their locating food.

Experiment 3

Question: Are bananas (or other fruit) and yeast both essential for the flies to live and reproduce? Can they live on banana alone, without the yeast added? Can they live on a mixture of yeast and water alone? What about other variations?

Hypothesis: Flies can live on fruit alone, but not yeast alone.

Methods: As a control, set up one vial as usual — one part banana flakes, one part water and a pinch of yeast. To a second vial add banana flakes and water as usual, but don't add yeast. In another vial mix yeast and water until it has a pasty consistency. Try other combinations: meat sprinkled with yeast, a vegetable sprinkled with yeast, a rotting wild fruit found outside like a crabapple or persimmon, both with and without added yeast, and a damp piece of bread or damp cracker sprinkled with yeast. Add eight to ten flies to each vial and wait two weeks. In which vials do the flies reproduce?

Result: Your result is a statement of your observations regarding which combinations allow the flies to reproduce.

Conclusion: The prediction or hypothesis is supported somewhat in that fruit to which you have not added yeast may support fruitflies. The flies eat yeast, but

fruit left outdoors may very well pick up airborne yeast spores that you don't see. Fruit that has not been outdoors and to which you've not added yeast probably will not support a fly population. The yeast must have something to grow on, so the mixture of yeast and water will not support flies. Yeast grows best on fruit, but it may grow well enough to support the flies on other things as well.

Experiment 4

Question: Does temperature affect the development time of the flies? How?

Hypothesis: If we put one vial of flies in a cold place, they will grow more slowly than flies left at room temperature.

Methods: Set up two or three new vials with banana flakes, water and yeast as described earlier. Add eight to ten flies to each (be consistent). Put one vial of flies in the refrigerator or outside if it's cool (but not cold enough to freeze them). Leave another at room temperature. If you have a place that's warmer than room temperature, but not more than around 100 degrees F (38° C), put another vial in there. The three vials should be as similar as possible in other regards. In which vial do larvae appear first? Pupae? New adults?

Result: Your result is a statement of the number of days it takes to reach each stage of development for each vial of flies. Use for comparison the number of days it takes to notice the first larva, the first pupa, the first new adult in each vial. Since larvae in the banana mixture are sometimes hard to see, you may want to use as your record the first larva you see crawling up on the plastic side of each vial to pupate. There's no mistaking that. You can record your counts on the table in Figure 14.5a and the histogram in Figure 14.5b. Figure 3.4 provides an example of a completed histogram.

Conclusion: The prediction in the hypothesis is confirmed. The warmer it is, the faster the flies will develop, although there is an upper limit. They can tolerate cold almost all the way down to freezing. How could you determine the upper limit of their temperature tolerance? You may get developmental abnormalities at higher temperatures before you get any mortality.

The students can make a graph with days across the horizontal axis and the number of pupae visible on the plastic along the vertical axis. The graph would have two lines, one for the cold group and one for the group at room temperature. The difference in the two lines would show the effect of cold. The graph would look similar to the one in Figure 6.5, which also compares the growth rates of two animals. A blank graph is provided in the Appendix.

The Effect of Cold on Fly Development Time

	Cool Flies	Room Temperature Flies	Warm Flies
Number of Days until Larvae Appear			
Number of Days until Pupae Appear			
Number of Days until New Adults Appear			

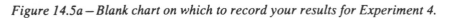

Figure 14.5a — Blank chart on which to record your results for Experiment 4.

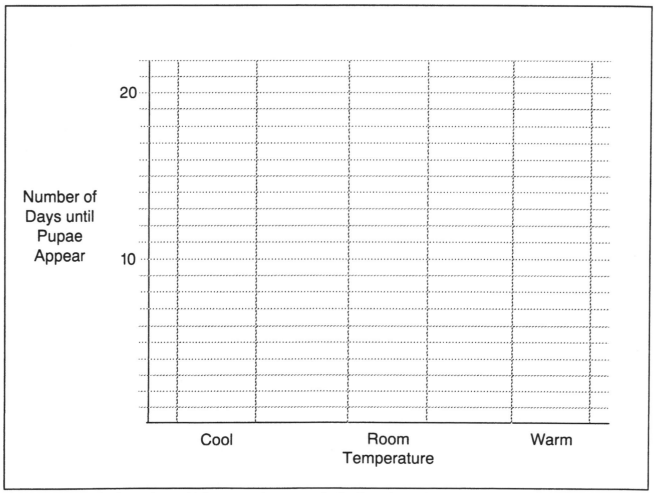

Figure 14.5b — Blank graph on which to record your results for Experiment 4.

Experiment 5

Question: Does cold affect the number of individuals surviving to pupation?

Hypothesis: We think that if we put one vial in the refrigerator, it will not make as many new flies as one left at room temperature.

Methods: Set up two new vials with banana flakes, water and yeast as described earlier and add eight to ten flies to each (an equal number to the two vials). Leave one at room temperature; keep one in the refrigerator. (You can use the same vials as in Experiment 4.) There is no need, for this experiment, to record any observations about the larvae. After you have begun to get pupae on the sides of one vial, count the number of pupae in that vial every day until you have gotten no new pupae for a period of five days. Use that as a measure of the number of adult flies you are going to get in the first generation of offspring in that vial. Do the same thing when pupae appear in your cold vial. Compare the counts for the two vials. Did you get more pupae in the vial that was kept at room temperature? Using several replicates would add meaning to this experiment, since no two vials are going to produce exactly the same number of adults even under identical conditions.

Result: Your result is a statement of your counts of pupae for each vial. You can record your results as a histogram (see Figure 3.4 for an example of a completed histogram). A blank graph for your results is provided in the Appendix.

Conclusion: The prediction is not confirmed. Temperature should not affect the number of pupae or number of adults, unless the temperature was so close to freezing that some were killed.

Experiment 6

Question: Does the size of the fly affect the development time?

Hypothesis: If we start one vial with big fruitflies and one with small fruitflies, the small ones will develop faster.

Methods: With a fly trap, capture two different sizes of fruitflies. Some fruitflies are at least twice as big as others. Start two vials at the same time, one with large flies and one with smaller flies. In which vial do you see larvae first?

Result: Your result is a statement of the day you first saw larvae, pupae and adults in each vial.

Conclusion: The prediction is not confirmed here. Fly species do differ in their development times, but in my experience, this variation does not necessarily correlate with size.

Experiment 7

Question: Does darkness affect the ability of a fly population to reproduce?

Hypothesis: If we put one vial of flies in a dark room, they will reproduce normally.

Methods: Set up two fruitfly vials identically, with banana flakes and yeast. Add eight to ten fruitflies to each (be consistent). Put one in an absolutely dark place — a box on a back shelf in a dark closet, under a dark towel. Leave the other one in a normally lit place. To add confidence in your results, do several replicates of each type of vial. Check both vials or group of vials after two weeks. Is there a difference?

Result: Your result is a statement of your observations.

Conclusion: The prediction is not confirmed, probably due to an inability to court successfully in the dark. Some of the male flies' courtship may be tactile (tapping the female with his front legs), but most of it is perceived visually by the female. If she can't see him, she won't be persuaded by his courtship activities to accept him. They probably will not mate, so there will not be offspring in the dark. What would happen if you put the two vials in the light and dark, respectively, after giving the adults a week to mate first and then removing the adults? Would the larvae and the pupae develop in the same way?

Experiment 8

Question: Are adult fruitflies attracted to light?

Hypothesis: Adult fruitflies are attracted to light.

Methods: Put at least twenty fruitflies into a terrarium at least 1 foot (30.4 cm) long with a lid. Put one end of the terrarium near a lamp that's turned on in a room otherwise uniformly lit or darkened. Leave the flies alone for an hour or more, then note their position. As a control, turn the lamp off, wait an hour or so and note the position of the flies.

Result: Your result is a statement of your observations.

Conclusion: The prediction is confirmed. Adult fruitflies are attracted to light and will be clustered at the end of the terrarium near the lamp when the lamp is on.

Experiment 9

Question: Do fruitflies have a tendency to walk upward, away from gravity?

Hypothesis: We think fruitflies have a tendency to walk upward, away from gravity.

Methods: Get two vials of flies and note the position of the flies inside the vials. In both vials most flies will probably be clustered at the top, on the underside of the foam stopper. Turn one of the vials upside-down and put it in a dark cabinet. As a control put with it the second vial of flies that you do not turn upside-down. Leave the vials in the dark for five minutes. (Put the flies in clean vials first if your banana mixture is very goopy, or the goop may drop in the upside-down vial.) When you open the cabinet, check the flies' position immediately before they have a chance to reorient themselves in response to the light. Did the flies in either vial change position?

Result: Your result is a statement of your observations regarding the positions of the flies after five minutes in the dark cabinet.

Conclusion: The prediction is confirmed. The flies in the vial that was turned upside-down will have changed their position. They will now be standing on the banana mixture, which is now at the top of the vial. The flies in the other vial will still be on the underside of the stopper. The only difference in the vials is that one was inverted, so the only explanation of the flies' move is a tendency to walk away from gravity.

CHAPTER 15

Aphids and Their Predators, Ladybug Beetles

Introduction

Aphids are tiny soft-bodied insects that suck plant juices and are major garden pests. Experiments in this chapter address questions about the aphids' feeding and their destruction of garden plants, their reproduction (the females usually reproduce without males) and the relationship between the aphids and ladybug beetles. Ladybugs are voracious predators of aphids and are sold through gardening catalogs for aphid control.

The teacher of one class that kept aphids had this to say about the class' experience: "I ask the children to name all the vowels and no one knows. But I ask them how many aphids were on their plants today and they know that. Everyone remembers because they held them and touched them and owned them."

Aphids are useful particularly for math exercises. The children can make histograms showing how the number of aphids increases each day for the class as a whole or for each student. Older children can calculate averages.

Figure 6 in the Postscript provides a range of questions and answers comparing the life cycles of the organisms discussed in Chapters 14 to 16. A list of the questions represented in Figure 6 is provided in Figure 7, which can be photocopied and handed out for the children to answer.

Materials

1. Sugar-snap pea plants (snow pea plants) or lettuce plants planted outside to attract aphids and ladybug beetles. Any other plant that you know will attract aphids will do.
2. Aphids.
3. Ladybug beetles.
4. Small paintbrush for moving aphids. Bristles should be about 1/2 inch (1.3 cm) long and 1/8 inch (.3 cm) across.
5. One young sugar-snap (snow pea) plant or lettuce plant for each child.
6. One plant container and soil for each child (peat pots, paper cups or yogurt cups—anything that will hold soil).
7. Fruitfly culture vials and foam stoppers (see Chapter 14 on how to get them) or other small containers with lids.

Background Information
Feeding of Aphids

Aphids live on plants and they feed by piercing stems and leaves with a long, strawlike mouth part and sucking the plants' sap. Leaves that support large numbers of aphids turn yellow and curl. A heavily infested plant may die.

Aphid Reproduction and Dispersal

Aphids' reproduction is unusual in a couple of different ways. What first caught my attention about them is that most aphid populations are all female and reproduce quite satisfactorily without males. This type of sexless reproduction is called parthenogenesis. All the offspring in such a population are female. Another unusual aspect of aphids' reproduction is that they give birth to live young most of the time instead of laying eggs like most insects. Children can actually see the baby aphids being born if they look carefully. The young aphids mature and begin cranking out their own babies at the ripe old age of one week. One female can have one hundred babies, so the population increases rapidly.

When a plant gets crowded, the aphids need some way to disperse to new plants. Most adult aphids have no wings, but frequent contact with other aphids (crowdedness) signals the females' bodies to produce female offspring that will be winged as adults. These winged female adults fly away singly to establish more populations of unwinged females. (The advantage of the dispersers' being all female and parthenogenetic is that it allows them to establish twice as many new colonies as they could if they had to pair up to reproduce.) This cycle of unwinged female populations expanding and finally dispersing via a winged female generation goes on all summer. Only in the fall are some male babies born. When they mature they mate with the females, which then lay fertile eggs instead of bearing live young. The eggs overwinter and hatch in the spring into another parthenogenetic all-female population.

Why Mate at All?

If reproduction without sex allows them to start more new colonies, why mate in the fall or ever? The sexual reproduction (mating) in the fall provides some genetic variability in the offspring. Siblings from sexual reproduction are not all identical, just as most human siblings are not identical. But sisters of a parthenogenetic or female-only reproduction are all clones of their mother, all genetically identical.

When all individuals in a population are genetically identical, the population is more vulnerable to environmental stress. Genetic variability in a population increases the likelihood that some individual will possess the traits necessary to weather any particular crisis.

Population Growth

Aphids are a useful tool in talking about uncontrolled population growth. Human population growth is unchecked in most of the underdeveloped countries, and we are rapidly filling up our planet. This is an issue your students will be confronted with sometime during their lifetimes, because the world population is expected to double in the next forty years.

The same would happen to any insect or animal population that was left unchecked. A frog may lay one hundred or two hundred eggs at once. What if each one of the eggs grew up and became the parent of one hundred more eggs? And each of those eggs grew up and did the same? Soon there'd be a million (100 x 100 x 100 = 1,000,000) frogs where not long before there were two. Birds, turtles, fish and raccoons eat tadpoles, and some die of starvation, so only a small fraction of tadpoles survive.

It used to be that due to disease and injuries only a fraction of human offspring survived to adulthood. Modern medicine has stopped that, and we're filling up the planet, just as frogs would if we took away all their predators.

What about aphids? Why is the world not covered with aphids? Because they have lots of predators. Ladybug beetles are their primary predator, which is why they are sometimes sold for controlling aphids. This lesson is an opportunity to show children (1) that an unchecked population

will increase rapidly and (2) that predation can provide population control.

Predation is one of the primary factors that can limit population growth in nature. Competition is another, which is explored in Chapter 9. What can limit human population growth? Birth control! If not that, it will eventually be starvation, disease or war.

Ladybug Beetles

Ladybug beetle adults and larvae are predators of aphids. There are many different species of ladybugs, and the adult coloration varies. Some are black with orange or yellow spots (see Figure 15.1). Ladybugs lay eggs on plants that harbor aphids. The eggs hatch after several days into tiny [1/16 to 1/8 inch (1.6–3.2 mm)] black caterpillarlike larvae (see Figure 15.2). Larvae of some ladybug species can eat up to five hundred aphids a day! Most larvae molt (shed their exoskeletons) three times as they grow. When the larvae are about 1/4 to 3/8 inch (.6–1 cm) long, they are ready to pupate. They affix themselves to a surface and remain immobile. The skin of the larva splits and the new skin underneath hardens as it becomes a pupa. Inside the pupal skin an adult is forming. It doesn't eat during this process of metamorphosis. After about five days, an adult will emerge from a split in the hard skin of the pupa. The characteristic spots of the adult ladybug appear gradually as the wings harden. The adult, like the larva, walks around the aphid-infested plant eating aphids. It never touches the aphids with its legs, but just walks right up to an aphid, grabs it with its tiny jaws and munches.

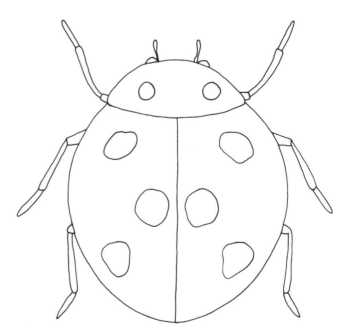

Figure 15. 1 — Adult ladybug beetle, 3/16 inch (4.8 mm) long.

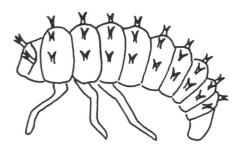

Figure 15.2 — Drawing of a ladybug larva.

The most outstanding features of aphids to young children are these:

1. The number of aphids on a plant can increase from one to fifteen overnight.
2. Aphids give birth to live young.
3. A dense population of aphids can sicken a plant.
4. Some aphids are winged and some are not.

How to Get and Keep Aphids and Ladybugs

Aphids

I don't know of anywhere to order live aphids, but they're easy enough to come by. I've never had a garden that wasn't plagued by aphids sooner or later. They're always on sugar-snap pea plants and always on leaf lettuce. In the South sugar-snaps can be planted in mid-February, or even earlier, and sprout in March. Lettuce is planted in early- to mid-March. Aphids appear on both in April (later in the North). You may need to start your plants indoors in the North and set them out when it's warm enough to get aphids before summer vacation. Ask someone at a local gardening supply store how early you can plant.

When the aphids first appear there are just a few. Look on the undersides of leaves and where there is new growth. Aphids come in lots of colors, but most I've seen are green or red. An adult is usually the size of the head of a pin, sometimes twice that size. They are pear-shaped (the narrow end is the head) and very soft-bodied (see Figure 15.3). Their legs are so thin they are barely visible. Aphid eyes are tiny black specks, which I didn't notice until a first-grader pointed them out to me.

To maintain aphids, just keep their plant alive, leave them on the plant and don't use any pesticides near them. Since they prefer tender growth and buds, don't prune back all the new shoots. There are many aphid species, and each species is restricted biologically to feeding on only one or a few particular types of plants. Its innately preferred plant species is called its host plant. Aphids will die or leave if placed on plants other than their host species.

When you need to collect aphids to put on children's plants or to feed ladybug larvae, you can collect them from a plant with a tiny paintbrush and a vial if you've gotten some vials for baby mantises or fruitflies (see Chapters 4 and 14). Put the open vial directly under the aphid. Then gently sweep the aphid into the vial and put the foam stopper in. You can also pick up an aphid (or any other tiny insect) with a paintbrush by touching the blunt end of the brush gently to the aphid. Its legs get tangled in the bristles and you can lift it easily and without damage. Then tap the paintbrush against the edge of the vial as though tapping the ash off of a cigarette. The aphid falls in the vial.

Ladybugs

If you want to do the experiments involving predation (Experiments 5 and 6), you'll need ladybugs. I've always been able to find at least a couple with the help of a class of students. Even first-graders probably know what a ladybug looks like. If you take a class into a natural area for a half-hour in warm weather, chances are someone will find one. Have them look at home and at recess for a week. They can also be ordered from a biological supply company, although garden supply sources are usually cheaper and send huge quantities (see Appendix for both). I keep beetles in vials with the wet end of a cotton swab in the vial for moisture held in place by the foam stopper (see Figure 15.4). A jar with a bit of moistened paper towel or cotton will do.

If you find a beetle it may lay eggs in the container. They wait about a week after mating before egg-laying. Another way to get eggs is to find them already laid. If you

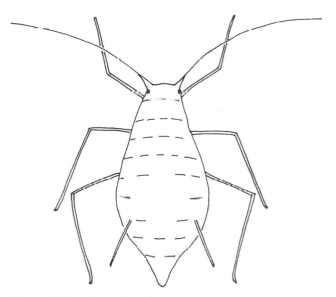

Figure 15.3 — Drawing of an aphid.

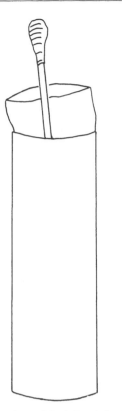

Figure 15.4 — Drawing of fruitfly vial with a cotton swab for moisture for ladybug larvae and adults.

Figure 15.5 — Ladybug eggs, 1/16 inch (1.6 mm).

Ladybug larvae and adults need aphids to eat. I have offered alternative diets but have not found any to be accepted. Although they can eat huge quantities of aphids, only a few aphids a day will keep them going. Like all "cold-blooded" animals, their food requirements are flexible because they need food mainly for growth and loco-motion, not for maintaining body temperature. You can collect aphids from a plant with a paintbrush, as described above, and then tap them into the ladybugs' vials. I feed ladybug larvae and adults by collecting aphid-covered buds from a thistle weed behind my house and putting a whole bud in with each predator.

Field Hunt

A garden is a good place to look for aphids but they can be found on many other plants as well, both cultivated plants and wild. Most encyclopedias should have photographs of aphids to show the children before you hunt. Gardening pest books do too, since aphids are one of the most common pests. Tell the children to check stems and leaves, especially the undersides and new growth.

carefully examine aphid-infested plants that have been outside, there's a good chance you'll find some ladybug eggs. The eggs look like a tiny cluster of short thick yellow cigars (white when about to hatch), all on end, with their sides stuck together more or less (see Figure 15.5). Each egg is about 1/16 inch (1.6 mm) long. The eggs of other beetles that may be attacking the plant instead of the aphids look similar, but chances are if you find eggs like these on an aphid-infested plant they're ladybug eggs. Check every day for a week or two. If you find them, leave them on the leaf. Put the leaf in an escape-proof container, such as a vial or small jar. The eggs are so tiny the air in the jar will last for a long time. After they hatch, the larvae stay clustered for a few hours, then disperse rapidly looking for aphids to eat. I usually let all but a few go and put the remaining ones in separate vials with one end of a cotton swab, as described for the adults. Ask the children how many want a larva for Experiment 5 or 6. Keep that many, if you have enough, or keep enough to do those experiments as a class.

If the children put their plants outside for some sunshine, they may get some ladybug eggs that way. It happened the first time I shared aphids with a class. A little blond girl named Rachel discovered eggs on her plant by herself after we brought the plants in and was delighted when she found out what they were. The next morning they hatched. Rachel was thrilled to be the owner of our only ladybug larvae.

Figure 15.6 — Tyewanda tamping down the soil after planting her sugar-snap pea plant.

Figure 15.7 — Valerie and Shawnta are trying to get an aphid on Shawnta's plant.

My son Alan (then three years old) tried to collect aphids from our garden on his own after watching me do it. He took the foam stopper out of the vial and began sweeping them jerkily into the vial with his paintbrush. He was knocking most of them onto the ground because the aphid's only defense is to simply let go and drop to the ground when disturbed. Another defense is that some aphids lure ants to defend them, by feeding the ants excess sugar that the aphids have sucked from the plants. The excess is secreted by the aphids as a liquid called honeydew, edible to the ants.

After a demonstration of how to pick up an aphid with a paintbrush, Alan tried again and got several into his vial.

Ladybugs are found almost anywhere outdoors. Have the children search plants and the ground. Ladybugs are found most easily perhaps by not looking, and being patient and waiting until one finds you.

Aphids and Ladybugs at School
Getting Ready

A month or maybe more before you plan to begin the lesson, plant some sugar-snaps or whatever plants you plan to use later in the classroom. Plant in pots and transfer them outside as weather permits. The purpose of this is to attract aphids so you'll have some to transfer to the children's individual plants in the classroom. After you've found aphids on your outdoor plants, you can start growing the children's plants in cups.

Observations and Activities

A good place to start involving the children is in planting their own host plants for their future aphids (see Figure 15.6). They can use paper cups, peat pots or plastic

yogurt cups. I generally use small milk cartons that the children collect themselves from lunches. Either potting soil or good soil from outside will do. The sugar-snap seeds will germinate faster if you soak them for twenty-four hours or so before planting. Label the cups with the children's names and, if possible, let each child fill his or her own cup with soil, leaving about 1 inch (2.5 cm) of space at the top of the cup. Let them plant a couple of seeds per child. (Even a toddler can do this.) If the soil is kept moist, the seeds should sprout within a few days. When a plant has at least two unfolded leaves, it's big enough for aphids. Most plants will be 3 to 4 inches (7.6–10.2 cm) tall about a week after planting. Don't let the plants get much bigger before putting the aphids on them, or the children may have trouble finding the aphids later.

The easiest way to introduce aphids to the children's plants is to use the paintbrush to gather a vial full of aphids from your source plant. Then, again using the paintbrush, put an aphid from the vial onto each child's plant. Or you can let the children transfer the aphids to their own plants. I've found third-graders can do it easily, if they do it one at a time. I show the first person how to do it, then he or she shows the second person and so on (see Figure 15.7).

Tell the children at this point that the aphids are sap-sucking insects with strawlike mouth parts. You may want to stop there and see how much the children discover on their own.

Figure 15.8 — Mena counts the aphids on her plant the day after putting her single aphid on it.

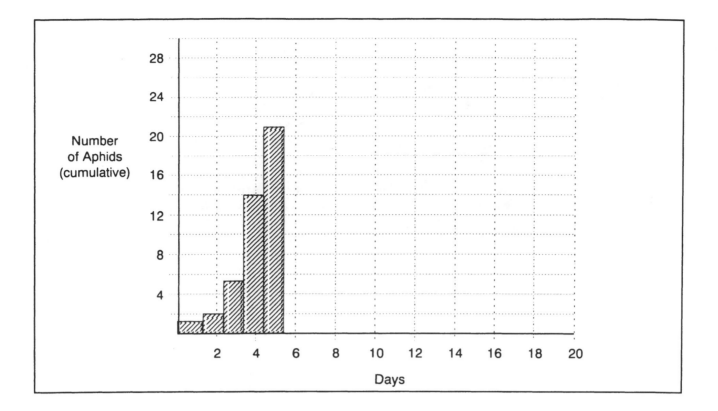

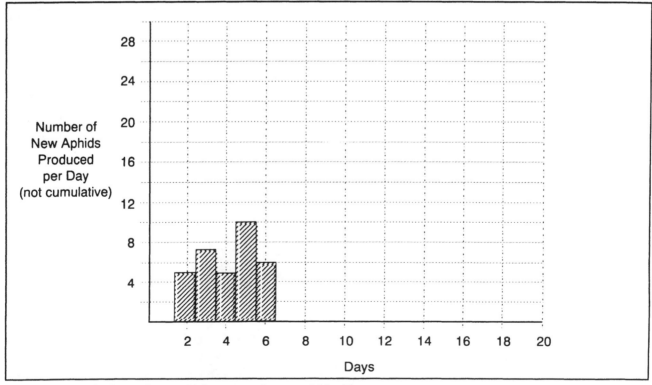

Figure 15.9 — Blank graphs on which to record your aphid tallies.

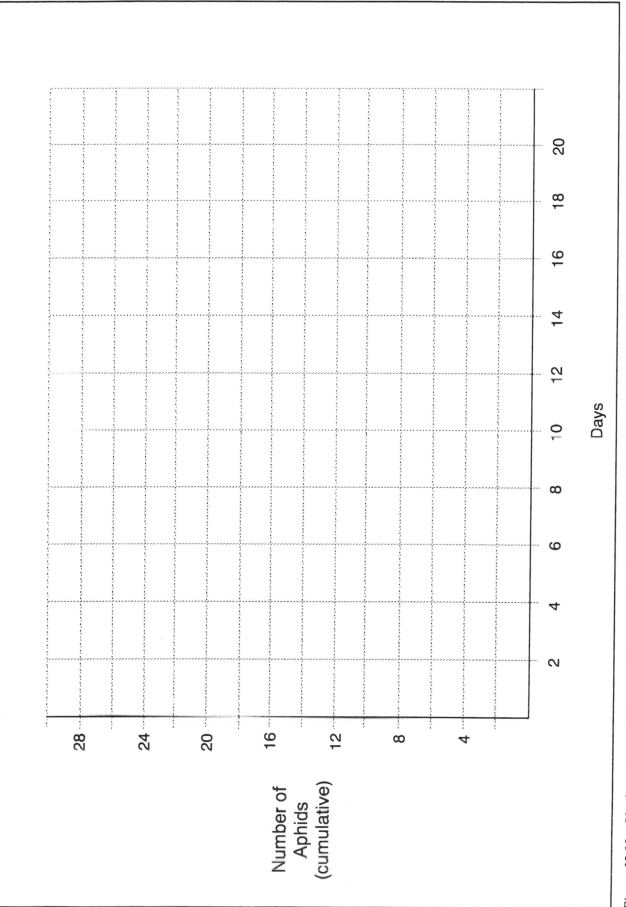

Figure 15.10 — Blank graph on which to record your aphid tallies.

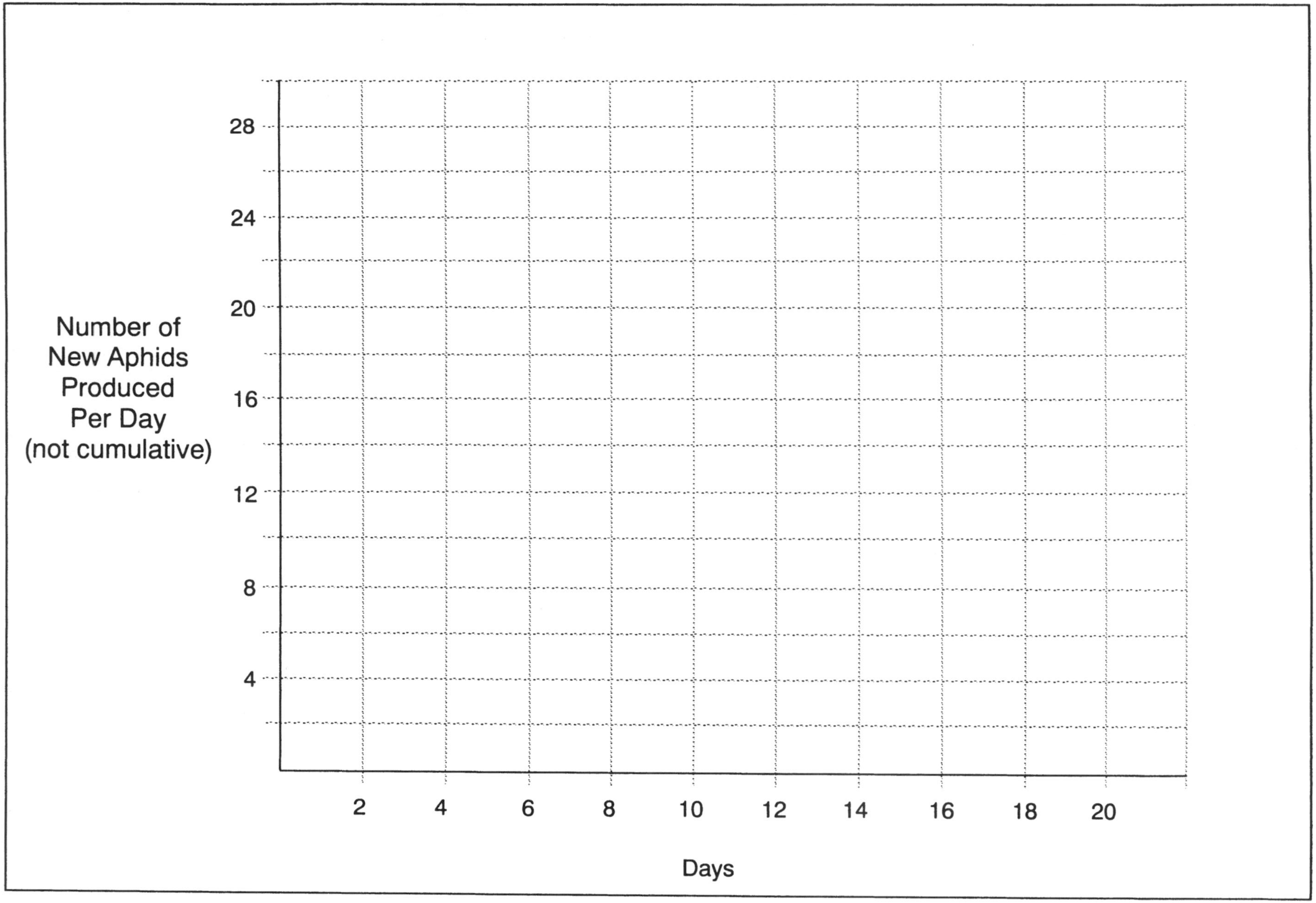

Figure 15.10 — Blank graph on which to record your aphid tallies.

The day after you introduce the aphids to the children's plants, have each child count the number of aphids on his or her own plant. Although each started with only one, most will have several more now. Most of the new ones will be babies. Some will be newly arrived winged aphids that flew in from outdoors.

They'll ask questions about the new arrivals. If the children are old enough to know that most animals mate to have babies, they may wonder how there can be babies with only one parent. This is a good time to give them a little information on the aphid life cycle, or at least the parthenogenetic part. Help them to notice that the aphids are giving birth to live young.

Have them count babies for a week or more (see Figure 15.8). If they're old enough each child can make a histogram, with the number of days on the horizontal axis and the number of babies (cumulative or per day) on the vertical axis. You can make a similar histogram of the class totals for each day. You can record your results on the histogram in Figure 15.10. Figure 15.9 provides an example of the completed histogram.

Have the children record the day when they first notice their original aphids' babies having their own babies. Compare records.

Experiments

Remember that the hypotheses I give are just examples. Most are written in the "if ... then" format, but they don't have to be. Your hypotheses will be the predictions made by the class or a particular child. Your result for each experiment will be a statement of how your animals reacted to your experimental setup. Your conclusion is a statement of whether your prediction was confirmed or not. For each experiment, adding replicates increases your confidence in the validity of your conclusion, but they may be omitted if tedious for young children.

Experiment 1

Since aphids are considered garden pests, one obvious question is this:

Question: What happens to the plant when it gets crowded with aphids?

Hypothesis: If the plant gets crowded with aphids, the plant will get sick.

Methods: Allow aphids to multiply unchecked on one plant. On another plant keep aphid numbers low as a control (for comparison). Rate the condition of the plants every day.

Result: Your result is the relative condition of the two plants after a period of several days.

Conclusion: A very crowded plant turns yellow, gets curled leaves and eventually dies.

Experiment 2

All animals have the problem of dispersal, as do humans. If a farmer has four children, and they have three or four children each, the offspring can't all inherit their parents' farm. How do animals handle this problem? If all the seeds from a maple tree sprouted under the tree, the competition for light, water and soil nutrients would be so fierce that very few or none would survive. So the seeds are equipped with wings to disperse via the wind. All living things, plant and animal, have some method whereby the young can spread out, or disperse, to avoid interfering with one another. Many seeds are dispersed by animals who eat them and later eject them unharmed with their feces. This is why fruits have fleshy edible parts. Other seeds have spurs that cling to animals' fur or human trousers and are thereby dispersed. Many animals simply wander or fly away when grown.

What do aphids do when they get crowded? Do they disperse? How? An aphid on the end of a stem has a long way to wander to a new plant. You might pose this question to the children. What do they think? If they're stumped, get them to think about how other insects, such as flies, beetles and dragonflies, disperse. Most fly away. They may or may not come up with suggestions, or hypotheses, but lead the conversation in such a way that someone (maybe you) proposes that you let the plants get too crowded and see what happens. If your plant starts to decline from lack of sunshine, the aphids may die before they get crowded. You may need to set it outside for a few hours a day if you don't have a sunny window.

Question: Will aphids disperse when they get too crowded?

Hypothesis: If we let one plant get too crowded, the aphids will somehow leave.

Methods: Let one or more plants get too crowded. Add new adults if you want to speed things up. Keep an uncrowded plant as your control (for comparison). Watch the aphids every day. This is the same setup as Experiment 1, but you're watching the aphids instead of the plant this time.

Result: Your result is a description of specifically what the children observed about the aphids on the crowded plant and on the uncrowded plant. Your anticipated result is that the females on the crowded plant will begin giving birth to young that will be winged as adults and will fly away. The aphids on the uncrowded plant will not have young that grow up to be winged.

To get this result, both your plants must get adequate sunlight and water so that the health of the plant is good other than the effects of crowding. Aphids don't reproduce enough on a sickly plant for it to work.

Conclusion: Aphids do have a way of dispersing when crowded.

The stimulus that causes this change to winged offspring may be an increased number of contacts between the mother and other aphids, or it may be some alteration in quantity or quality of sap.

If you can't get the answer by this approach, try it from the other end. That is, put a fresh plant outside and see how new aphids get to it. You may need to put out several or wait a while. If it's warm outside, eventually you'll get a winged aphid. Have the children make hypotheses about how they think the aphid will get there. If they've made a prediction, the observation of what really happens will make much more of an impression on them.

Experiment 3

The sap of a plant travels in vessels similar in principle to our blood vessels although there is no heart. If you cut off a stem, you stop the flow of sap in that stem. What happens to the aphids if you cut off the stem and the flow of sap?

Question: What will aphids do if the stem is clipped?
Hypothesis: If the stem is clipped, the aphids will starve.
Methods: Clip a stem with aphids on it and keep an eye on the aphids over the next couple of days. Watch the aphids on a still attached stem for comparison, as your control.
Result: Your result is a description of the aphids' behavior on the cut stem and on the attached stem.
Conclusion: The aphids will leave the cut stem or die. If another stem is available, they find it and climb it from the soil up. Aphids should stay on an unclipped stem, provided the plant is healthy. A clipped stem can't sustain aphids.

Experiment 4

A first-grader, Courtney, became interested in transferring her aphids to other types of plants and making hypotheses about whether or not the plants would be accepted.

Question: Will my aphid stay on grass from the lawn?
Hypothesis: If I transfer an aphid to a grass plant, it will stay.

Methods: Put an aphid or aphids on the grass. The grass must be healthy and rooted in soil. Transfer an aphid to another pea plant simultaneously as a control. If the aphids leave both plants, then being handled may have caused the exit. If only the aphid on the grass leaves, then the grass is probably not a host plant of that aphid species.
Result: Your result is a description of the response of both transferred aphids. Does each stay or leave?
Conclusion: It depends on the species of aphid and plant.

Experiment 5

You may want to begin this experiment without telling the children that the ladybugs will eat aphids.

Question: Will ladybugs eat aphids? Can ladybugs control aphid population growth?
Hypothesis: If we put ladybugs on a plant, they'll get rid of some of the aphids.
Methods: Give each child who wants one either an adult or a larval ladybug. They may need help getting the predators onto the stem with the aphids. Show one student how to do it, then he or she shows a second student and so on. This way there are always only two at the table. Let them take the plants back to their desks and watch what happens right away because sometimes the ladybug leaves. After they've seen the ladybug in action, then they can put the plant back on a windowsill to get some sun. Keep another similarly infested plant free of ladybugs for comparison as a control. Wait a few days. Compare the health of infested and uninfested plants. Which plant seems healthier?

If the children don't see any predation occurring on the plant, you can enclose the ladybug and aphids in a vial together and watch. In this event, the students will have to speculate about the outcome of the second question.

You can also enclose the end of a live stem, with aphids and a ladybug, in a vial with a foam stopper. The stopper keeps the insects in without crushing the stem, which is still attached to the rooted plant. This works well to contain wandering ladybugs, but children usually wind up breaking the stem by careless handling of the vial.
Result: Your result will be the children's observations about the effect of ladybugs on the aphid population.
Conclusion: Ladybugs eat aphids voraciously. If the plants are heavily infested in the beginning, the one without ladybugs will eventually die. The ladybugs should reduce the aphid population on the other plant, thereby saving the plant. If the ladybugs won't stay on the

plant, they'll certainly eat aphids in a container. Because ladybugs are effective in controlling aphids, they are a help to gardeners.

Experiment 6

You may want to talk about gardening without toxic pesticides here. Do the children think that ladybugs can do as good a job in protecting the plant as an insecticide could do?

Question: Which is more effective in controlling aphids, ladybugs or chemicals?

Hypothesis: Ladybugs (or chemicals) are more effective.

Methods: You probably don't want to use a toxic chemical with children. Instead, use a spray bottle to spray an infested plant with alcohol or soapy water (one application). To another similarly infested plant add a few ladybugs. After a few days, which has more aphids?

Result: Your result is a description of what happened when ladybugs or other agents were applied to the aphid populations. The result depends in part on how thoroughly you spray and on whether or not the ladybugs stay on the uninfested plant.

Conclusion: Ladybugs can be as effective as some sprays in controlling aphids.

What advantages do ladybugs have over toxic chemical sprays? What about soapy water and alcohol? (Alcohol and soapy water are not toxic as long as the vegetables are washed, while the chemicals sold as pesticides can persist even through washing because they are often incorporated into the flesh of the vegetable.) Chemicals sold as pesticides are probably the most effective aphid killers, but you have to weigh their effectiveness against their toxicity to humans and to the other living things outside. The children can weigh the advantages and disadvantages of each method of aphid control and make recommendations.

CHAPTER 16

Insect Metamorphosis on a Macro Scale: Mealworms to Beetles

Introduction

Most of this chapter focuses on *Tenebrio* beetles, with a quick glimpse at flying beetles. The outstanding feature of *Tenebrio* beetles is their illustration of the insect life cycle on a much larger scale than what we see with fruit flies. The *Tenebrio* larvae, commonly called mealworms, grow to about 1 inch (2.5 cm) long, which is ten times longer than fruitfly larvae. All three life stages of the beetle — larvae, pupae and adult — can be handled and inspected freely (see Figure 16.1).

These beetles, or their larvae (mealworms), are often available at pet stores as food for amphibians and larvae. Full-grown praying mantises (see Chapter 12) enjoy the adult beetles and eat mealworms like corn on the cob, grasping one end in each front leg.

The activities and experiments with *Tenebrio* include exploratory behavior, habitat choices, growth rates, food choices and more. I've included a list of questions for flying beetles, which can be caught at certain times of year with a porch light or lamp outside.

Figure 6 in the Postscript provides a range of questions and answers comparing the life cycles of the organisms discussed in Chapters 14 to 16. A list of the questions represented in Figure 6 is provided in Figure 7, which can be photocopied and handed out for the children to answer.

Materials

For Tenebrio:
1. A larva for each student or group to watch through metamorphosis, plus twenty or so for various experiments. Available from pet stores or a biological supply company (see Appendix).
2. A dishpan or other container of similar size with no lid. This can be ordered with the mealworms.
3. Oat bran or wheat bran to fill the container half full. Oat bran is preferred. Bran without additives can be found in the hot cereal section of most grocery stores, at health food stores or ordered with the mealworms.
4. A raw potato.
5. Strips of newspaper.
6. A petri dish 3 1/2 inches (9 cm) in diameter for each student or group (available at a science hobby store or biological supply company, see Appendix).
7. Refrigerator or other cool place for Experiments 1 and 9.
8. Construction paper for Experiments 3, 4 and 5.
9. A hot water bottle, bowl of ice and baking tray for Experiment 6.
10. Alternate food and a box for Experiment 8.
11. A box for Experiment 11.

For flying beetles:
12. A porch light or lantern to attract them at night.
13. A net or jar to catch them.

Figure 16.1 — Malcolm expertly displays his two adult Tenebrio *beetles.*

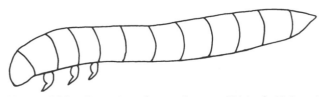

Figure 16.2 – Drawing of a mealworm, 3/4 inch (1.9 cm) in length.

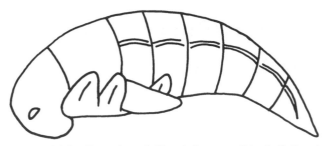

Figure 16.3 – Drawing of a Tenebrio *pupa, 1 inch (2.5 cm) in length.*

Background Information

Tenebrio are the most useful beetle for classrooms that I know of, and it is certainly an easy one to keep going generation after generation. Each child can keep his or her own larva to raise to adulthood in a petri dish with a small amount of bran and a cube of raw potato. The wormlike larvae are soft, light brown and easily viewed and handled at their maximum length of about 1 inch (2.5 cm). They have six short legs as do all insects. The larvae don't have three body parts, but the adult beetles do. Children will want to know if their larvae have mouths and eyes, which they do, as labeled on Figure 16.2. The students will also want to know the gender of their larvae, but you can't tell that until you watch them mate as adults.

The larvae are very lethargic. When they do move, they move slowly and clumsily. Their exoskeletons are shed or molted about five to seven times as they grow. The duration of the larval period varies depending on temperature and food availability, but lasts about ten weeks under ideal conditions. It can last several weeks longer. When a larva molts for the last time, the soft new exoskeleton underneath has the shape of a pupa. This change from larva to pupa is its first metamorphosis, which means "changing form" (see Figure 16.3). (The teacher of hearing-impaired third-graders keeping mealworms told me that the first time metamorphosis was witnessed in the class was an occasion of great celebration among the students.)

The pupae don't move much unless handled, and they do not eat. Two to three weeks after pupation, an adult beetle about 5/8 inch (1.5 cm) long emerges from the pupal exoskeleton (see Figure 16.4). The adults are almost white right after metamorphosis, but soon turn dark brown. I've never seen one fly, but they crawl constantly.

The adults mate a few days after emergence. At this point you can tell boys from girls because the male crawls on the female's back. You can see the tip of his abdomen curved downward to reach the tip of her abdomen, to transfer the sperm to her.

The female beetles lay eggs about seven to ten days after emergence from the pupal exoskeleton. The eggs hatch about fourteen days later into tiny larvae, which are not really visible in the bran for several weeks.

How to Get and Keep Beetles
Tenebrio *(Mealworms)*

If you order *Tenebrio* beetles from a biological supply company, they come with instructions and a supply of bran for food. I keep mine in a plastic dish tub over half full of bran. They need a fresh slice of raw potato on the surface of the bran every three days or so for moisture. Other than that I haven't touched my culture in several months, and it is thriving with adults, larvae and pupae. My kids play in it sometimes, fishing out the beetles. Once in a while I take out a beetle to feed a praying mantis or a larva to feed a toad.

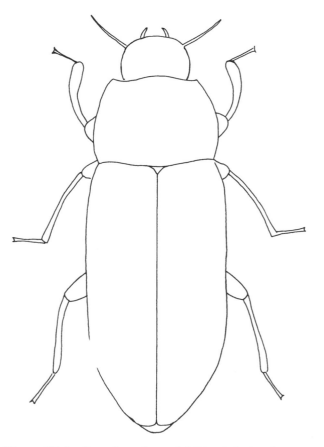

Figure 16.4 – Drawing of an adult Tenebrio *beetle.*

The adults don't live very long, so there are dead adults in the culture. I never remove them, and it doesn't seem to make any difference. They just dry out.

When the bran under the surface begins to get powdery, or if the culture seems too crowded, start a new one by transferring some larvae and/or pupae to a new pan of bran.

Children will want to know where the beetles and larvae are found in nature. *Tenebrio* flourish in places where large quantities of grains are stored, such as on farms. They are seldom found in kitchens. In nature, they live under the bark of dead trees. I can't tell you positively how to tell *Tenebrio* apart from the many other kinds of beetles that live under the bark of dead trees, so it's best to order them.

Flying Beetles

I've never seen *Tenebrio* beetles fly, although all beetles have wings. One way to attract flying beetles is to turn on a porch light at night, because many of them are attracted to light. You may be able to catch one with a plastic jar, but an insect net will make it easier. Or you can make a funnel trap with light as bait (see Chapter 2).

You may be able to identify your beetle with *A Field Guide to the Beetles* or *A Field Guide to the Insects*, both in the Peterson Field Guide series. Neither book includes all the beetles. If a field guide doesn't tell you what to feed it, you can still keep it alive for at least a week with a wet paper towel in the jar. That's long enough to do the activities suggested here.

Beetles at School
Getting Started

If you want the children to watch *Tenebrio* beetles go through complete metamorphosis, it's best to start with small larvae. They can watch the larvae grow to full size before pupating. The population you get from a biological supply company is usually an assortment of adults, larvae and pupae. You may want to ask how many small larvae you can expect. If you want a small larva for each child, you may have to order your beetles several months in advance and let them reproduce. Or you can always start with large larvae. The smallest larvae I'm able to find in my culture are about the length of a child's fingernail. Larvae smaller than that are too hard to see in the bran.

Each child will need for his or her mealworm a petri dish with a lid or other similar container like a baby-food jar, 1 tablespoon (15 ml) of bran and a small chunk or slice of potato for moisture. The children enjoy scooping the bran into their own dishes and selecting their own mealworms. Use a grease pencil to write names on the petri dishes (plastic petri dishes crack with too much pressure).

Observations and Activities
Tenebrio

After setting up a dish for each child, have the children measure the mealworm every other day or so and record the date and length in a journal. Have them record the dates their larvae metamorphose into pupae.

After all have metamorphosed into pupae, make a list of all the larvae's final length measurements before pupation. Were they all about the same length before pupating? How much variation was there, if any? Can a larva be induced to pupate at a somewhat smaller size than average by removing it from its food source?

Have the children record the dates their pupae metamorphose into adults and calculate the duration of the pupal stage. Make a class list of these calculations. Were the pupal stages of the same duration? How much variation was there, if any? If there was variation, help them calculate an average and state a range, for example, "The longest pupal stage was Kelly's, with x days. The shortest was Pat's with y days."

Exploratory Behavior of *Tenebrio*

Here are some questions to help students notice the exploratory behavior of an adult beetle. Have each child put an adult beetle on top of his or her bare desk.

What does the beetle do? Sit still? Move around constantly?
Walk around the perimeter of the desk? Or walk in a straight line and fall off?
How does a beetle react to an obstacle (petroleum jelly, a pencil laid in front of it, water or a child's hand)? Does it turn around and take a new direction? Climb over or through? Try to go around?

Compare its behavior to that of other animals in this book in the same setting, like a roly-poly or a millipede.

How does the adult beetle behave when exploring a new place with food? Get a square box about 1 foot (30.4 cm) in diameter. Put a pile of wheat or oat bran in each corner. Put a beetle or beetles (adults or larvae) into the middle of the box.
Do the beetles go directly to a pile? Or do they seem to find it by accident?
Do they stay in the pile once they find it?
Does one beetle, when put in the box alone several times, go over and over to the same pile?
Does a second or third beetle go to the same pile as the first one?
Do they prefer a pile with a potato slice to a pile without one? (Give them a day or two to make this choice.)

Flying Beetles

Get a very fine thread and glue one end of it to the beetle's thorax, which is the body segment behind the head. Attach the thread in front of the wings. Glue the other end of the thread to something suspended in the air, like the end of a yardstick.

How long does the beetle fly without landing?
Does it fly counterclockwise or clockwise?
Does it change direction frequently?
Does it fly so the thread is tight or loose?
How does it land?
Can it land on a moving target?
How small an object will the beetle land on?
What stimuli cause it to start flying?
Is there a pattern to the flight?
If you put something under the flying beetle's feet, does it stop?

Experiments

Remember that the hypotheses I give are just examples. Most are written in the "if ... then" format, but they don't have to be. Your hypotheses will be the predictions made by the class or a particular child. Your result for each experiment will be a statement of how your animals reacted to your experimental setup. Your conclusion is a statement of whether your prediction was confirmed or not. For each experiment, adding replicates increases your confidence in the validity of your conclusion, but may be omitted if tedious for young children.

Experiment 1

Question: How does temperature affect the speed of development of *Tenebrio* larvae?

Hypothesis: We think mealworms kept in the cold won't grow at all.

Methods: Keep one group of larvae at room temperature. Keep another group in a cooler environment; a refrigerator is ideal. An air-conditioned room and a non-air-conditioned room might make a difference. Or you can put one group of larvae outside if it's cool as long as the temperature is above freezing.

Result: Your result is a statement of your measurements on particular days and relevant observations.

Conclusion: The prediction is not confirmed. The larvae develop more slowly at cooler temperatures (see Figure 16.5). They may also molt fewer times and pupate at a smaller size than larvae under ideal conditions. You can make a graph like Figure 16.5 showing the difference in the two growth rates, using the blank graph in Figure 16.6.

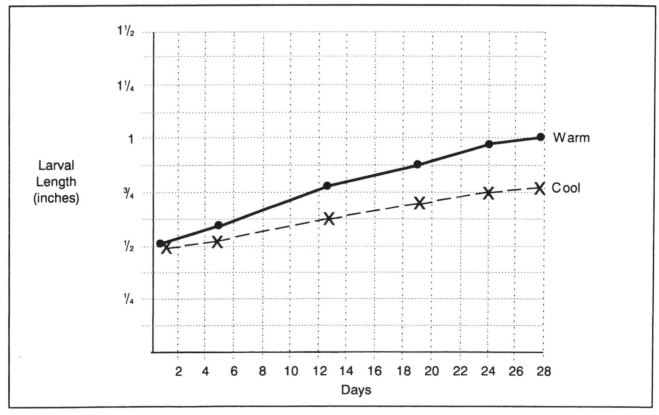

Figure 16.5 — Line graph showing larval growth rates in two different temperature environments.

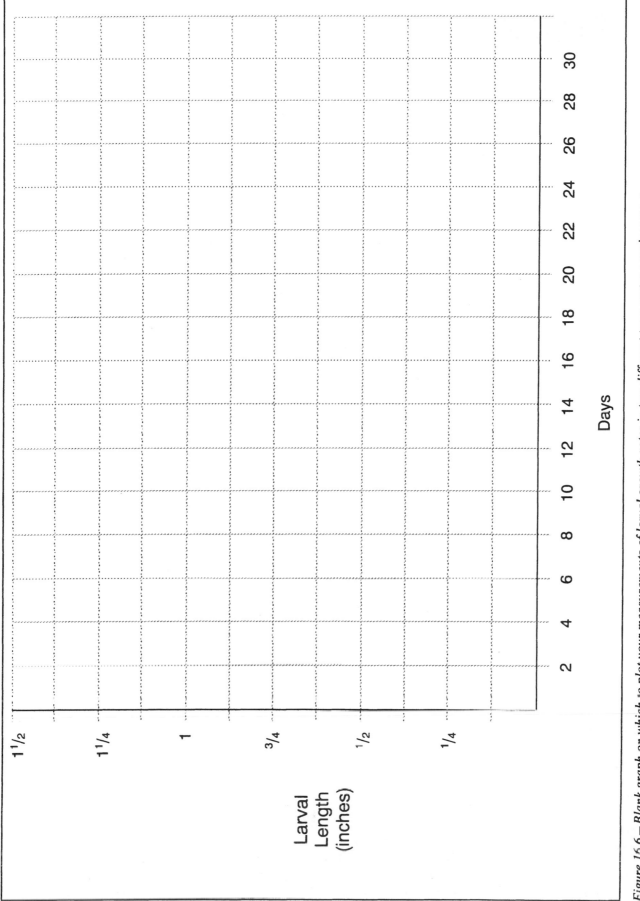

Figure 16.6 — Blank graph on which to plot your measurements of larval growth rates in two different temperature environments.

Experiment 2

Question: How does food supply affect the speed of development of *Tenebrio* larvae?

Hypothesis: We think larvae that don't get enough to eat will get sick.

Methods: Select two groups of similar-sized larvae. Provide one group of larvae with more than enough bran at all times. Feed the other group intermittently. For example, surround them with bran every other day or every third day. On intervening days, remove them from the bran entirely. Handle them gently to make sure that abuse is not the cause of any observed slowing of growth. To be certain that handling is not the cause of any observed difference between the two groups, you'd need to handle the larvae remaining in the bran also. Provide moisture (a potato chunk) for all.

Result: Your result is a statement of your measurements on particular days and any relevant observations. You can plot your measurements for these two groups on a graph (see Figure 16.5 for an example). A blank graph for your measurements is provided in the Appendix.

Conclusion: The prediction is not confirmed. Those fed intermittently will grow and develop more slowly than those fed continually.

For each of the following four experiments, you should have at least ten replicates because not every larva and beetle will make the same choice. Your conclusion will be in the choice of the majority. For Experiments 3 to 5, each beetle or larva should be in a dish alone, so they won't influence each other's behavior. If each child has his or her own petri dish and larva or beetle, then each child's dish will be one replicate. You can record your results for Experiments 3 to 7 on a table similar to the one shown in Figures 3.7 and 3.8. A blank table for your results is provided in the Appendix.

Experiment 3

Question: Do *Tenebrio* (beetle or larvae) prefer dampness or dryness?

Hypothesis: Beetles and larvae will choose dampness over dryness.

Methods: Provide a damp surface and a dry surface in each container (petri dish or other). The texture should be the same on the two sides. I use two half-circles of paper in a petri dish, one damp and one dry. With paper, you have to keep the two sides apart a little so the dry paper won't wick water from the other. Tape down the edges of the paper so the larvae or beetles can't crawl under it. You can also use wet and dry sand. In this case make a foil barrier between wet and dry (under the surface).

Put a beetle in the middle of each container and after a half-hour record their positions. After you've done beetles, try larvae.

Result: Your result is a statement of the number of beetles on the damp side and the number on the dry side, as well as the number of larvae choosing each side. You can record your results as a histogram (see Figure 3.4 for an example of a completed histogram). A blank graph for your results is provided in the Appendix.

Conclusion: The prediction is not confirmed. In my experience, adult beetles prefer the dry side. They may initially suck water from the wet side if they are dehydrated, but most will eventually wind up on the dry side. On the other hand, the larvae do not show a strong preference (in my experience) for either the wet side or the dry side.

Experiment 4

Question: Do *Tenebrio* (beetles or larvae) prefer light or dark?

Hypothesis: Beetles and larvae prefer light to dark.

Methods: Cover half of the lid of each petri dish with black construction paper, so that one half of the dish is in deep shadow (see Figure 16.7). Leave the floor of the dish bare. Put one beetle in the middle of each dish and put the half-covered lid in place. Record the location of the beetles after a half-hour or longer. Then repeat the procedure with larvae.

Result: Your result is a statement of the number of beetles under the black construction paper and the number in the light, as well as the number of larvae choosing each side. You can record your results as a histogram (see Figure 3.4 for an example of a completed histogram). A blank graph for your results is provided in the Appendix.

Conclusion: The prediction is not confirmed. A majority of adult beetles choose the dark side. In my experience the larvae do not show a strong preference for either side.

Experiment 5

Question: Do *Tenebrio* (beetles or larvae) prefer a dark or a light substrate?

Hypothesis: Beetles and larvae prefer a light-colored substrate.

Figure 16.7 — Craig assesses his beetle's choice of light versus dark.

Methods: Cover half of the floor of each petri dish with black construction paper and half with white construction paper. Tape the edges down so the beetles and larvae can't crawl under. Put one beetle in the middle of each dish. Wait a half-hour or longer and record their choices. Then repeat the procedure with one larva per dish.

Result: Your result is a statement of your beetles' choices and your larvae's choices. You can record your results as a histogram (see Figure 3.4 for an example of a completed histogram). A blank graph for your results is provided in the Appendix.

Conclusion: The prediction is not confirmed. Adult beetles tend to prefer a dark substrate. This preference helps protect them from predators. My captive mantises have trouble spotting a beetle on a dark floor or the dark edge of a terrarium. When I put beetles in a terrarium with a dark edge, they run to the dark part and stay there. A beetle on the floor of an all-white container with a mantis is dead meat. In my experience

the larvae have no preference between a light and dark substrate, which makes sense because they are equally visible on either.

Experiment 6

Question: Are *Tenebrio* adults attracted to cold or warmth?
Hypothesis: The beetles are attracted to warmth.
Methods: Get a long baking tray and put a hot water bottle or a heating pad under one end of it, a tray of ice cubes under the other end. Wait a half-hour or more for the tray to get cool on one end and warm on the other. Put several beetles in the middle. Wait at least a half-hour or so to record the results.
Result: Your result is a statement of your beetles' choices. You can record your results as a histogram (see Figure 3.4 for an example of a completed histogram). A blank graph for your results is provided in the Appendix.
Conclusion: The prediction is not confirmed. Most beetles prefer the cool end.

Experiment 7

Question: Do *Tenebrio* adults in a petri dish "bunch" (huddle together) or stay separate? Does moisture affect the outcome?
Hypothesis: Beetles will not huddle together or bunch in a dry or moist container.
Methods: Get two containers like petri dishes. Put a damp substrate in one and leave the other dry. If you use paper for the damp substrate, tape the edges down. Put two or more beetles into each container, without bran (see Figure 16.8). Wait a half-hour or so to check on them. How many of them are in contact with another individual?
Result: Your result is a statement of your animals' reaction in each dish.
Conclusion: Adult beetles will usually bunch or huddle together in a dry dish, but not in a damp dish. Contact with another individual reduces water loss from body surfaces.

Experiment 8

Question: Do *Tenebrio* adults like other foods as well as bran?
Hypothesis: They might like cookies.
Methods: Get a square box about 1 foot (30.4 cm) in diameter. Put one food item in each corner, for example,

Figure 16.8 — Jennifer recording observations of her beetles on a damp substrate.

oat bran, wheat bran, sawdust, a crumbled cookie, flour, sugar, salt, loose dry soil or other things the children suggest. Give the beetles enough time so that most of them have gravitated to one pile or another.

Result: Your result is a statement of your beetles' choices.

Conclusion: Of the items suggested above, sugar and salt are the least acceptable to the beetles, in my experience. They will usually burrow into a pile of bran and sometimes into the others.

Experiment 9

Question: Does a chilled beetle move more slowly than a warm beetle?

Hypothesis: A chilled beetle will move more slowly than a warm beetle.

Methods: Make a grid on a sheet of paper with squares about 1 1/2 inches (3.8 cm) in diameter. Put the paper inside a box. Put on the grid an adult beetle straight from your culture container. How many grid lines does the beetle cross in thirty seconds? Now replace that beetle with one that's been chilled in a freezer for about one minute (longer if it's chilled in a refrigerator) and repeat the procedure. (The time required to chill the beetle adequately may vary depending on the size of the container and the temperature of the freezer.)

Result: Your result is a statement of the number of grid lines crossed by each beetle in thirty seconds.

Conclusion: The prediction is confirmed. A chilled beetle crosses fewer grid lines than a warm beetle. Chilling reduces the body temperature of a cold-blooded animal and makes them move more slowly.

Experiment 10

Question: Can a beetle walk faster on a slick surface or a rough surface?

Hypothesis: A beetle can walk faster on a rough surface.

Methods: Mark a starting point on two surfaces, one a very slick surface like smooth plastic and one a more grainy surface like wood or smooth cloth. Put a beetle at each starting point, set a time and poke both beetles from behind to get them moving. After thirty seconds or less, stop them and measure the distance covered by each beetle. Do beetles have trouble walking on slick surfaces?

Result: Your result is a statement of the distance covered by each beetle.

Conclusion: The prediction is confirmed. *Tenebrio* beetles have more trouble than many other insects walking on slick surfaces. They sometimes walk and walk while not moving forward at all. They're adapted for living in grain piles and under bark, where slick surfaces are not an issue.

Experiment 11

Question: Which is better at staying on its feet, a roly-poly or a *Tenebrio* beetle?

Hypothesis: Roly-polies are better at staying on their feet.

Methods: Put a beetle and a roly-poly in a flat smooth-floored box. Which one turns over first? Begin again nine more times. Which one flips over first more?

Result: Your result is a statement of which one flips over more and any relevant observations.

Conclusion: The prediction is confirmed. *Tenebrio* beetles are the clumsiest animals I know. They flip over constantly with no provocation and lie helplessly flailing the air with their legs. But in grain piles, flipping over is not a problem. Roly-polies, on the other hand, are more accustomed to flat surfaces at least on occasion and so have evolved the ability to avoid constant flipping.

Postscript:
Making Connections among the Chapters

Lots of the creatures in this book share certain behaviors. That's to be expected, especially among those that share a habitat or share a food source. Most predators have certain things in common, as do most of the under-log creatures. Most of the latter are scavengers, eating decomposing plant or animal material.

Seeing the trends or common elements among chapters helps students extrapolate to creatures not in this book. If wolves and cheetahs both asphyxiate their prey before eating them, then maybe lions do too. Or if turtles and lizards both like to sun themselves, then maybe snakes do too.

Creatures Found in
and under Logs

The most outstanding common thread I see is among the under-log creatures. Coming from the same habitat, it's not surprising that they all prefer conditions like those under a log when offered a choice. I think what is surprising to children, or really to students of any age, is that these lowly creatures have "sense" enough to have any preference at all. I've never heard a child verbalize this, but I think most of us assume that creatures like insects are found where they are because they're born there. Before I got to graduate school I'm sure I thought that. And it's true that most invertebrates don't really have sense enough to make real decisions. But they possess an innate attraction to the conditions most suited to their own particular physiology. This prevents them from wandering away from the log where they hatched. Or it helps them find another log if they somehow get displaced.

What are the conditions under a log? Damp, dark, cool, covered. In the experiments in this book, four under-log creatures were offered a choice between a damp place and a dry place. Roly-polies, earthworms, crickets and millipedes all prefer dampness. The millipede and earth-worm chapters suggest offering a choice between cool and warm — both animals tend to prefer cool. Can the students predict what crickets and roly-polies might prefer? Three of the under-log animals show a preference for darkness. In general, the under-log creatures tend to choose the same conditions in which we find them in nature. See Figure 1, a table that summarizes the similarity of their choices. To fill out every block in the chart, you'll need to apply instructions from one chapter to another. For example, the roly-poly chapter does not have an experiment to offer them a choice between cool and warm, but the millipede chapter does, so apply the instructions for millipedes to roly-polies. Figure 2 is a blank table for the children to fill out. What would the students guess about under-log animals that aren't in the book, such as centipedes or snails or termites?

Flying Insects and Light

Some animals are attracted to light. Most of them are flying animals, such as fruitflies, moths and flying beetles. One benefit of this attraction is that it causes them to walk out into the open or to climb where they may become airborne more easily. Can the children make predictions about other flying insects, like houseflies, dragonflies or adult ant lions?

Similarities and Differences
among Predators

There is a common element of prey recognition shared by most of the predators in this book. Most are generalist predators, which means they'll eat just about any prey that is small enough and not noxious. The toads, the praying mantises and the spiders are all generalist predators, and they all recognize an item as prey by the fact that it's moving. None of them will notice or attack an insect that isn't moving regardless of how fresh it is. The same is true of most of the aquatic predators in Chapters 2 and 9, unless they are very hungry. Ant lions too will not recognize prey that is not moving, but will toss out a dead thing like it's a tiny pebble.

The ladybug beetle is the exception, and that's because ladybugs are not really generalist predators. Ladybugs eat soft-bodied insects, usually aphids and scale insects, neither of which move much. A ladybug will plow along a stem of aphids like a lawn mower, eating every one it comes to. The aphids just sit there, making no attempt to get out of the way. The ladybug recognizes its prey by some means other than by movement. Since they eat mostly aphids, they may recognize the aphids' shape, soft body or taste. Ladybugs I have kept in captivity have refused fruitflies, which are about the same size as aphids.

Predators as specialized as ladybugs are unusual, because in nature it doesn't generally pay to be finicky. An eat-what's-available strategy usually pays off better for predators. Aphids are a relatively safe bet, though, because they are so abundant on their host plants, and the ladybug eggs are laid and hatch right on the same plants.

Can the children extrapolate to other predators? What about predatory lizards and salamanders or predatory ground beetles (all generalists)? Do the children think they recognize prey by its movement?

Predatory behavior varies among animals in lots of other ways too. Some predators, like ladybug beetles, wander around looking for prey. Others, like orb weaving spiders, are sit-and-wait or ambush predators. (Not all are clearly one or the other. Most aquatic predators do both. Toads do both.)

Some predators, like toads and frogs, swallow prey whole. Some, like mantises, eat it in small pieces, while some, like ant lions, suck the insides out.

Some predators poison their prey, some don't. Some predators store prey.

Following is a list of questions and answers summarizing these similarities and differences (see Figure 3). Figure 4 is a set of the same questions without answers to photocopy for the students.

	Damp or Dry Substrate	Well-Lit or Deep Shadow	In House or Out of House	Cool or Warm	Light or Dark Substrate	Other
Roly-Polies	Damp	Dark	Not tested	Not tested	Not tested	
Earthworms	Damp	Dark	Not tested	Cool	Not tested	
Crickets	Damp	Prefer dark tube, but sometimes prefer well-lit end of terrarium	In	Not tested	Not tested	
Millipedes	Damp	Dark	In	Cool	Not tested	

Figure 1 — Summary of choices made by under-log creatures. Choices may vary with species.

	Damp or Dry Substrate	Well-Lit or Deep Shadow	In House or Out of House	Cool or Warm	Light or Dark Substrate	Other
Roly-Polies						
Earthworms						
Crickets						
Millipedes						

Which animals made choices that you might expect, given the conditions in their natural habitat?

Which ones didn't? _____

Do you have any ideas about why they didn't? _____

Figure 2 — For summarizing choices made by under-log creatures. Your results may vary considerably from mine, if you use different species of animals or if your conditions are slightly different.

The Effects of Cold on Growth Rates

Chapters 8, 13, 14 and 16 all had experiments addressing the effect of either food or temperature on the growth rate of young. Since all the animals in this book are cold-blooded (all animals except birds and mammals are), all responded to cooler temperatures and food deprivation by growing more slowly. Warm-blooded animals would be much more likely to respond to either with impaired health or death. Use Figure 5 to summarize your results.

Insect Reproduction

The animals in the last section of the book will all reproduce easily in captivity—fruitflies, aphids and *Tenebrio* beetles. But their life cycles vary considerably. The flies and beetles lay eggs, but the aphids give birth to live young. The aphids, along with some other animals in the book, have incomplete metamorphosis. Their young are nymphs, or miniature replicas of their parents, instead of larvae. The beetles and flies, and others earlier in the book, go through complete metamorphosis. The larva metamorphoses as a pupae into an adult that looks completely different.

Which animals in the last section have the shortest life cycle? Which have the longest? Following this section you'll find a list of questions and answers to help the children compare these animals (see Figure 6). Figure 7 is a set of the same questions without answers to photocopy for the students.

Your students may see other trends. Encourage them to make other connections among chapters.

Photocopy Figure 4 and have students answer the following questions, choosing their answers from among these predators: wandering spiders, web-building spiders, ant lions, mantises, ladybug beetles, giant water bugs, backswimmers, diving beetles, dragonfly nymphs, toads and frogs.

1. **Which of the predators are generalists (will take almost any prey of the right size)?**
   All except ladybug beetles.

2. **Which of the predators are specialists (will take only one or maybe two prey types, rejecting others of similar size)?**
   Ladybug beetles

3. **Which predators did you see take the most different kinds of prey?**
   Could be anything except ladybug beetles and maybe ant lions because of the size restriction.

4. **What advantage might there be in being a generalist predator instead of a specialist predator?**
   A generalist seldom passes up available prey, so generalizing makes them more likely to get a meal.

5. **What disadvantage might there be in being a generalist?**
   A generalist predator might attack prey it can't handle or can't digest and perhaps be injured. It also must be equipped physiologically and anatomically to handle a variety of prey. A jack-of-all-trades is often not as good at any one job as a specialist.

6. **What advantage might there be to a specialist predator?**
   Its body is specialized physiologically and anatomically for catching and handling only one prey type. So it probably utilizes the prey type more efficiently than a generalist would.

7. **What disadvantage might there be to a specialist predator?**
   If its prey species disappears, it's in trouble. That's why you find few specialist predators, and their prey are always superabundant.

8. **Did any of the predators reach satiation (get full and refuse more prey)?**
   Toads and the aquatic predators become sated quickly on large prey.

9. **Did any continue to take one prey after another for an extended period, without refusing any?**
   Ladybugs and ant lions will eat for a long time, because their prey are so small. Mantises will also eat small prey for a long time and will sometimes continue to strike even when full, eating only part of the prey, then dropping it. Spiders often wrap prey and save them for later when full.

10. **Which predators ate only moving prey?**
    Toads, frogs, mantises, ant lions, most spiders, aquatic predators usually but not always.

11. **Did any accept dead prey?**
    Aquatic predators when very hungry, dragonfly nymph usually, mantises when prey is jiggled (sometimes).

12. **Which predators did you see wander around looking for prey?**
    Wandering spiders, ladybug beetles, some aquatic predators. Frogs and mantises sometimes pursue prey a short distance once they see it, but don't wander much. Toads often wander, but sometimes sit and wait.

Continued on next page

Figure 3 — Looking for similarities and differences among predators.

Figure 3 continued from previous page

13. **Which predators seemed to be mainly sit-and-wait or ambush predators?**
    Ant lions and web-building spiders; mantises and frogs most of the time. Toads and the aquatic predators sometimes ambush prey.

14. **What advantage might wandering predators have over ambush predators?**
    They encounter more prey.

15. **What disadvantage might wandering predators have?**
    They expend more energy than ambush predators and also make themselves much more visible to larger predators who might eat them.

16. **What advantage might there be to the sit-and-wait strategy?**
    Ambush predators expend less energy and keep themselves more concealed from larger predators than do the wandering predators.

17. **What disadvantage might there be to the sit-and-wait or ambush strategy?**
    Ambush or sit-and-wait predators encounter fewer prey than wandering predators.

18. **Which prey have traps?**
    Ant lions and web-building spiders.

19. **Are those with traps sit-and-wait predators?**
    Yes.

20. **What disadvantages and advantages are there to traps?**
    They take a lot of energy to construct and repair. They restrict the predator to prey in one small area. The advantage is that they are very efficient at catching whatever prey do come into that small area.

21. **Which predators ate the whole body of the prey, but piece-by-piece?**
    Mantises, ladybug beetles, diving beetles, dragonfly nymphs.

22. **Which predators sucked out the prey's insides, leaving an empty carcass?**
    Ant lions, spiders, giant water bugs, backswimmers.

23. **Which predators inject poison and/or digestive juices into their prey?**
    The same ones that suck out their insides.

24. **Do any predators store their prey for the future?**
    Web-building spiders.

25. **Which predators did you like best? Why?**

26. **Can you think of other similarities and differences among the predators?**

Answer the following questions, choosing your answer from among these predators: wandering spiders, web-building spiders, ant lions, mantises, ladybug beetles, giant water bugs, backswimmers, diving beetles, dragonfly nymphs, toads and frogs.

1. Which of the predators are generalists (will take almost any prey of the right size)?

2. Which of the predators are specialists (will take only one or maybe two prey types, rejecting others of similar size)?

3. Which predators did you see take the most different kinds of prey?

4. What advantage might there be in being a generalist predator instead of a specialist predator?

5. What disadvantage might there be in being a generalist?

6. What advantage might there be to a specialist predator?

7. What disadvantage might there be to a specialist predator?

8. Did any of the predators reach satiation (get full and refuse more prey)?

9. Did any continue to take one prey after another for an extended period, without refusing any?

10. Which predators ate only moving prey?

11. Did any accept dead prey?

12. Which predators did you see wander around looking for prey?

Continued on next page

Figure 4 — Looking for similarities and differences among predators in the book.

Figure 4 continued from previous page

13. Which predators seemed to be mainly sit-and-wait or ambush predators?

14. What advantage might wandering predators have over ambush predators?

15. What disadvantage might wandering predators have?

16. What advantage might there be to the sit-and-wait or ambush strategy?

17. What disadvantage might there be to the sit-and-wait strategy?

18. Which prey have traps?

19. Are those with traps sit-and-wait predators?

20. What disadvantages and advantages are there to traps?

21. Which predators ate the whole body of the prey, but piece-by-piece?

22. Which predators sucked out the prey's insides, leaving an empty carcass?

23. Which predators inject poison and/or digestive juices into their prey?

24. Do any predators store their prey for the future?

25. Which predators did you like best? Why?

26. Can you think of other similarities and differences among the predators?

In which of the two chapters did you find an effect of cold on the growth rate of the young?

Chapter 8   Tadpoles _____

Chapter 13   Baby Mantises _____

Chapter 14   Fruitflies _____

Chapter 16   Mealworms _____

Other: _____

If you made graphs for each of the above experiments, which graph showed the greatest effect of cold?

Did any of the animals seem harmed or sick because of the cold?

Would a baby mammal placed in a cold environment without protection (no mom or thick fur) be more likely to be harmed by the cold?

Figure 5 — Comparing results of the experiments that tested the effects of cold on growth rates.

Photocopy Figure 7 and have students answer the following questions.

1. **Which three of these four animals lay eggs that hatch into larvae: fruitflies, aphids, *Tenebrio* beetles, ladybug beetles?**
   Fruitflies, both beetles.

2. **Which one does not lay eggs?**
   Aphids.
   What does it do instead?
   Aphids give birth to live young.

3. **Which one has young that look like miniature adults, instead of larvae?**
   Aphids.
   What are such young called?
   Nymphs.

4. **Do larvae usually look like their parents?**
   No.

5. **Do nymphs usually look like their parents?**
   Yes.

6. **Do larvae pupate and metamorphose?**
   Yes. Their development is called complete metamorphosis.

7. **Do nymphs pupate?**
   No, they molt several times as they grow but there is no abrupt major change in body form. Their development is called incomplete or gradual metamorphosis.

8. **Can you name another animal in this book that has nymphs instead of larvae?**
   Crickets, mantises, dragonfly nymphs, giant water bugs, backswimmers, water boatmen (all the aquatic hemipterans in Chapter 2).

9. **What other animals in this book have young called larvae?**
   Toads, frogs, ant lions, diving beetles.

10. **Which animals in Chapters 14, 15 and 16 had the fastest development time (egg or birth to adult)?**
    Aphids.

11. **Which had the longest development time?**
    Tenebrio beetles.

12. **What advantage is there to having larvae (called complete metamorphosis)?**
    Because the larvae are different physically, they often have a different diet and habitat than the adult, one where food may be more plentiful so the young can grow fast. So in a way, the larvae are specialized for exploiting a habitat where food is plentiful for growth, while adults are specialized for dispersal or spreading.
    Animals with incomplete metamorphosis must accomplish both tasks with one body form. The advantage of "incomplete metamorphosis" is that they avoid pupation, which takes a lot of energy and time and often leaves the animal vulnerable to predators. Pupae are usually more or less immobile.

Figure 6 — Insect reproduction.

1. Which three of these four animals lay eggs that hatch into larvae: fruitflies, aphids, *Tenebrio* beetles, ladybug beetles?

2. Which one does not lay eggs?

   What does it do instead?

3. Which one has young that look like miniature adults, instead of larvae?

   What are such young called?

4. Do larvae usually look like their parents?

5. Do nymphs usually look like their parents?

6. Do larvae pupate and metamorphose?

7. Do nymphs pupate?

8. Can you name another animal in this book that has nymphs instead of larvae?

9. What other animals in this book have young called larvae?

10. Which animals in Chapters 14, 15 and 16 had the fastest development time (egg or birth to adult)?

11. Which had the longest development time?

12. What advantage is there to having larvae (called complete metamorphosis)?

Figure 7 — Insect reproduction.

Appendix

Biological Supply and Scientific Equipment Companies

Carolina Biological Supply Company
2700 York Road
Burlington, NC 27215
800/227-1150 (technical assistance)
800/334-5551 (orders)
(This is the place I have used exclusively, because it's located nearby.)

Ward's Natural Science Establishment, Inc.
5100 West Henrietta Road
P.O. Box 92912
Rochester, NY 14692-9012
800/962-2660
    or
812 Fiero Lane
P.O. Box 5010
San Luis Obisbo, CA 93404-5010
800/872-7289

Frey Scientific
100 Paragon Parkway
Mansfield, OH 44903
800/225-FREY (corporate office)

Nasco Science
901 Janesville Avenue
Fort Atkinson, WI 53538-0901
800/558-9595
    or
4825 Stoddard Road
Modesto, CA 95352-3837
209/545-1600
(Nasco has less available than Carolina and Ward's.)

Praying mantises and ladybug beetles are available from the following company, as well as many other gardening supply catalogs (especially those focusing on organic or pesticide-free gardening):

Gardens Alive!
5100 Schenley Place
Lawrenceburg, IN 47025
812/537-8650

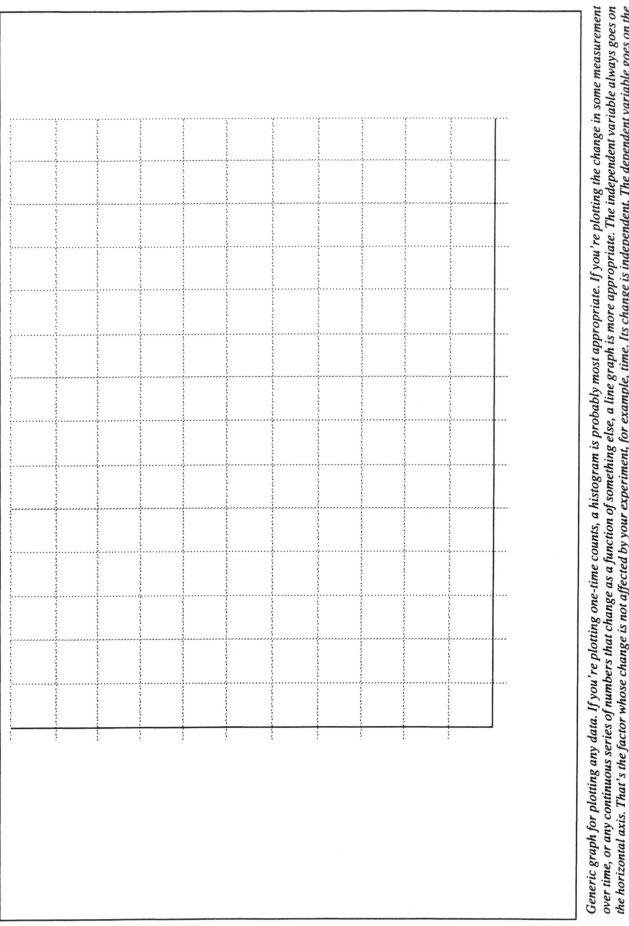

Generic graph for plotting any data. If you're plotting one-time counts, a histogram is probably most appropriate. If you're plotting the change in some measurement over time, or any continuous series of numbers that change as a function of something else, a line graph is more appropriate. The independent variable always goes on the horizontal axis. That's the factor whose change is not affected by your experiment, for example, time. Its change is independent. The dependent variable goes on the vertical axis. Its change depends on the change in the independent variable. For example, the growth of larvae depends on the passage of time.

A generic table for recording any results.

Bibliography

Chapter 2

Barnes, Robert D. 1974. *Invertebrate Zoology*. W. B. Saunders Co., Philadelphia, London, Toronto.

Borror, Donald J., and Richard E. White. 1970. *A Field Guide to the Insects of America North of Mexico*. (The Peterson Field Guide series.) Houghton Mifflin Co., Boston.

Carolina Biological Supply Company. 1990–91. *Biology/Science Materials: Catalog 61*. Carolina Biological Supply Co., Burlington, N.C.

Conant, Roger. 1975. *A Field Guide to Reptiles and Amphibians of Eastern and Central North America*. (The Peterson Field Guide series.) Houghton Mifflin Co., Boston.

Johnson, Sylvia A. 1989. *Water Insects*. Lerner Publications Co., Minneapolis.

Lawrence, Gale. 1984. *A Field Guide to the Familiar*. Prentice-Hall, Inc., Englewood Cliffs, N.J.

McClung, Robert M. 1970. *Aquatic Insects and How They Live*. William Morrow and Co., New York.

Parker, Steve. 1988. *Pond and River*. Eyewitness Books, Alfred A. Knopf, Inc., New York.

Pennak, Robert W. 1978. *Fresh-Water Invertebrates of the U.S.* John Wiley and Sons, New York.

Reid, George K. 1967. *Pond Life: A Guide to Common Plants and Animals of North American Ponds and Lakes*. (The Golden Field Guide series.) Golden Press, Western Publishing Co., Racine, Wis.

Roth, Charles E. 1982. *The Wildlife Observer's Guidebook*. Prentice-Hall, Inc., Englewood Cliffs, N.J.

Smith, Hobart M. 1978. *Amphibians of North America*. (The Golden Field Guide series.) Golden Press, Western Publishing Co., Racine, Wis.

Stokes, Donald W. 1983. *A Guide to Observing Insect Lives*. Little, Brown and Co., Boston, Toronto.

White, Richard E. 1983. *A Field Guide to the Beetles of North America*. (The Peterson Field Guide series.) Houghton Mifflin Co., Boston.

Chapter 3

Levi, H. W., and L. R. Levi. 1968. *Spiders and Their Kin*. (The Golden Field Guide series). Golden Press, Western Publishing Co., Racine, Wis. This book has two pages in the back on pill bugs, sow bugs and the other "wood lice."

Raham, Gary. 1986. Pill bug biology: a spider's spinach, but a biologist's delight. *The American Biology Teacher* 48(1): 9–16.

Chapter 4

Andrews, William A. 1973. *A Guide to the Study of Soil Ecology*. Prentice-Hall, Inc., Englewood Cliffs, N.J.

Hess, Lilo. 1979. *The Amazing Earthworm*. Charles Scribner's Sons, New York.

Hogner, Dorothy Childs. 1953. *Earthworms*. Thomas Y. Crowell Co., New York.

McLaughlin, Molly. 1986. *Earthworms, Dirt, and Rotten Leaves: An Exploration in Ecology*. Atheneum, New York.

Chapter 5

Alexander, Richard D. 1961. Aggressiveness, territoriality, and sexual behavior in field crickets (Orthoptera: Gryllidae). *Behavior* 17: 130–220.

Andrews, William A. 1974. *A Guide to the Study of Terrestrial Ecology*. Prentice-Hall, Inc., Englewood Cliffs, N.J.

Borror, Donald J., and Richard E. White. 1970. *A Field Guide to the Insects of America North of Mexico*. (The Peterson Field Guide series.) Houghton Mifflin Company, Boston.

Carolina Biological Supply Company. 1982. *Carolina Arthropods Manual*. Carolina Biological Supply Co., Burlington, N.C.

Earle, Olive Lydia. 1956. *Crickets*. William Morrow and Co., New York.

Hogner, Dorothy Childs. 1960. *Grasshoppers and Crickets.* Thomas Y. Crowell Co., New York.

Johnson, Sylvia. 1986. *Chirping Insects.* Lerner Publications, Minneapolis.

Milne, Lorus, and Margery Milne. 1980. *The Audubon Society Field Guide to North American Insects and Spiders.* Alfred A. Knopf, Inc., New York.

Porter, Keith. 1986. *Discovering Crickets and Grasshoppers.* Bookwright Press, New York.

Wyler, Rose. 1990. *Grass and Grasshoppers.* Messner, Englewood Cliffs, N.J.

Zim, Herbert S., and Clarence Cottam. 1987. *Insects: A Guide to Familiar American Insects.* Golden Press, New York.

Chapter 6

Barnes, Robert D. 1974. *Invertebrate Zoology.* W. B. Saunders Co., Philadelphia, London, Toronto.

Levi, H. W., and L. R. Levi. 1968. *Spiders and their Kin.* (The Golden Field Guide series). Golden Press, Western Publishing Co., Inc., Racine, Wis.

Preston-Mafham, Ken. 1990. *Discovering Centipedes and Millipedes.* Bookwright Press, New York.

Chapter 7

Alexopoulos, Constantine J. 1962. *Introductory Mycology.* John Wiley and Sons, New York.

Carolina Biological Supply Company. 1986. *Techniques for Studying Bacteria and Fungi.* Carolina Biological Supply Co., Burlington, N.C.

Ellis, Harry. 1992. It's slimy! It's alive! *Wildlife in North Carolina* 56(6): 24–28.

Farr, M. L. 1981. *How to Know the True Slime Molds.* William C. Brown Co., Dubuque.

Lincoff, Gary H. 1981. *The Audubon Society Field Guide to North American Mushrooms.* Alfred A. Knopf, Inc., New York. This has an excellent and thorough section on identifying slime molds, with color photographs of plasmodia and sporangia.

Stephenson, S. L. 1982. Slime molds in the laboratory. *American Biology Teacher* 44(2): 119–120, 127.

Stephenson, S. L. 1985. Slime molds in the laboratory II: Moist chamber cultures. *American Biology Teacher* 47(8): 487–489.

Stevens, R. B.(ed.) 1981. *Mycology Guidebook.* University of Washington Press, Seattle.

Chapter 8

Conant, Roger. 1975. *A Field Guide to Reptiles and Amphibians of Eastern and Central North America.* (The Peterson Field Guide series.) Houghton Mifflin Co., Boston.

Martof, Bernard S. et al. 1980. *Amphibians and Reptiles of the Carolinas and Virginia.* University of North Carolina Press, Chapel Hill.

Smith, Hobart M. 1978. *Amphibians of North America: A Guide to Field Identification.* (The Golden Field Guide series.) Golden Press, Western Publishing Co., Racine, Wis.

Stewart, M. M. 1956. The separate effects of food and temperature differences on the development of marbled salamander larvae. *Journal of the Elisha Mitchell Scientific Society* 72: 47–56.

Chapter 9

Barnes, Robert D. 1974. *Invertebrate Zoology.* W. B. Saunders Co., Philadelphia, London, Toronto.

Borror, Donald J., and Richard E. White. 1970. *A Field Guide to the Insects of America North of Mexico.* (The Peterson Field Guide series.) Houghton Mifflin Co., Boston.

Johnson, Sylvia A. 1989. *Water Insects.* Lerner Publications Co., Minneapolis.

McClung, Robert M. 1970. *Aquatic Insects and How They Live.* William Morrow and Co., New York.

Parker, Steve. 1988. *Pond and River.* Eyewitness Books, Alfred A. Knopf, Inc., New York.

Pennak, Robert W. 1978. *Fresh-Water Invertebrates of the U.S.* John Wiley and Sons, New York.

Reid, George K. 1967. *Pond Life: A Guide to Common Plants and Animals of North American Ponds and Lakes.* (The Golden Field Guide series.) Golden Press, Western Publishing Co., Racine, Wis.

Stokes, Donald W. 1983. *A Guide to Observing Insect Lives.* Little, Brown and Co., Boston, Toronto.

White, Richard E. 1983. *A Field Guide to the Beetles of North America.* (The Peterson Field Guide series.) Houghton Mifflin Co., Boston.

Chapter 10

Banks, Joan Brix. 1978. Ant lion. *Ranger Rick's Nature Magazine* 12(8): 28–29.

Burton, Maurice, and Robert Burton. 1974. *Funk and Wagnalls Wildlife Encyclopedia.* Funk and Wagnalls, Inc., New York.

Zim, Herbert S., and Clarence Cottam. 1987. *Insects: A Guide to Familiar American Insects.* Golden Press, New York.

Chapter 11

Comstock, J. H. 1948. *The Spider Book.* Comstock Publishing Co., Inc., Ithaca, N.Y.

Kaston, B. J. 1972. *How to Know the Spiders.* William C. Brown Co., Dubuque.

Land, M. F. 1971. Orientation by jumping spiders in the absence of visual feedback. *Journal of Experimental Biology* 54: 119–139.

Lavine, S. A. 1966. *Wonders of the Spider World.* Dodd, Mead and Co., New York.

Levi, H. W. and L. R. Levi. 1968. *Spiders and their Kin: A Golden Guide.* Golden Press, Western Publishing, Inc., Racine, Wis.

Milne, Lorus, and Margery Milne 1980. *The Audubon Society Field Guide to North American Insects and Spiders.* Alfred A. Knopf, Inc., New York.

Moffett, Mark W. 1991. All eyes on jumping spiders. *National Geographic,* September 1991.

Rovner, J. S. 1989. Wolf spiders lack mirror-image responsiveness seen in jumping spiders. *Animal Behavior* 38: 526–533.

Chapter 12

Conklin, Gladys. 1978. *Praying Mantis, the Garden Dinosaur.* Holiday House, New York.

Earle, Olive. 1969. *Praying Mantis.* William Morrow and Co., New York.

Hess, Lilo. 1971. *The Praying Mantis, Insect Cannibal.* Scribner, New York.

Johnson, Sylvia A. 1984. *Mantises.* Lerner Publications, Minneapolis.

Lavies, Bianca. 1990. *Backyard Hunter: The Praying Mantis.* Dutton, New York. This book has fantastic photographs of every life stage.

Milne, Lorus, and Margery Milne. 1980. *The Audubon Society Field Guide to North American Insects and Spiders.* Alfred A. Knopf, Inc., New York. This book can be useful in distinguishing species.

Zim, Herbert S., and Clarence Cottam. 1987. *Insects: A Guide to Familiar American Insects.* Golden Press, New York.

Chapter 13

Conklin, Gladys. 1978. *Praying Mantis, the Garden Dinosaur.* Holiday House, New York.

Earle, Olive. 1969. *Praying Mantis.* William Morrow and Co., New York.

Hess, Lilo. 1971. *The Praying Mantis, Insect Cannibal.* Scribner, New York.

Johnson, Sylvia A. 1984. *Mantises.* Lerner Publications. Minneapolis.

Lavies, Bianca. 1990. *Backyard Hunter: The Praying Mantis.* Dutton, New York.

Chapter 14

Carolina Biological Supply Company 1982. *Carolina Arthropods Manual.* Carolina Biological Supply Co., Burlington, N.C. This booklet tells how to culture houseflies indoors (get them to reproduce indefinitely) under sanitary conditions.

Carolina Biological Supply Company 1988. *Carolina Drosophila Manual.* Carolina Biological Supply Co., Burlington, N.C.

Cunningham, John D. 1970. *First You Catch a Fly.* McCall Publishing Co., New York. This book is full of ideas about things to do with fruitflies and houseflies.

Milne, Lorus, and Margery Milne. 1980. *The Audubon Society Field Guide to North American Insects and Spiders.* Alfred A. Knopf, Inc., New York. Look up Drosophila, not fruitfly.

Chapter 15

Borror, Donald J., and Richard E. White. 1970. *A Field Guide to the Insects of America North of Mexico.* (The Peterson Field Guide series.) Houghton Mifflin Co., Boston.

Burton, Maurice, and Robert Burton. 1974. *Funk and Wagnalls Wildlife Encyclopedia.* Funk and Wagnalls, Inc., New York.

Johnson, Sylvia A. 1983. *Ladybugs.* Lerner Publications, Minneapolis.

Roth, Susan A. (ed.) 1987. *Controlling Lawn and Garden Insects.* Ortho Books, Chevron Chemical Company, San Francisco.

Watts, Barrie. 1987. *Ladybug.* Silver Burdett, Morristown, New Jersey.

White, Richard E. 1983. *A Field Guide to the Beetles of North America.* (The Peterson Field Guide series). Houghton Mifflin Co., Boston.

Zim, Herbert S., and Clarence Cottam. 1987. *Insects: A Guide to Familiar American Insects.* Golden Press, New York.

Chapter 16

Borror, Donald J., and Richard E. White. 1970. *A Field Guide to the Insects of America North of Mexico.* (The Peterson Field Guide series.) Houghton Mifflin Co., Boston.

Carolina Biological Supply Company 1982. *Carolina Arthropods Manual.* Carolina Biological Supply Co., Burlington, N.C.

Cunningham, John D. 1970. *First You Catch a Fly.* McCall Publishing Co., New York. The questions I've used for flying beetles came from this book about flies.

White, Richard E. 1983. *A Field Guide to the Beetles of North America.* (The Peterson Field Guide series.) Houghton Mifflin Co., Boston.

Index

T